The Song-Writers Idea Book

40 strategies to excite your imagination, help you design distinctive songs, and keep your creative flow.

SHEILA DAVIS

Writer's Digest Books

Cincinnnati, Ohio

Sheila Davis, a gold-record lyricist, teaches at The New School for Social Research in New York and conducts songwriting seminars around the country. She is the author of *The Craft of Lyric Writing* and *Successful Lyric Writing*.

Songwriters Idea Book. Copyright © 1992 by Sheila Davis. Printed and bound in the United States of America. All rights reserved. No part of this book may be reproduced in any form or by any electronic or mechanical means including information storage and retrieval systems without permission in writing from the publisher, except by a reviewer, who may quote brief passages in a review. Published by Writer's Digest Books, an imprint of F&W Publications, Inc., 1507 Dana Avenue, Cincinnati, Ohio 45207; 1(800)289-0963. First edition.

Library of Congress Cataloging in Publication Data

Davis, Sheila
    The songwriters idea book / Sheila Davis.
        p. cm.
    Includes index.
    ISBN 0-89879-519-2
    1. Lyric writing (Popular music) I. Title.
MT67.D253   1992
808'.066782—dc20   92-23322
                                                                    CIP
                                                                    MN

Designed by Sandy Conopeotis

*Every good idea and all creative
work are the offspring of the
imagination.* . . .
*The debt we owe to the play of
imagination is incalculable.*

CARL JUNG

This book advances an original theory: Namely, that writing style predicts one's personality type and brain dominance — and vice versa. Every theory of course piggybacks on the thinking of others. So I must acknowledge those seminal thinkers without whom my hypothesis could not exist. First and foremost, Carl Jung on whose theory of psychological types my own notion of the relationship between language and cerebral function squarely rests.

I am indebted to Katharine C. Briggs and her daughter Isabel Briggs Myers who together created the Myers-Briggs Type Indicator® (MBTI), a pioneer psychological instrument based on Jung's theory of type. Their idea to supplement Jung's three scales of polar-opposite cognitive functions and attitudes with a fourth scale of orientations was essential to my envisioning the type/brain models which have become fundamental to my teaching methods.

The insight of another illustrious thinker scaffolds my theory of writing style and brain function: Giambattista Vico, the 18th century philosopher, was the first to realize that *Metaphor, Metonymy, Irony* and *Synecdoche* were not mere figures of "speech," but rather the four master figures of *thought*. My theory links those master figures to both Jung's personality types and to brain lateralization function.

Of course my hypothesis would not exist without the neurological discoveries of such eminent researchers as Broca, Wernicke, Sperry, Bogen, Gazzaniga, Geschwind, et al. Their pioneering studies paved the way for the sophisticated techniques that continually yield exciting new clues to the brain's organization of language.

I want especially to acknowledge the talent and tenacity of my students whose role-model lyrics enliven this book. They rose to the challenge of tough criticism to polish the rough edges of those lyrics until they fulfilled their potential.

And finally a "thank you" to my husband, mentor, and meticulous editor, whose cogent comments on my manuscript sent me back yet again to polish my own rough edges.

B uilding a successful songwriting career demands three attributes: talent, technique and *sustained* creativity. Talent of course is something one is born with. It's what Irving Berlin called "having the knack."

My first two books — *The Craft of Lyric Writing* and *Successful Lyric Writing* — aimed to support that knack by laying a foundation of craftsmanship — those timeless principles on which our standards were built. This book, like my advanced classes, presumes that you're familiar with the major music forms and the basic tenets of rhyme, rhythm and plot development. So we start beyond the basics. We'll address here the third requisite — sustained creativity. This book aims to put you in closer touch with your individual creative process.

The core material of *The Songwriters Idea Book* features forty strategies to spark your imagination and keep your creative flame burning. It's illustrated by over one hundred role-model lyrics produced by writers trained in whole-brain thinking and writing. These songwriters not only know their right brain from their left — which hemisphere does what, and when and how to use it — they know a lot about their individual thinking styles, generally called brain dominance. They've learned how to access their right brain's ability to be spontaneous, imaginative, visual, metaphoric — to tease out intuitions and come up with original concepts. And they've learned how to access their left-brain's structural ability to help shape their thoughts into sequential order and the ideal form, and with its resident editor to detect the discrepancy, weed out the redundancy, and transform a promising first draft into a polished final.

Their lyrics "work" on the printed page without the crutches of melody or synthesized rhythm track because each coherently expresses an individual slant on a universal concept with genuine feeling — combining the best of both brains.

We all possess enormous creative potential. But, like solar power, to be effective it must be harnessed. I believe that you'll find the whole-brain approach to songwriting both challenging and rewarding. And like my students who've gained success in every area of songwriting — pop, country, children's market, cabaret and theater — you will gain a new mastery of your creative process that will lead to success in *your* chosen marketplace.

PART ONE

A Digest of Songwriting Theory

Throughout the book I'll allude to such common songwriting terms as *the bridge*, or *the attitudinal plot*, or *trailing rhyme*. For your convenience, Part I supplies you with a digest of the major principles of songwriting structure and development.

From time to time you may want a more detailed description of a particular element such as *meter* or *time frames*, so I'll refer you to those pages in *The Craft of Lyric Writing* and *Successful Lyric Writing*—hereafter referred to as *CLW* and *SLW*—which go into a subject in depth.

An Overview of Lyricwriting Principles

Before we plunge into the forty strategies for generating ideas, let's briefly review the main terms, principles and guidelines for successful songwriting.

The Essential Lyric Framework

Make sure your lyric contains:

- *A Genuine Idea*
  About convincing human beings in believable situations
  That expresses one clear attitude or emotion
  That's substantial enough to be set to music
  That strikes a common chord
  That puts the singer in a favorable light
  That millions will want to hear again

- *A Memorable Title*
  That is identifiable after one hearing
  That summarizes the essence of the lyric's statement
  That's one of a kind

- *A Strong Start*
  That pulls the listener into the song
  That establishes the Who, What, When and Where in the first few lines

- *A Satisfying Progression*
  That arranges elements in a meaningful sequence
  That develops an idea from something, through something, to something
  That draws some conclusion—either stated or implied

- *The Appropriate Music Form*
  That supports and enhances the lyric's purpose
  That delivers the desired effect

  (The three major song forms will be detailed in the next section.)

The Three Song Plots

Song plots come in three levels of complexity:

- *Attitudinal*: ("Unforgettable") In which a single emotion or attitude is expressed.
- *Situational*: ("Torn Between Two Lovers") In which the attitude has been given a situational framework.
- *Story* Song: ("Coward of the County") In which the plot events have a beginning, middle and end.

The Major Development Techniques

- *Meaningful Sequence*: ("The First Time Ever I Saw Your Face") Places the details in ascending order of importance.
- *Foreshadowing*: ("Class Reunion") Suggests a plot development before it occurs.
- *Imagery*: ("Gentle On My Mind") Arranges word pictures in a manner that creates a purposeful effect.
- *The Return*: ("In the Ghetto") Brings back at the end some key word, phrase, line or entire section used at the beginning.
- *Conflict*: ("Coming In and Out of Your Life") Puts the singer at odds with some internal or external force.
- *Ironic Tension*: ("Send in the Clowns") Contrasts what *seems, ought,* or *used to be* with what *is.*
- *Surprise*: ("Harper Valley PTA") Surprises the listener at the end by means of such devices as the *Discovery, Twist* or *Turnaround.*
- *Pun*: ("On the Other Hand") Exploits the multiple meanings in a single word or phrase.
- *Scene Method*: ("It Was a Very Good Year") Creates vignettes to symbolize the meaning.
- *Question Plot*: ("Guess Who I Saw Today, My Dear?") Presents a question in the first verse that isn't answered until the last.
- *Conversational Debate*: ("Baby, It's Cold Outside") Uses a duet to dramatize opposing viewpoints.

The Plot Spine: Viewpoint, Voice, Time Frame, Setting

Four major plot choices—viewpoint, voice, time frame and setting—interconnect to form the spine of your lyric. Each of the VVTS (vits) must be clear and consistent to give your lyric a strong backbone. Here's an overview of plot options.

Because the majority of pop songs are either attitudinal or situational, the predominant viewpoints we hear are first and second person—with the emphasis on *I* and *you* respectively. The third-person narrates the story song. Most lyrics

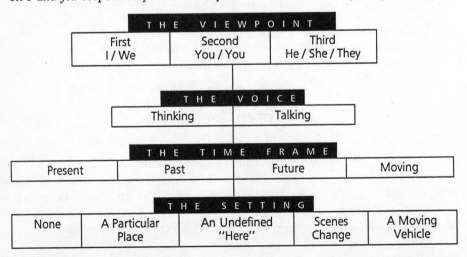

THE VIEWPOINT		
First I / We	Second You / You	Third He / She / They

THE VOICE	
Thinking	Talking

THE TIME FRAME			
Present	Past	Future	Moving

THE SETTING				
None	A Particular Place	An Undefined "Here"	Scenes Change	A Moving Vehicle

find the singer in the *thinking voice*—either reflecting on an experience or emotional state or addressing some absent person, place, or thing in her mind. In the *talking voice* the singer is holding a face-to-face conversation with a singee. How you handle one element will affect the others. The goal is to control each of the four so that they work together to form a unified and coherent lyric:

> Get a fix on the VVTS.
> Once you set them,
> Don't forget them.
> If they change, be sure to show it
> So your listener's sure to know it.

For an explanation of each element in the VVTS, see *SLW* pages 46-49.

A Rundown on Rhyme

Rhyme—A definition: Two or more words are said to rhyme when each contains the same final accented vowel and consonant sound with a different consonant preceding that vowel. The three most common types of rhyme—of one, two and three syllables—are called *Major Accent* rhyme; all other instances of perfect rhyme are called *Minor Accent* rhyme. Sound links that don't meet the requirements of perfect rhyme are called *Near Rhyme*.

Perfect Rhyme—Major Accent

Masculine (1-syllable):	rain/retrain; bronze/swans
Feminine (2-syllable):	ballast/calloused; *sad to/had to
Trisyllabic (3-syllable):	beautiful/dutiful; *monotonous/forgotten us
Mosaic*:	untie/one tie; feminine/lemon in

*One in the pair consists of two or more words.

Perfect Rhyme—Minor Accent

Broken:	beanery/keener re-/(ception)
Trailing:	part/started; love/above me
Apocopated:	told me/bold; singer/ring
Light (Weakened):	me/tenderly; bring/remembering
Contiguous:	What's the *diff if* I live or die
Internal:	The final *scene* of a Balan*chine* ballet
Linked:	*bond*/Sammy *Cahn* Delight

Near Rhyme

Unstressed:	gĭvĕn/héavĕn; hóllŏw/wíllŏw
Assonance:	wine/time; cra*ve*/ga*te*
Consonance:	boa*t*/skir*t*; drea*d*/tra*de*
Para rhyme:	s*cene*/s*ign*; *cave*/*curve*
Feminine para:	*bear*de*d*/*boar*de*d*; re*seal*/re*sell*
Augmented:	see/plea*d*; pen/dren*ch*; say/gra*ve*;
Diminished:	pligh*t*/sigh; year*s*/we're; drown*ed*/town

Other Sound Effects

Alliteration:	At night awake he *w*onders *w*hen
Onomatopoeia:	*Boom, boom, boom* went the big bass drum
Word Derivatives: (Polyptoton)	How do we *teach* what must be *taught*?
Phonetic Intensives:	"You nick da skin/You clip-a da chin" (Sondheim)

Non Rhyme (Traditionally considered a flaw)

Identity:	*day*/to*day*; *leave*/be*lieve*; *know*/*no*

Note: For more theory, definitions and examples of rhyme, see *CLW* pages 185-212 and *SLW* pages 113-121.

The Top-Ten Writing Principles

Simplicity: Keep to one idea, and eliminate subplots. The plot of a well-crafted lyric can be summarized in a short sentence.

Clarity: Include key pronouns to make clear who is doing the talking or thinking. Give every pronoun—*him, her, they, them* and especially *it*—a clear and close antecedent. If the lyric changes time frames, settings or viewpoint, show it in a transitional line.

Compression: Make every word count. Eliminate empty qualifiers *(very, just)*, -*ly* adverbs like *slowly/sadly*, and meaningless modifiers (*morning* sunrise).

Emphasis: Use short, strong one-syllable words. Place important words at the *end of the line.* Prefer active-voice verbs over passive voice: "Your kiss fooled me," not "I was fooled by your kiss." Be mindful that the present tense is stronger than the past, and that first and second person create greater listener identification than third. Rhyme only those words you want to stress.

Consistency: Keep the tone and the language style the same throughout. Keep your theme words such as *rain* consistently literal (real rain) or consistently figurative (trouble); don't shuttle between two meanings within the same lyric. Be sure your lyric has only one *you*; for example, in "Moon River" the river is the sole *you* that is consistently addressed.

Coherence: Remember that meaning is not retroactive: *Precede* every reaction or effect with a reason or cause. Maintain a logical chronology from line to line—morning, noon, night—and an ascending emotional order: "ev'ry minute of the hour, ev'ry hour of the day, ev'ry day of the week."

Specificity: Choose the particular (apple) over the general (fruit); concrete (the roses you bring) over the abstract (little things you do). Try to *show* an emotion, rather than tell it. (Strategy No. 16 will detail the ways and means).

Repetition: To satisfy the listener's need to recognize the familiar, repeat important words and/or lines for emphasis—especially the title (" 'Ol man river/ 'dat 'ol man river . . .").

Unity: Treat elements with a length that's appropriate to their importance. Weave the elements of time, action and place into a harmonious whole to produce a single general effect.

Genuine Feeling: Write about situations and emotions you understand. There is no substitute for sincerity: be true to be believed.

The Key Decisions

Choose the Gender: Will the expressed emotion be given a male or female sensibility? For certain subjects, gender makes a vast difference. The lyric may of course work well for either gender. Consider before you write.

Select the Viewpoint: Will the lyric be set 1) In first person with the emphasis on "I"; 2) In second person with the emphasis on "you"; 3) In third person with the emphasis on "he," "she," or "they"? If your lyric changes viewpoints (which is rare), be sure the change is purposeful and clear.

Decide the Voice: Will the singer be *thinking* (an interior monologue) or *talking* (a dialogue)? In thinking lyrics the singer may be: 1) Alone and thinking; (2) With someone and thinking; 3) Addressing an absent person, place or thing; or 4) Addressing the *collective you*. A *talking* lyric is a (second-person) conversation with someone present. Decide the voice and keep it consistent.

Define the Time Frame: Is your action set in the 1)Nonspecific present—an undefined moment; 2) Habitual present—an ongoing action or emotion; 3) Particular present—a onetime action; 4) Simple past; 5) Historical present—a past action told in present-tense verbs; 6) Future tense? Decide. Keep your eye on the clock; if it moves, *state* it.

Set the Scene: Where is the singer doing the thinking or talking—in a barroom, bedroom, boardroom? Even if the lyric doesn't state where, you should know where. If the scene changes, show it.

Identify the Tone: What is the singer's emotional attitude toward the events—wistful, spiteful, grateful, etc.? Consistency of tone is essential; stay with one tone all the way.

Pick the Diction: Is your character educated? Street smart? Poetic? Know your character and keep the language style consistent.

Determine the Song Form: What do you want your audience to feel? Form creates effect. Which of the three major song forms will best deliver the effect your seek? Choose before you begin to write.

Become the Character: Do you truly believe in the character and the situation you are creating? Only when you do, will your audience.

Know Your Audience: Rock songs, country songs, R&B songs, children's songs, cabaret songs all have special audiences. Know the audience for which you are writing. It determines to a great extent the diction and style of your lyric and the sound of your music.

WrapUp

That's a lot to keep in mind as you write. But somehow you can manage to do it all—if not in the first draft, well, by the final one. And that's the one that counts. Now we examine the three major song forms.

The Three Major Song Forms

Three distinct musical forms provide the structure for the majority of popular songs: The verse/chorus (v/c), the AABA and the AAA. Each form includes a number of variations.

The Verse/Chorus Form

Rap aside, the dominant pop song form continues to be the verse/chorus. The following diagrams, along with titles of some well-known songs in that form, will help you visualize the musical and lyrical frameworks of each. The basic verse/chorus is comprised of two musical sections: The chorus embodies the main musical motif, the lyric's main message and the song's title; the first verse acts as introduction to the chorus, with subsequent lyric verses developing the plot. A lyric message that bears repetition is best treated in the verse/chorus form. The form is also ideal for plots that feature a change of time frame and/or setting. Generally either one or two verses precede the first chorus with the song's title generally placed in the chorus' first line, less frequently in its last line. (The asterisk indicates the use of the title at the beginning of the chorus.)

1. The classic verse/chorus with first-line title.

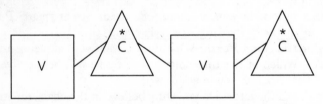

Tie a Yellow Ribbon
Material Girl
Don't Cry Out Loud

Nobody Does It Better
She Believes in Me
Sunrise, Sunset

2. The verse/chorus with last-line title.
Although this placement can generate hit songs, the melodies tend to be less independently successful because the song's title lacks a link to the chorus' opening musical motif.

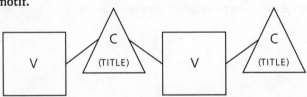

Wind Beneath My Wings
The Search Is Over

Separate Lives
What's Forever For?

3. The verse/chorus/bridge form.

This variation has a third (optional) section called a bridge, a 4-8 bar section that serves as a contrast to both the verse's words and chorus' melody; the bridge generally arrives after the second chorus. But that's a tradition, not a rule: There are no rules, only useful guidelines.

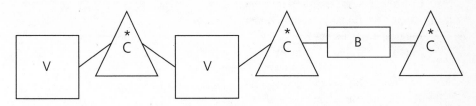

Touch Me in the Morning
Just Once
Somewhere Down the Road

Private Dancer
Up Where We Belong
Stranger in My House

4. The verse/climb/chorus form.

This variation has a climb—a pre-chorus 2-8 line (or bar) section—that musically and lyrically seems to push out from the verse and climb up to the chorus; the form may or may not also contain a bridge.

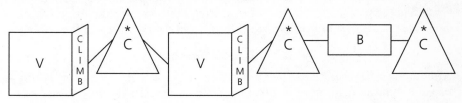

Rhythm of the Night
Heartbreaker
Solid (As a Rock)

I Made It Through the Rain
If Ever You're in My Arms Again
How Am I Supposed to Live Without
  You?

The following lyric is a student example of the classic verse/chorus form with top-line title and was recorded by the multi-platinum artist Ray Peterson.

Song Form: Example No. 1 (Verse/Chorus)
THE STRENGTH OF OUR LOVE

We built our love out of trust.
Now it's grown stronger than steel.
When troubles rain down on us
They can't weaken the love that we feel.
Like the old oak tree that leans with the wind,
Our love is able to bend.
The night depends on the sun to rise
And we count on love to survive.

THE STRENGTH OF OUR LOVE can withstand anything—
The weight of a mountain, the force of a storm.
Together we face what life brings.
Thank God for THE STRENGTH OF OUR LOVE.

Like the lark, we return every spring
To our favorite place where we met.
You can still make my heart sing,
There's a lifetime of harmony left.
Like the evergreens that always look new,
Our love continues to bloom.
Tossed and turned by the winds of change,
We're even stronger today.

THE STRENGTH OF OUR LOVE can withstand anything—
The weight of a mountain, the force of a storm.
Together we face what life brings.
Thank God for THE STRENGTH OF OUR LOVE.

By Rick Swiegoda and Thornton Cline
© *1990 Blue Valentine Music/Clientele Music. Used with permission.*

▲ Comment

The lyric illustrates the often-heard writing principle that content dictates form: This sentiment requires a full repetition of its statement. Like many first-line-title choruses, it brings back the title at the end for closure and memorability.

The AABA Form

After the verse/chorus, the AABA form is most frequently chosen by songwriters—especially in the fields of country, cabaret and theater. Its flowing musical statement makes it best-suited to convey one moment's feeling; it thus requires a consistent time frame (usually the nonspecific present), one viewpoint, and an unchanging setting. Traditionally, the form embodies four 8-bar sections with the title either starting *or* concluding the A section. Because the bridge (B-section) functions as a contrast to the A's, the best-crafted songs respect the tradition not to recycle the title there.

1. The classic AABA.

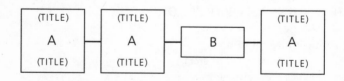

Over the Rainbow   Body and Soul
Yesterday   Send in the Clowns
Here You Come Again   Just the Way You Are

2. The *extended* AABA.

A longer variant that meets the demands of our 3-4 minute records I've dubbed the extended AABA: It lengthens the classic four-section form to six sections. The last and third A generally consists of all new or mostly new words, some of which may reprise a line from the first A. Similarly, the second bridge may be all new words or a repeat of the first A—if its statement bears such a repetition.

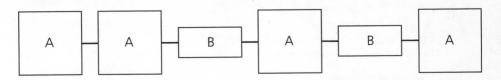

Memory	Do You Know Where You're Goin' To?
Longer	Out Here On My Own
When I Need You	Saving All My Love For You

3. The *augmented* AABA.

Song forms are constantly being modified by inventive writers. A case in point is Sting's variation on the classic AABA in his memorable mid '80s hit "Every Breath You Take"; he added a third section which composers would term a "C." I've dubbed this variant the augmented AABA. Stephen Sondheim's Broadway scores invariably feature augmented AABA's—as did his songs for Madonna in the film *Dick Tracy*.

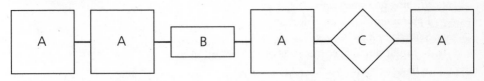

Every Breath You Take	Broadway Baby
Could I Leave You?	Sooner or Later
I'm Still Here	More

Here's an augmented AABA which has earned well-deserved kudos from New York critics and at the time of this printing boasts two recordings—by jazz artist Marlene VerPlanck and cabaret diva Margaret Whiting.

Song Form: Example No. 2 (AABABA)
THE LIES OF HANDSOME MEN

I believe in star signs.
And I believe in film romances.
I believe in fantasy.
And I believe with just one glance
He's crazy 'bout my eyes,
'Cause I believe THE LIES OF HANDSOME MEN.

I believe in witchcraft.
And I believe in Cinderella.
I believe in gypsies.
And I believe I cast a spell
That sends him to the skies.
'Cause I believe THE LIES OF HANDSOME MEN.

Somewhere in a corner of my mind
I'm not a fool, completely blind.
Even though he's hooked me on his line,
I find the pleasure has been mine.

I believe in love songs;
They seem to know just what I'm feeling.
I believe in Prince Charming;
(I never guess he's double-dealing).
How my spirits rise
Believing in THE LIES OF HANDSOME MEN.

Somewhere in a dark and lonely place
The truth and I meet face to face.
Even though his highness disappears
I keep some lovely souvenirs.

I believe in heroes.
And I expect that happy ending.
Wishing on some rainbow,
I pretend he's not pretending.
Someday I'll grow wise
But right now I need THE LIES OF HANDSOME MEN.

By Francesca Blumenthal
© 1988 Quentin Road Music. Used with permission.

▲ Comment

In the hands of a genuine craftswoman, the effortless flow of rhyme belies the claim by some lyricists that perfect rhyme prevents the attainment of genuine feeling. In a WBAI radio interview, Margaret Whiting, in characterizing the response of audiences from New York to London to her performance of the song said, "The 'Lies of Handsome Men' is the greatest thing that ever's happened to me!" What finer compliment could a songwriter receive.

The AAA Form

The AAA musical form evolved from composers setting to music the uniformly shaped stanzas of hymns and Irish and Scotch poetry. The form is still a staple with folk singers and other poetically minded lyricist/composers. Its longer length—averaging 16 bars—allows for short self-contained scenes or vignettes, thus making it ideal for a changing time frame or setting. The song usually averages three to five verses. Like the verse/chorus and the AABA, it's also open to variation.

1. The AAA with a top-line title.

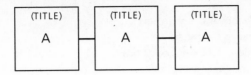

First Time Ever I Saw Your Face   Do That to Me One More Time
It Was a Very Good Year   Try to Remember
Where Have All the Flowers Gone   By the Time I Get to Phoenix

2. The AAA with a last-line title.

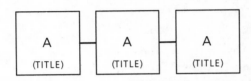

My Cup Runneth Over   Gentle On My Mind
Ladies of the Canyon   The Rose
I Walk the Line   Desolation Row

3. The AAA with a closing refrain.
Many AAA songs feature a repeated line or two (often ironic) at the end of each stanza, called a refrain, which may or may not embody the title.

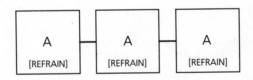

Annie's Song   Bridge Over Troubled Water
Harper Valley PTA   Blowin' in the Wind
Ode to Billie Joe   The Times They Are A'Changin'

Here's an example of my own with a last-line title. Though starting out life as a verse/chorus lyric, it evolved through the collaborative process into an AAA. It was recorded in the seventies by Shirley Bassey (in the *Something Else* album) and in 1990 found its way into the musical *Words Fail Me*, which the Lincoln Center Library videotaped for their research archives.

Song Form: Example No. 3 (AAA)
I'M NOT THERE

Down the corridors of misty dreams
I chase the strange elusive scenes
Of childhood days in playground games
And overhear the angry names that
Once were hurled in early years and
Echo still in unshed tears, but
I'M NOT THERE, no, I'M NOT THERE.

In the attic of my memory
I see the faded tapestry of
Tangled threads from daisy chains
Collected in the sudden rains
Of summer days gone quickly by—
I turn my face away and sigh, but
I'M NOT THERE, no, I'M NOT THERE.

I pass through brightly lighted doors
To join the dance on crowded floors
Until the throbbing rhythm numbs and
Once more empty night becomes
Another link that slipped the chain and
Never can be found again, but
I'M NOT THERE, no, I'M NOT THERE.

On a day that hasn't dawned as yet
Perhaps someone I've never met
Will say, "I'll tell you who you are:
You are the one I've waited for."
And when I look into those eyes that
Strip me bare of all disguise
Then I'll be there.
Yes, I'll be there.

Lyric by Sheila Davis/Music by Michael Leonard
© 1968 Solar Systems Music/Fluttermill Music. Used with permission.

▲ Comment

The lyric employs the development device of *the scene* and its last verse illustrates the principle that a title doesn't need to be rigidly repeated from verse to verse when an evolving plot demands otherwise. Many a student first-draft never takes flight because the writer stiffens it wings with inappropriate "shoulds" and "musts." Creativity requires flexibility and chance taking.

WrapUp

Throughout the book, you'll be reading over one hundred examples of these three major forms and all their variants. If, before moving on, you want more details on the forms, each is treated to extensive discussion in *SLW* (pages 20-45) and *CLW* (pages 30-80).

PART TWO

Personality Type, Brain Dominance, and the Creative Process

Coming up soon are forty strategies to help you generate song concepts. But first, we'll take a look at the source of all your creativity—your brain-dominance style. The objective: Whole-brain writing.

What do I mean by whole-brain writing? Simply that the ideas and images supplied by the "creative" right brain have been shaped and edited by the structural left brain into a unified lyric. A first draft often delivers less than its promised potential. Virtually all of the more than one hundred lyrics that will illustrate the upcoming strategies went through several revisions before they could appear on the printed page as "role models." But lyrics, after all, are not produced whole from an automated machine; they evolve in stages from a cerebral process.

This chapter will give you a clearer picture of the creative process in general and your individual process in particular. First you'll identify your "type"— that is, your natural style of behaving and thinking—by means of a short questionnaire: The DPS (Davis Personality Scale), a personality assessment instrument based on Carl Jung's theory of *Psychological Types*. Then we'll examine your type in relation to your songwriting style.

Although every brain is unique, members of each type group tend to produce writing that shares characteristic strengths as well as characteristic potential weaknesses. Armed with this new awareness of how your type/brain dominance shapes your rough first draft, you'll have a much clearer picture of how to achieve a polished final draft.

Identifying Your Personality Type and Brain Dominance

The short questionnaire on page 17 that you're about to answer asks you to rate your everyday ways of thinking, acting and deciding—not how you believe you *should be* or *wish you were* or how you *plan to change*, but how you actually behave. The questionnaire is in no way a "test." There is no right or wrong answer because there is no good, better or best type. All thinking styles are essential to a balanced functioning of the world.

As you read each set of four polar-opposite statements, you may think that the most desired response is a balanced middle ground between two extremes. It isn't. Strong preferences create strong, achieving personalities—an Einstein, a Bernstein, a Baryshnikov, a Schwarzkopf. The objective is to indicate as honestly as you can your preferences—however mild or extreme.

First read each pair of polar opposites. Then on the scale beneath them, mark two (2) Xs, one on each side of the -0- on the dot that indicates where the degree of your preference lies. Be sure to give a preference to one end of the scale over the other, however slight; for example I-8, E-9. I suggest you use a pencil rather than a pen: As you gain a better understanding of type terms, you may want to modify some of your initial responses. Stop reading a minute and take the questionnaire now. After you fill in your four-letter type, I'll define the letters I/E, S/N, T/F and J/P.

What the Letters Mean

Now that you've identified your type, what do those four letters signify? The I/E scale represents two opposite sources of energy—*Introverting*, that is, being energized from within by reflection; *Extraverting*, being energized from without by interaction. The S/N scale represents two opposite means of perception—*Sensing*, knowing via the five senses, or *iNtuiting*, knowing via unconscious insights. ("N" is used for Intuiting as "I" already stands for Introverting.) The T/F scale represents two opposite means of coming to conclusions—by *Thinking*, which is objectively based on logic; or by *Feeling*, which is subjectively based on people-centered values. The J/P scale represents two opposite behavioral styles—*Judging*, which is organized, purposeful and decisive; or *Perceiving*, which is unstructured, flexible and open-ended.

Extraverting (E), Introverting (I), Judging (J) and Perceiving (P) are the four *attitudes* we have toward life; Sensing (S), Intuiting (N), Thinking (T) and Feeling (F), the four *functions* by which we learn and decide. Because these eight terms are used around the world to refer to Jungian psychological types, I'll be using them throughout the book interchangeably with the capital letters that represent them.

DAVIS PERSONALITY SCALE (DPS)

I

I'm attracted to an inner world of enduring concepts and ideas. I seek clarity, enjoy solitude and work well alone. I tend to delve deeply into my interests.

E

I'm attracted to people, places and things. I'm outgoing, talkative, sociable and work well with others. I thrive on variety and action.

I: 15 . . . . 10 . . . . 5 . . . . 0 . . . . 5 . . . . 10 . . . . 15 :E

S

I'm attuned to the here and now and trust information gathered by my five senses. I am observant, practical, realistic, detail oriented, and put my faith in facts.

N

I am intrigued by patterns, theories and relationships, am impatient with routines and structure, and place belief in the future and its possibilities.

S: 15 . . . . 10 . . . . 5 . . . . 0 . . . . 5 . . . . 10 . . . . 15 :N

T

I tend to base my decisions on objective criteria and logical analysis. I am inclined to be critical of society's customs and beliefs. I excel at organizing ideas. I value competence.

F

I tend to base my decisions on my personal value system and the effect of my actions on others. I enjoy pleasing people. I value harmony.

T: 15 . . . . 10 . . . . 5 . . . . 0 . . . . 5 . . . . 10 . . . . 15 :F

J

I take an organized approach to life and like things decided. I'm inclined to be painstaking, industrious, orderly, persistent and cautious.

P

I take a flexible approach to living and like to keep options open. I tend to be spontaneous curious, tolerant, adaptable to change and chance taking.

J: 15 . . . . 10 . . . . 5 . . . . 0 . . . . 5 . . . . 10 . . . . 15 :P

Now, starting with the first pair of opposites, the I/E scale, and working in sequential order, write on the line below the capital letter signifying the higher score of each pair. You will then see your 4-letter type. (For example, INFP).

I consider myself to be an _____ .

Type and the Brain

Now let's look at the way that type mirrors brain function. This stylized model points up the distinctive nature of the two hemispheres:

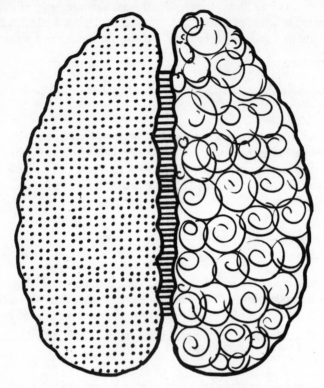

Adapted from *Left Brain, Right Brain* (1989).

The left has tight, vertical, nonoverlapping cells needed for fine motor movements; the right has horizontal, overlapping and more widely spaced cells needed for visual/spatial tasks. The left brain can be compared to a microscope that provides a closeup of the details — the parts; and the right brain compared to a telescope that provides a broad view of the possibilities — the whole. Whole-brain thinking integrates the part and the whole.

In the model on page 19, the eight sets of descriptive phrases identify major characteristics of our eight functions and attitudes. Their inherent polar-opposite relationship forms a kind of invisible X: Introverting and Thinking in the upper left cerebral cortex contrast with their opposites, Extraverting and Feeling in the lower right; similarly, Intuiting and Perceiving in the upper-right cerebral cortex contrast with Sensing and Judging in the lower left.

First read the two descriptive lists *vertically* to gain a sense of the distinctive nature of the two hemispheres: your literal, logical, sequential left brain, in contrast to the imaginative, visual, holistic right brain. Then, to better appreciate the antithetical nature of the four pairs — I/E, S/N, T/F and J/P, compare the descriptions of each pair by reading them alternately line by line.

THE FOUR ATTITUDES & FOUR FUNCTIONS
A SYMBOLIC BRAIN MODEL

The Left-Brain Microscope	The Right-Brain Telescope
Introverting (I)	**Perceiving (P)**
Private/reflective	Inquiring/flexible/open-ended
Focuses energy inward	Broad vision/approximate
Interest in concepts	Follows the flow
Develops ideas alone	Juggles multiple projects
Requires reflection time	Works spontaneously/needs freedom
Considers before answering	Mindless of time
Sets own standards	Energized at last minute
Seeks underlying principles	Resists closure
Thinking (T)	**Inuiting (N)**
Impersonal/objective/just	Imaginative/insightful/theoretical
Analytical/critical	Figurative/visual/abstract
Challenging/questioning why	Innovative/future oriented
Values clarity/coherence	Changing/radical
Logical/reasoned	Recognizes patterns
Detects discrepancies	Sees the big picture
Seeks meaning	Wonders "what if?"
Enjoys independence	Synthesizes
Cause/effect thinking	Random/amorphous
Sensing (S)	**Feeling (F)**
Realistic/practical/factual	Personal/subjective/humane
Literal/syntactic/concrete	Accepting/appreciative
Traditional/present oriented	Accommodating/agreeable
Consistent/conservative	Values empathy/compassion
Matches by function	Persuasive
Sees the small detail	Sees similarities
Makes statements	Seeks harmony
Breaks into parts	Enjoys affiliation
Sequential/structured	Value-based thinking
Judging (J)	**Extraverting (E)**
Organized/industrious/decisive	Sociable/active
Narrow focus/precise	Focuses energy outward
Follows a schedule	Interest in people/things
Deals with one thing at a time	Develops ideas in action
Works from lists/plans/goals	Plunges into experience
Time conscious	Readily offers opinions
Completes tasks early	Needs affirmation
Seeks closure	Avoids complex procedures

As this model suggests, you possess all these qualities which you use in varying degrees every day, both consciously and unconsciously. Taking the DPS you discovered that you tend to use one of each pair of opposites more than the other, thus creating your type/brain dominance profile. That profile can range from an all-left or all-right preference — ISTJ and ENFP respectively — to fourteen other types whose preferences are split between the two hemispheres. Now that you have a better understanding of what the letters I, E, S, N, T, F, J and P represent, I recommend that, before moving on, you look back at the DPS to see if you want to modify your ratings on any of the four scales. A slight shift in preference could change your type.

Visualizing Your Type and Cognitive Style

On page 21 are two models that enable you to visualize your mental process. The first shows how the eight attitudes and functions relate to general areas of the brain. The second illustrates the four cognitive styles: the cerebral dominant Intuitive/Thinker (NT), the right dominant Intuitive/Feeler (NF), the limbic dominant Sensing/Feeler (SF), and the left dominant Sensing/Thinking (ST). (The term "limbic" comes from the limbic system, the ancient part of the brain under the cerebral cortex).

When you feel confident about your DPS results, you're ready to envision your four-letter type and your two-letter cognitive style as they function in your brain. Shade in the four wedges representing your four favored attitudes and functions with a colored pen or pencil, leaving your four less-favored wedges blank; then shade in your cognitive style — NT, NF, SF or ST.

As we begin to discuss the creative process in terms of right- and left-brain function, you'll be better able to "picture" your individual thinking style at work.

WrapUp

Rest assured that every type can and does write successful songs. Though you share common characteristics with other members of your type, you are unique. And it is your uniqueness that you want to develop to the utmost.

Your Personality Type: _____

Your Cognitive Style: _____

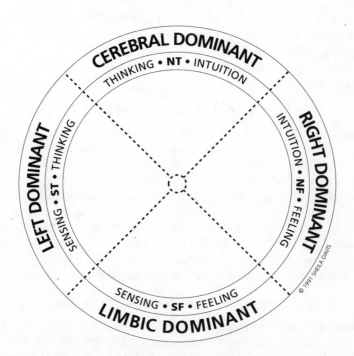

Tracking the Four-Step Creative Process

Experts in the burgeoning field known simply as *Creativity* suggest that it's a multi-step process. I've identified the four steps as *Associate, Incubate, Separate* and *Discriminate*. How we activate the songwriting process, and in what order we proceed, seems to be a matter of our type. Naturally, what counts is the destination: A whole-brain song. You can activate the process in either a right-mode or a left-mode way.

To *Activate* — The Right-Mode Way

We've all experienced that sudden insight that arrives unbidden while showering, walking, driving: Motion appears to put the right-brain into gear. Some songwriters choose to activate the process with such activities as free writing, doodling, or noodling at an instrument. This gives the storehouse of unconscious images and insights a chance to rise to the surface of the conscious mind.

It's as Randy Travis says, "I just pick up a guitar and sing till I hear something I like. . . ." Lyricist Billy Steinberg clearly values his unconscious, "I try to write without thinking. When you're on the phone, do you ever doodle on a pad and draw strange things that you aren't consciously thinking about? This is much like how I start my best song lyrics." Mike Stoller of the fabled team of Lieber and Stoller described the collaborators' approach, "It was like spontaneous combustion. . . . I would just play riffs [at the piano] and Jerry would shout lines, almost like automatic writing."

To Access the Right Mode: Be physically active. Noodle at an instrument. Doodle on a pad. Extravert: Verbally brainstorm. And honor the random.

To *Activate* — The Left-Mode Way

Other writers prefer to start the process with a concrete "part" and work from the part to the whole. Michael McDonald, for example, likes to rhythmically structure: "I usually write around a certain melodic rhythmic figure that is going to be the bottom theme of the song. Everything is an offshoot from that." Comedy writer Dave Frishberg finds his structuring element in a newfound title: "I start out with a title and premise and then try to map out the scheme of what will happen in the lyric. I plan how I will arrive at the punch line or the climactic lyric moment and then *construct* the lyric to make it happen." (emphasis mine)

To Access the Left Mode: Think "part." Narrow the options. Choose a title or motif or chord progression. Devise a structure. Work step by step.

To *Associate* — A Right-Mode Step

When the lyric concept or music motif has announced itself, unconsciously, or consciously, let it expand, that is, let it connect to other random thoughts and sounds. For example, Tom Waits says, "Sometimes I'll turn on the tape recorder and start playing, just making up words before I have any words. . . . I'll [even] do it in Spanish, anything that makes a sound. Then I'll listen to it and put words to it." That's free associating! Paul McCartney summed up the Beatle's right-brain process by admitting, "There's a lot of random in our songs . . . writing, thinking . . . then bang, you have the jigsaw puzzle."

To Access the *Associate* Mode: Be spontaneous. Brainstorm for related lyrical ideas and/or rhymes allowing words to connect without censure. Let your music flow freely. Resist closure.

To *Incubate*—A Right-Mode Step

Sometimes the first associations fail to fuse. Creativity can't be rushed. Your concept may simply need incubating time. This step in the process can be enhanced by meditation or movement: Veteran lyricist Mitchell ("Stardust") Parish told me, "Once I had the title, I'd walk around with it for a while to let it percolate." Richard Rodgers claimed, "I usually get the approach sitting in a chair or walking around outdoors. Then I'll do the tune on a piece of paper or at the piano."

My teaching experience has verified that many writers start to write too soon—especially J-types: In their hurry to come to closure, they may zip past this essential step. The first draft shows it: The lyric's all surface and no depth. Not enough time was taken to create a believable situation and develop a genuine character who feels a real emotion. We hear rhymes without reason. I encourage you to believe that the more time you spend incubating, the less time you'll spend revising.

To Access the *Incubate* Mode: Walk around with it. Imagine. Become the character. Feel what the singer's feeling. Sleep on it.

To *Separate*—A Left-Mode Step

After the initial "aha" and the whoosh of associated ideas comes the separating process, both musically and lyrically. After incubation, shift to the left-mode to structure ideas, determine the form, to *separate* into parts—verse/climb/chorus/bridge and so on. Stephen Sondheim consciously practices the separating process: "I write on legal pads in very small writing . . . I find it very useful to use a separate pad for each section of the song. "Then comes the winnowing down process of 'how much can this song take?' You can make points, A, B and C, but you don't have room for D, E and F. As you do that, you eliminate certain colors and it becomes more apparent what the song should be about."

Separating also embodies contrast: Cynthia Weil told me, "In a bridge I try to say something I haven't said before—taking the story one step further." Discussing musical form, Jimmy Webb suggests, "The chorus should always have a different melodic and chordal character than its verse . . . Sometimes it is advisable to modulate the end of a verse to a different key—often high—to set up the chorus. . . ."

To Access the *Separate* Mode: Break into parts. Contrast the parts. Sequence ideas. Put causes before effects. Solidify rhyme scheme and meter.

To *Discriminate* — A Left-Mode Step

And last comes *discrimination*, that essential of all art — making fine distinctions. By accessing our helpful critical editor, we can detect the flaw, prune the redundancy, revise the awkward phrase, and thus transform a mediocre first draft into a marvelous final. Johnny Mercer clearly enjoyed this part of the process, "I type dozens of alternative lines. And I look at these alternatives, and I gradually weed out the poor ones until I think I've got the best lyric I can get." Rupert Holmes asserts, "The biggest part of being a good lyricwriter is learning to be a good editor." John Prine agrees, "You don't write, you edit."

To Access the *Discriminate* Mode: Seek clarity. Unify the time frame, voice, viewpoint and tone. Distinguish figurative from literal. Perfect the syntax.

The Ongoing Process

That's just the first go 'round. Your song, of course, needs a response from an audience. Then, after some critical feedback, the revision process will again spiral through *discriminate/separate* and yet again, *incubate/discriminate* and on and on until you feel 100 percent satisfied that you've polished the lyric to its ultimate best.

WrapUp

As you begin to relate your process to your type, you may understand why you find some steps more enjoyable than others. (As do we all!) Perhaps you'll even want to try a different mode of activating a song. Though you may have a favorite "system," trying it another way will help you increase the creative flow.

How Your Type Influences Your Work Habits

Every aspect of your type influences your songwriting in some manner. Here we'll examine how your primary source of energy, E or I, affects the collaborative process and how your favored decision-making style, J or P, influences your work mode—when, how often, and maybe even how much you write. A few guidelines will suggest how to get the best out of your personal style.

Extraverts, Introverts and Collaboration

The Extraverted Style

Extraverts thrive on face-to-face collaborating because conversation (for them) stimulates the flow of ideas. E's often don't know what they think till they hear themselves say it. Siedah Garrett characterized the E preference when she admitted, "My reason for co-writing is that if I sat down in a room by myself, it would be quiet for a very long time!"

An E-Guideline: Try to structure your writing time so that it serves your energy needs. Voice-activated extraverts, for example, can benefit, when alone, from taping themselves talking aloud as they move around the house, or walk or drive, and the natural E-avesdropper would be wise to travel with a pocket pad for converting those overheard one-liners into hook choruses.

The Introverted Style

Introverts, on the other hand (or brain), do their best thinking in private: Dean Pitchford, in discussing his work habits with collaborator Tom Snow said, "Tom and I each happen to do our best work alone and we spend very little time together in a room."

Introverts—who in this country are outnumbered three to one—tend to feel shy about saying that they work better by themselves, as if it were a flaw. But, introversion, like red hair or black eyes, is a natural genetic alternative, not an anomaly.

An I-Guideline: So Introverts, honor the fact that you require, for your best writing, to write apart. Seek composers who similarly like to write a tune or set a lyric without any distractions. Respect your natural style and make it work for you as it works for Pitchford and Snow (and worked for Rodgers and Hammerstein).

The J/P Polarity and Personal Work Habits

Your preference for either the J or P style tends to predict how and when you write best. Time-oriented, routine-loving J's often set up a regular writing schedule. Fred Ebb—of the Broadway team of Kander and Ebb—said: "Johnny Kander and I work daily from ten to four. Even when we're not working on a specific project, we still work daily on whatever comes to mind." J's are often self-described "morning types": Alan Jay Lerner claimed, "I never begin a new song at any time of the day other than early morning."

The right-brain counterpart, P's, find schedules confining: Kim Carnes says, "I'm not a nine-to-five writer who can sit in a room and say, 'Hey, we're gonna write today!' " P's prefer spontaneity and flexibility and tend to work best in a last-minute burst of energy. Cole Porter (clearly an EP) said: "I have no hours. I can work anywhere. I've done lots of work at dinner sitting between two bores. I can feign listening beautifully and work. That's the reason I like to go out!"

A J/P Guideline: Remember there's no right or wrong or better way. Honor *your* way: Try to identify the pattern of your creative needs and arrange your work sessions—structured or spontaneous—for your optimum creative output.

Type and Writer's Blocks

Virtually all writers have experienced that frustrating moment when they can't find the right rhyme or line or chord. With luck, it passes quickly. Then there's another kind of extended fallow period when we fear we may never come up with another idea. Both are instances of that ancient bugaboo known as writer's block. But both can be avoided as you learn to sense when the right brain is the wrong brain—or the left brain is the right brain.

The Temporary Block: The Causes and Solutions

Too Narrow a Focus—A J-Mode Left-Brain Block: Because J's like to stay with a task until it's completed, they doggedly sweat out a block (and in the process make themselves miserable): Diane Warren confessed, "I'll have the whole song almost done and I'll need one line at the end of a bridge or something. Logically, I should just walk away and take a drive. . . . But I'm a masochist . . . I'll work three days on that one line and it drives me nuts!" If Diane had heeded her (right-brain's) message and headed for the freeway, she'd have probably gotten the needed line before reaching the corner—and had three days to write another three hits!

Similarly, Marty Panzer admitted to me how self-defeating it is to stay in a stuck place, "Sometimes I'll sit with pencil and paper in hand, and ten hours will go by and nothing will happen. And finally I go shave and while the radio is playing and my mind is on a hundred other things, the one line that I've been trying all day to get will come right to mind." That's how the resourceful unconscious works when given the chance.

The trick is to become aware of where in your brain you are. Whenever you get that stuck feeling, it means it's time to shake up the neurons a little: You've stayed too long in a left-mode close-up on a *part* when you need a wide-angle look at the *whole*. The flexible Ps take a more spontaneous approach when they feel blocked: Carole King suggests, "Get up and do something else. Then you come back again and trust that it [whatever's missing] will be there." "Trust" is the key. And that technique is called "bracketing."

Bracketing—A Right-Mode Incubating Solution: In bracketing, you say to your uncooperative left-brain, "I'll put a bracket around that [line], [chord], [rhyme]"— you name it—"I'll move on, and come back to it later." Bracketing suggests that you *trust* your process, that you *know* that the missing word or note awaits at a lower layer of consciousness, and that if you just relax, it'll eventually bubble to the surface. And that's exactly what it does. Smokey Robinson summed the P-bracketing approach, "If the song isn't flowing in the *right* direction, I'll just put it down; don't try to force it." (Italics mine, and pun intended).

Sleep on It — A Right-Mode Incubating Solution: Like bracketing, 'sleeping on it' can be considered a significant aspect of the right-brain incubating mode. It gives the creative process something essential that it needs. Sting, who as we know from his hit album, *Synchronicity,* is a follower of Jungian theory, commented, "Original ideas begin in the unconscious. . . . Our logical minds are in compartmented boxes, and those boxes are disturbed when one is asleep . . . and [when we're] not being logical, an idea can flow from one rigid box into another. . . ."

The extraordinary insights and creative inspirations that have emerged while the mind is presumably asleep have been well documented. Composer Burton Lane, in discussing the genesis of "When I'm Not Near the Girl I Love," told me, "I dreamed that tune." The previous day he'd been trying to come up with a melody to Yip Harburg's title, but had been unsuccessful: "A tune woke me up in the middle of the night . . . but I didn't connect the melody then with that title. And that wasn't the first time it's happened. Many times it will come out and I don't realize that it's a tune for the thing I've been thinking about!"

An Overload of Options: The Right-Mode Block

Just as intensive concentration on a problem can cause a left-brain jam, extensive openness to the possibilities can cause a right-brain overload. P-types often suffer from right-brain mental clutter (as evidenced by their paper-strewn desks and overstuffed files). Because they're adept at seeing alternative solutions, they sometimes find it difficult to sort through all their treatment options for a given lyric or melody and come to closure on one.

Organizing — The J-Mode Separating Solution: A P-mode overload requires a J-mode solution: A shift to the organizing area in the lower left brain for sorting out and winnowing down. It means spiraling back to the *Separate* process. So P's it's time to neaten your desk, answer your mail, alphabetize your files, weed out your ideas, narrow your options — and choose *one.*

A Different Kind of Type-Caused Block

Sometimes writers feel that their creative juices have simply dried up. This is another kind of block caused by an aspect of our dominant function. Each type seems to produce its own characteristic self-limiting injunction that cuts down on productivity: The intuitive can get blocked by a need to be original; the feeling type by an excessive fear of boring or not pleasing an audience; the sensate by an overzealous focus on the mechanics of writing and doing it "right"; and the thinker by a goal to come up with an important or "great" song. Becoming aware of your own self-critical inner voice can help you to purposefully countermand it. Why not stop reading for a few minutes to think about any unfinished songs you may have. Can you identify why you haven't finished them? Mull it over. Then think of some recent top-ten records that you consider unoriginal, boring, imperfect, and less than "important" songs. Might it be worthwhile to give your unfinished lyrics another look? Possibly they've had all the incubating time they need and are now ready to be brought to life.

Filling the Well

Every outpouring requires an inpouring: The creative well needs to be filled up periodically in order to have something to draw from at writing time. A few sources of replenishment include reading good literature and poetry; going to films, theater and museums; and, of course, listening to a wide range of musical and lyrical styles. Consider, too, that taking a walk, watching TV, and chatting on the phone are not "goofing off," but rather a necessary (incubating) break in the creative process.

Honor your favorite way to fill the well, or try a new one. Yip Harburg said, "I do something physical—walk, hit a golf ball around, go to the zoo. . . ." Franne Golde suggests, "Go see friends, read the newspaper, go to the beach. You got to feed yourself." Valerie Simpson offers a thought you might want to pin on your wall: "If you don't try to force it, a song will find the proper moment to come to life." Exactly.

WrapUp

Here's a brain model that helps you picture the four modes of the creative process—*associate, incubate, separate, discriminate*—and suggests some ways to access each. (You'll find detailed descriptions of the right-brain techniques on pages 32-34.)

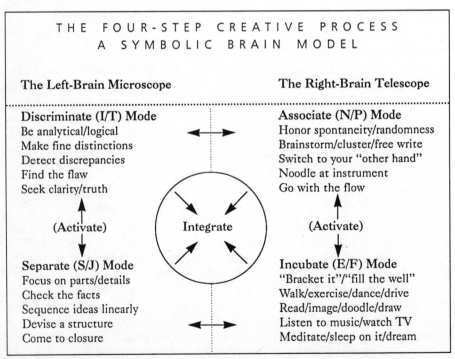

THE FOUR-STEP CREATIVE PROCESS
A SYMBOLIC BRAIN MODEL

The Left-Brain Microscope   **The Right-Brain Telescope**

Discriminate (I/T) Mode   **Associate (N/P) Mode**
Be analytical/logical   Honor spontaneity/randomness
Make fine distinctions   Brainstorm/cluster/free write
Detect discrepancies   Switch to your "other hand"
Find the flaw   Noodle at instrument
Seek clarity/truth   Go with the flow

(Activate)   Integrate   (Activate)

Separate (S/J) Mode   **Incubate (E/F) Mode**
Focus on parts/details   "Bracket it"/"fill the well"
Check the facts   Walk/exercise/dance/drive
Sequence ideas linearly   Read/image/doodle/draw
Devise a structure   Listen to music/watch TV
Come to closure   Meditate/sleep on it/dream

© 1991 Sheila Davis

How Your Type Shapes Your Lyrics

Just as your favored attitudes (introversion or extraversion) tend to shape your work style, so do your favored functions (sensing or intuition and thinking or feeling) tend to shape your language style. Here are the major ways in which the functions combine to effect a first draft—along with some helpful hints on how to revise the flaws—or better yet, to avoid them. As you might surmise, the revision generally requires tapping the function that is the polar opposite to your favorite.

The Sensing Style

Common Characteristics: Because sensates are here-and-now realists with acute powers of observation, their lyrics often embody names, numbers and places ("Do You Know the Way to San Jose?"/"99 Miles From LA"); are set in the present tense ("Piano Man"); and are made memorable with small concrete details ("Chestnuts roasting on an open fire").

The Sensate/Thinker (ST) tends to write from an objective distance with a clearly structured beginning, middle and end ("It Was a Very Good Year"). STJs often exhibit a dry wit and satiric flair ("It Ain't Necessarily So"). The Sensate/ Feeler (SF), more than any other type, is given to story songs ("16th Avenue"/ "Taxi"). Conservative SFJs tend to express society's traditional values ("Easter Parade"/"God Bless America").

Potential Problems and Solutions: Because sensates like to do things "the right way" and believe "rules" were made to be followed, some may adhere too strictly to their chosen rhyme scheme, rhythm pattern and song form, producing a possible singsong monotony. Regarding rhythm, S-types benefit from a reminder that songs are made up of sound *and silence:* cutting out padded words like *just, very, really* will create more space for holding notes; rhythmic monotony can also be eliminated by consciously varying the meter from verse to chorus to bridge. The "telegraphing" of a rhyme can be avoided with a little purposeful delay. (*SLW,* pages 103-121, provides detailed guidelines and exercises on rhythm and rhyme.)

The Sensate's emphasis on "itemizing facts" can result in a lyric that lacks a clear emotion, point or meaning. For the revision, Sensates will need to access their intuitive perception with its knack for seeing possibilities. An SFJs second draft often needs to explain the implication of a plot that contains a series of factual details without a clear *point.* Sensates, just ask yourself, "What does my song *mean?* What message do I want to send? With what universal situation do I want the listener to identify?"

The Intuitive Style

Common Characteristics: Intuitives are imaginative, future-oriented, hopeful thinkers whose language is usually more abstract than concrete ("Imagine"), who like to pursue the possibilities beyond the reach of the senses ("Over the Rainbow"), and are attracted to fantasy ("Yellow Submarine").

Intuitive/Feelers (NFs) are considered the most "poetic" (metaphoric) of the types. Their lyrics often feature "confessional" revelations ("I'd Rather Leave While I'm in Love"). Idealistic INFJs often write songs that inspire others ("You'll Never Walk Alone"/"Climb Every Mountain").

Intuitive/Thinkers (NTs) are given to asking questions rather than making statements ("What Are You Doing the Rest of Your Life?") NTs are inclined to see the ironic aspect of a situation ("Send in the Clowns") and to be critical of society's mores ("Who Will Answer").

Potential Problems and Solutions: Because intuitives (Ns) think in insightful leaps rather than in a step-by-step process, their lyrics may lack a linear ordering of events and omit important plot details. These factors can combine to make their first drafts difficult to follow. NF plots often suffer from a blurring of multiple emotions—where the singer's feelings from both "then" and "now" have not been differentiated. Drafts of ENFPs—whose four dominants all reside in the right (holistic) brain—may especially lack clarity because of the use of fused literal/figurative language, mixed viewpoint or voice, and poor sequencing of ideas. (The right-brain doesn't own a watch!)

Intuitive/feelers will need to spend some time using the left-brain's linear, structured, realistic, sequencing abilities. The NF will benefit from asking herself such questions as 1) Is the singer male or female? 2) Is she or he talking or thinking? 3) Is the singee present? 4) Where exactly are they? 5) *What one single emotion does the singer feel?* 6) Do I mean "rain" literally or figuratively (as "trouble")?

Having to focus on small details and think analytically can prove stressful to NFs, but this step in the process is necessary to make their lyrical insights and feelings understood and appreciated.

How the I/E and J/P Preferences Affect Lyric Content

I/E and J/P attitudes not only affect the collaborative process and work habits, they also influence the lyric's style and content.

The I/E Effect: Extraverted lyricists tend to write about interpersonal situations and use the talking voice as though the "you" were present ("Big Shot"/"Come in From the Rain"). Introverts are inclined to be more reflective and prefer the thinking voice ("Yesterday"/"Gentle On My Mind").

The J/P Effect: The laid-back, "we'll see" attitude of the Intuitive/Perceptive style is reflected in the lyrics by frequent use of words such as *if, maybe, perhaps, someday*. Occasionally, a first draft may have the singer indecisive with the listener left wondering, "And so . . . what's the conclusion?" So N/Ps will then need to give the lyric a clearer, more forceful ending.

Conversely, the lyrics of Js, who like to live by a set of systems, may be studded with words like *never, always, should, don't, must*, and so on. SJs especially need to be mindful that their fondness for absolutes might render first drafts negative, or dogmatic or preachy. For example, the first draft of an ISTJ (who can be pessimistic) may end up with an overly defeatist conclusion, like "I'll *never* get over you." So Js, bear in mind that listeners are more drawn to a character struggling to overcome adversity—as in "I'm *trying* to get over you"—than to one who's given in to despondency.

ESFJs can have a tendency to exaggerate emotions—confusing overstatement with depth of feeling. They may also create "stereotypes" rather than believable characters. The cure: Spending more time in the introverting/intuiting mode to ponder what a real human being would feel and say and do in the plot situation. This will result in a more credible revision.

WrapUp

The post-first-draft challenge to all: Clarify amorphous emotions, augment sensate facts with insightful meaning, put events in linear order, come to a clear conclusion, and avoid preachiness. As the role-model lyrics will make evident, every type has the ability to do just that and thus turn out successful final drafts.

Right-Brain, Left-Brain Techniques: Defining Our Terms

In the upcoming strategies, you'll practice various right- and left-brain exercises and techniques designed to help you switch hemispheres at will. Here we'll define the most significant brain shifters.

Right-Brain Shifters to Access "The Whole"

Free Associating/Brainstorming

These two terms are virtually synonymous. Essentially, they draw upon the right-brain's ability to see similarities and to make the odd connection. Finding the unsuspected link has been called the key to creativity. A quality that facilitates random discovery is a spirit of playfulness, a willingness to "goof around." Brainstorming requires suspending our left-brain editor in order to let the right brain do its thing—free associate. So we'll be goofing around.

Imaging

The ability to image plays a significant role in the process of creativity. Many creative thinkers have held that images form the matrix of thought. Although people differ greatly in their ability to produce images, the skill can be facilitated by solitude and relaxation—and baroque music. (More on that soon.) Accessing the right-brain's images and then putting them into words helps bridge the two hemispheres. Research studies have provided extensive evidence to support the theory that developing the skill of producing mental pictures develops mind/brain power.

Clustering

Clustering is a right-brain prewriting technique popularized by Gabriele Lusser Rico in her important book *Writing the Natural Way*. I recommend clustering as a way to generate ideas that reflect your true concerns. Clustering is a form of brainstorming on paper—letting uncensored ideas radiate from a central "nucleus" word or phrase. Through free association, it draws upon random thoughts and stored experiences. (For a picture of the process and examples of the results, see *SLW*, pages 124-127.)

Free Writing

The process of free writing enables an uninhibited right-brain flow of thoughts by requiring the pen or pencil to stay on the paper without the inhibiting "lift-up pause" caused by analytical thinking. By keeping your writing instrument moving, the mind can—for a two- or three-minute period—let randomness take the initial thought wherever it might want to go. This technique can prove useful in providing spontaneous associated ideas on your song topic before you actually start the lyricwriting process.

Other-Hand Writing

In *The Power of Your Other Hand*, author/artist Lucia Cappacionne offers an effective means to access the unconscious level. In the coming strategies, I will occasionally suggest that when stuck for a line or a phrase, you transfer your pen or pencil from your dominant (writing) hand to your nondominant hand. Your writing may look messy, but the potential discoveries that can result more than compensate. Since brain researchers have suggested that we enhance our ability to crisscross the hemispheres through ambidextrous activities, using your "other hand" may yield additional dividends.

Left-Brain Shifters to Access "The Part"

Systematize/Compartmentalize

To access your step-by-step organizational S/J mode: Make lists, organize your lyrics in alphabetical or chronological order, review your agenda, schedule appointments. In other words, break elements/problems into their component parts and think sequentially.

If you're working on a new lyric, examine each section and ask yourself: 1) What information does the first verse convey? 2) Does the second verse say something new? 3) Does the bridge use a strong contrast device and add more new information? 4) Does the title summarize the essence of the lyric?

Analyze/Criticize

To produce a whole-brain lyric, the final step, *Discriminate*, is arguably the most important. Developing your thinking function requires sharpening your critical faculties: the ability to discriminate between literal and figurative, to identify a mixed metaphor and unmix it, to recognize and weed out redundancies, to revise poor syntax.

A good way to get yourself into the Introverted/Thinking I/T mode is to analyze a hit lyric. Choose one from a favorite cassette or CD. But because listening to music engages the *right* brain, which for analysis is the *wrong* hemisphere, don't play the record: *Read* the lyric. This is not the time for *feeling* (reacting to whether you like or dislike the lyric) but for *thinking*—being objective and analytical. Using the first chapter's "Digest of Writing Theory" as a checklist, try to identify such elements as the song form, the viewpoint, the development device, the types of rhyme used. Be critical and discriminating. (Simply because a lyric's been recorded doesn't make it whole-brained.) Are there any inconsistencies in viewpoint, time frame or setting? Are there any dangling participles? It's a rare lyric that couldn't have been improved with a little more analytical thinking.

Write Small

Many Is and Js write small, carefully formed letters; it reflects the tighter nonoverlapping connections of the left-brain cells. Conversely, the handwriting of perceptives and extraverts tends to be larger and looser, reflecting the right-brain cellular connection that's more widely spaced and overlapping. Thus a concerted effort to write small, neat letters engages the concentrated and focused abilities of the left hemisphere. Remember this technique when you're feeling unfocused or "spacey."

Preconditions for Creativity

The Mind/Body Connection

Each stage of creativity requires that the mind be in a suitably receptive mental state. To achieve that state requires that the body be in good physical shape. In addition to the value of periodic exercise, research studies have discovered our basic need to take a break in activity every 90 to 120 minutes. For optimum mental performance, we need to honor that need. So be alert to your body's signals—inattention, hunger, fatigue. A good rule of thumb: When you're nervous, meditate; when you're hungry, eat; when you're tired, nap.

The Power of Music: Go for Baroque

One of the major ways to promote relaxation and improve concentration is through baroque music—a technique now widely used in American classrooms thanks to the pioneering research of Bulgarian educator Georgi Lozanov. Research experiments have verified that 20 percent more subject matter can be covered in the same amount of time with longer retention when largo (slow) movements of baroque works are played in the background! Largo/adagio music has a tempo of about 60 beats per minute (BPMs), and because it tends to sync up with the heartbeat, produces an alpha state, the most conducive for centered thinking.

Record stores now feature baroque/adagio or baroque/largo cassettes with such popular selections as Albinoni's Adagio, Pachelbel's Canon and Bach's Air for the G String—three selections that top the baroque Top 40. To help promote a state of heightened awareness for better absorption and retention, I recommend that as you read this book you play baroque music in the background. The goal is centeredness—a readiness to alternately *per*ceive and *con*ceive and thus integrate the part and the whole.

Pen/Pencil and Paper or PC

Although in the upcoming exercises I may make more references to pencil and paper than to a PC keyboard, a computer will serve equally well—if not better. Keep that in mind if your MO is PC. I've found that the ability to quickly scroll, delete, block and relocate enhances my whole creative process—whether priming rhymes for a lyric, planning a seminar, or editing a book. The reduction in paper clutter alone has been a definite plus of keyboard creativity.

WrapUp

You may now feel a desire to put down the book for a bit (especially if you're an E). If so, take a break—if only to stare into space. Or, you might want to get more familiar with those four steps in the creative process—*associate, incubate, separate, discriminate*—and decide to reread this section with some Bach in the background. Be attuned to the message from your mind/body, and honor it. And whenever you're ready for the first strategy, turn the page.

PART THREE

Title Strategies: A Key Word

Coming up with a fresh title has been long considered a smart way to start a song. Irving Berlin claimed that "The public buys songs, not because it knows the *song*, but because it knows and likes the title idea." Sting says, "I write titles and work backwards from there." Jimmy Webb agrees: "I almost *have* to do it that way."

The first six of the twelve title strategies reflect the principle of *specificity*: To pick the particular over the general and the concrete over the abstract. My analysis of the title features of standards—the most enduring and memorable songs—yielded an interesting fact: The titles often contained some key word that produced an image in the mind—a color, a place, a name, a date.

These first six strategies will encourage you to develop the skill of writing in concrete language. Translated into type/brain talk, it will require that you use your left-brain sensing function to think in specifics—details (parts) rather than in generalities (wholes)—which may or may not come easily, depending upon whether your preference is for sensing or intuiting. You'll soon see.

A Color Title

The Purpose

The purpose is twofold: To help you think in concrete images rather than in abstractions and to utilize a time-honored device with built-in memorability that makes for a distinctive title.

Some Color Titles

Yellow Taxi	Purple Rain
Green Tambourine	Nights in White Satin
Pink Cadillac	My Old Yellow Car
Goodbye Yellow Brick Road	Little Green Apples
Deep Purple	Blue Suede Shoes
Purple People Eater	Yellow Submarine
Black or White	Little Red Corvette
Cherry Pink and Apple Blossom	It's Not Easy Being Green
White	The Lady in Red
Tie a Yellow Ribbon 'Round the Ole	Black Denim Trousers and
Oak Tree	Motorcycle Boots

Prewriting Suggestions

You might start with a slow walk around your home, noticing familiar objects from a new perspective. Think small: *teapot, wallclock, matchbook.* . . . If that doesn't yield something, try the same narrow-focus approach while taking a walk or shopping. Or you might find a title by free associating. On an unlined piece of paper, cluster from one color at a time. Let random ideas radiate from that color until you get that "Aha!" feeling. That'll mean you've hit upon a phrase that evokes from you a genuine emotion to support your title.

Now the question is: Who is saying the title to whom, and why. You'll need to create a mini-scenario—a situation you believe in with a character with whom you can identify.

Small Craft Warning

Challenge yourself to avoid the cliché of *blue/blues* used as a metaphor for *sad*— that is unless you can create a title as distinctive as "A Pink Cocktail for a Blue Lady," or "Don't It Make My Brown Eyes Blue." If you're hooked on blue, try to use it literally as the hue, rather than figuratively as the feeling. In Part V you'll have lots of opportunity to exercise your skills in figurative language.

Color Title: Example No. 1 (AABA)
BLACK AND WHITE MOVIE

Give me a BLACK AND WHITE MOVIE
Where you know what's what.

The good guys get love,
The bad guys get shot,
The rich girl's cold,
The poor girl's not.
Don't want to give away the plot
But it's different as the day from night
When the movie's made in black and white.

Give me a BLACK AND WHITE MOVIE
Where the tough girls sin,
The hero's brave as Errol Flynn,
The villain sneers
A leering grin,
And you always know who's gonna win.
It's easy telling wrong from right
When the movie's made in black and white.

It's not that I don't like pictures
In every tint and hue.
(It's not that I have any strictures
Against red or green or blue.)
But I hate all those shades of meaning—
That psycho-significant stuff
That comes with each full-color screening:
Life is complicated enough!

Give me a BLACK AND WHITE MOVIE
Where the sweet girls smile
But don't give in
Till they walk down the aisle:
The music swells in movie style,
The bridesmaids stride in double file
The groom wears black. The bride wears white
And everything turns out all right
When the movie's made in black and white.

By Francesca Blumenthal
© 1988 Quentin Road Music. Used with Permission.

▲ Comment

Developing the title's pair of opposites, the writer unites the lyric with a series of antitheses: bad/good, rich/poor, hero/villain and so on. "Black and White Movie," which resulted from a class assignment, became the linchpin concept of the writer's award-winning cabaret revue "Life Is Not Like the Movies." Like all convincing lyrics, the emotion expressed reflects the writer's ideology: Francesca Blumenthal is enamored of black and white movies which is how she could write a sixteen-song revue around the theme.

Color Title: Example No. 2 (AAA)
GREEN STATELY MANSIONS

Lord, do you see me
Walkin' down this long and lonely road?
Lord, do you hear me
Cryin' out to you to ease my load?
Lord, reassure me
That you're there, and some day I will find
The GREEN STATELY MANSIONS
That I see shining in my mind.

Lord, don't you know me?
Can it be I'm nothing in your eyes.
Lord, won't you show me
That my name's engraved upon the skies.
Lord reassure me
That you're there, and someday I will find
The GREEN STATELY MANSIONS
That I see shining in my mind.

I've been a loser
At the games that people need to play,
Tho' I'm a loser
I have kept my faith along the way.
So Lord, reassure me
That you're there, and someday I will find
The GREEN STATELY MANSIONS
That I see shining in my mind.

© 1980 May Caffrey. Used with permission.

▲ Comment
This lyric emerged from the writer's clustering from the word "green." The process produced the words, *Green Pastures* (the title of a 1930 Pulitzer Prize-winning play with a Biblical theme), which led to the thought *More Stately Mansions* (a novel), which led to the fusion of the two, "Green Stately Mansions." The appropriate AAA form was set to appropriately hymnlike music; the result, a new Christian song.

WrapUp
Two more color titles—"My Brown-Skin Baby" and "Red and Green Season Again"—act as role-model lyrics for other devices. You may want to check them out now (in the index, pages 243-244) for additional treatment ideas. In case your initial color hunt nets nothing, remember *Roget's Thesaurus*; it lists dozens of exotic tints to blend into a title: Perhaps you'll find an intriguing shade of meaning in *hazel, khaki, chestnut, terra cotta, marigold, Oxford grey, Kelly green....*

A City, State or Foreign Place Title

The Purpose

Like color titles, place titles exert the appeal of the concrete and specific. And of course it's the specific (rather than the general) that leads to the universal.

Some State Titles	Some City Titles
Alabamy Bound	New York State of Mind
Moonlight in Vermont	Amarillo by Morning
Deep in the Heart of Texas	By the Time I Get to Phoenix
California, Here I Come	Way Down Yonder in New Orleans
The Jersey Bounce	Shuffle Off to Buffalo
Carolina in the Morning	Galveston
Massachusetts	Hooray for Hollywood
Louisiana Hayride	99 Miles From LA
California Dreamin'	Moon Over Miami
Midnight Train to Georgia	St. Louis Blues

Some Foreign Titles	
Come Back to Sorrento	April in Portugal
April in Paris	Brazil
On the Isle of Capri	A Rainy Night in Rio

The Strategy's Advantage

It's a funny thing about "place" song titles: They often endure. Many have gone on to become the official or semi-official city or state anthem: "New York, New York," "California, Here I Come," "Georgia on My Mind," "I Left My Heart in San Francisco," "Oklahoma!" — to name a few.

Prewriting Suggestions

The plot of most place songs seems to break down into three major categories: remembering the place with either joy ("Moonlight in Vermont") or regret ("Galveston"); heading to, or back to, the place ("New York, New York," "California, Here I Come"); and singing its praises ("Chicago"). One way to go about the title hunt would be to pick one of those plot lines and work from there. Another would be to get out an atlas and choose a place that hasn't be over-musicalized and perhaps link the name alliteratively; for example, "Nantucket Nights," or "Meet Me in Monterey" — you get the idea. Then decide who is doing what there and why.

The role-model songs show the diversity of style that this simple title device can evoke; the first, a country song and the second, a cabaret song.

Place Title: Example No. 1 (Verse/Chorus)

IT'S HARD TO FIND A NAPKIN IN NASHVILLE

I was new in Nashville, fresh from New York City,
A Yankee boy on my first day down South,
Munchin' fried potatoes, grits and grilled tomatoes
Needin' something fast to wipe my mouth.

The napkin holder next to me was empty.
I asked the waitress, "Please bring two or three."
She came back ten minutes later (I'd almost grown to hate her)
And she stood there empty-handed tellin' me:

"IT'S HARD TO FIND A NAPKIN IN NASHVILLE.
Songwriters use 'em all for writing songs.
If we come across A NAPKIN IN NASHVILLE,
'Fore we use it, first we try to sing along."

I scowled as I headed for the pay phone.
She giggled as the grits dripped from my chin.
I looked through the yellow pages, (seemed to take me ages),
Found the number, and thank God someone was in. He said:

"Restaurant and Hotel Supply of Nashville.
What can we do for you on this fair morn?" I said,
"I can't believe what's happ'nin'; I just gotta find a napkin.
Never needed one so bad since I was born." He said:

"IT'S HARD TO FIND A NAPKIN IN NASHVILLE.
Songwriters use 'em all for writin' songs.
If you come across A NAPKIN IN NASHVILLE,
'Fore you use it, you should try to sing along."

"No, no, you'll never FIND A NAPKIN IN NASHVILLE,"
Yelled the crowd that gathered 'round me as I talked.
"Don't go lookin' for no NAPKINS IN NASHVILLE
If you want 'em, Yankee, bring 'em from New York."

© 1985 Dr. Joe Waldbaum. Used With permission.

▲ Comment

As a sensate/thinker, Dr. Joe quite naturally emphasizes the parts rather than the whole as in the time frame *(this fair morn)*; the name *(Restaurant and Hotel Supply of Nashville)*; the number *(ten minutes)*; and in such sensate images as *fried tomatoes, napkin holder, pay phone, yellow pages* and *grits dripped from my chin.* By overstating the songwriting myth that lyrics are often written on napkins (match-covers and envelopes), Dr. Joe drew upon his natural (STJ) tendency to satirize. It was clear to the workshop group when he read the first draft of "Napkins" that Joe Waldbaum had a special style and that the song was going to "happen." It turned out to be the first of a group of satirical country songs that gave the Manhattan podiatrist the hope that he could become the singer-songwriter that he has now become. At this writing, Dr. Joe has sold his practice, bought a van, and is singing and strumming his way across the country.

Place Title: Example No. 2 (AABA Variant)
ACAPULCO

(This is sung in a calypso rhythm by a woman of a certain age.)
I took a trip to ACAPULCO,
Found a deal in some brochure.
Then it rained in ACAPULCO
So I signed up for a tour.
I thought, 'This is gonna bore us,'
As we lined up for the ride.
There was this fellow waiting for us,
"*Buenas días,* I'm your guide."

The other tourists all were members
Of some ladies sisterhood.
They'd seen a whole lot of Decembers
Next to them I looked damned good!
So, as we drove out of the city
This deep voice by my side
Said, "Senorita, you're so pretty,
Let me be your guide."

Climbing up some ruins
(I think it was in Yucatan)
He described those Aztec doin's;
I felt faint and grabbed his hand.
The other ladies far below us
Look as small as mice
Just when our guide was gonna show us
Rites of maiden sacrifice.

So he led me to the altar
Beneath a blazing Aztec Sun.
I thought, this is no time to falter,
It's not as if you were a nun!
He continued with his story
As he stretched out by my side.
I said, "I know *this* territory,
Let *me* be *your* guide."

Now I'm back from ACAPULCO;
My accounts are in arrears.
But I brought home from ACAPULCO
Several stunning souvenirs.

Didn't buy a big sombrero
In fact, I hardly spent a dime.
(The very thought of shopping
Seemed an awful waste of time.)

But I've a tan without one strap mark
And a sultry golden glow
And a tattoo on my shoulder
Reading "Made in Mexico."
I'll buy some baskets in Azuma
And some bowls on the West Side.
I made a trade with Montezuma
And brought home my guide!

▲ Comment

Though Francesca shares with Dr. Joe a preference for the sensation function, hers is linked to her preference for feeling as opposed to his for thinking. So romance sets the tone here, rather than satire. Like most of Francesca's lyrics, this one has been added to the repertoire of a number of cabaret singers. Because it was written expressly for a sophisticated Manhattan audience, the lyric can indulge itself in such "localisms" as *Azuma* (a chain of New York stores featuring imported housewares and apparel) and *the West Side*, another allusion to Manhattan. If your target marketplace however is national (pop), be careful to avoid allusions to local places or people that a broad audience would find unfamiliar and thus miss your intended meaning.

WrapUp

There may be no place like home, but the place that you're going to, or the place you've been to, or the place you've only fantasized about may make a far more entertaining subject for a song.

A Day, Month or Number Title

The Purpose

This strategy draws again upon the appeal of the specific. As you've just seen in two role-model lyrics, specificity comes naturally to the sensate writer. So, if you're an intuitive, you may need to work a little harder to think in such concrete details as names and numbers. Some suggestions on how to go about it are coming up. First, here are some well-known songs that feature three common specifics:

Some Day Titles	Some Month Titles
Sunday Kind of Love	June in January
Saturday Night Fever	I'll Remember April
Sunday, Monday and Always	April in Portugal
Monday, Monday	June Is Bustin' Out All Over
Rainy Days and Mondays	April Showers
Ruby Tuesday	Come September
Friday's Child	See You in September
Come Saturday Morning	September in the Rain

Some Number Titles	
One Less Bell to Answer	Heaven on the Seventh Floor
Tea for Two	Riot in Cell Block Number Nine
Two for the Road	Sixteen Tons
Knock Three Times	Eighteen Yellow Roses
Three Times a Lady	50 Ways to Leave Your Lover
Three Coins in the Fountain	When I'm Sixty-four
Five Minutes More	Seventy-six Trombones
Sweet Little Sixteen	Down in the Depths on the 90th
At Seventeen	Floor
Pennsylvania 6-5000	Try 100 Ways
Flight 309 to Tennessee	

Prewriting Suggestions

Because these three strategies all embody a similar type of literal term, they can all be approached by the brainstorming process. For example, you could begin by writing down in the middle of a blank page a day or month that hasn't produced a well-known song and see what connections you make. Just as with place names, alliteration links well to days/months ("Mine Till Monday," "See You in September"). Remember in the brainstorming process anything goes: Don't edit any idea before it has a chance to hit the page.

Regarding numbers, it might prove fruitful to think of categories that contain numbers; for example, addresses, phone numbers, ID's, license plates, ages, and so on. You're limited only by self-imposed restrictions on your imagination.

Guideline

As always, your title needs to be fused to a genuine emotion and a genuine character who feels something that an audience will respond to.

Example No. 1: A Day Title (AAA)
SUNDAY MORNING LOVE

As I lie here watching you sleep
And I wait for you to open your eyes,
I wonder if my fabulous Saturday night
Will end with Sunday goodbyes.
I hope you wake up thinking
The same thing I'm thinking of—
SUNDAY MORNING LOVE.

I know you enjoyed the dinner I made—
And that second bottle of wine.
And you seemed to feel what I was feeling
When our feelings started to climb.
So I hope you wake up thinking
The same thing I'm thinking of—
SUNDAY MORNING LOVE.

Or was it only another Saturday fling,
That you're gonna quickly forget.
Or has something very special begun?
There's no way of telling yet.
If only you wake up thinking
The same thing I'm thinking of—
Then maybe week after week
After month after year we'll make
SUNDAY MORNING LOVE.

© 1990 Richard W. Lippman. Used with permission.

▲ Comment

This lyric evolved from Exercise 12, page 59, in *SLW*. The choice in that exercise was to revise its muddled thinking/talking voice or to write an entirely new lyric based on the same plot line—the morning after. The writer chose to start from scratch and use the thinking voice. It's interesting that in his treatment, Richard Lippman, a sensate/thinking (ST) writer, left behind the abstract title "Let Me Pretend" written by an intuitive/feeling (NF) writer and chose to express the morning-after situation in concrete terms, "Sunday Morning Love."

Example No. 2: A Number Title (Verse/Chorus)
EIGHT

The workin' week is over,
Yeah, it's finally done.
Been longin' for the weekend
And it's finally come.

Friday night is our night, baby.
Now that it's near,
I'm countin' down the hours
Till the moment you're here.

I can see you gettin' ready,
See you tiein' your tie.
See you buttonin' your buttons,
See you zippin' your fly.
I can almost smell you comin'
With that sweet ol' cologne.
I know you're gonna be here
And you know I'll be home
I'll be here waitin',
Anticipatin'

'Cause when it's EIGHT
You'll come flyin' through the gate
I don't think that I could wait
Another minute for you.
Exactly EIGHT.
Thank the Lord, you're never late!
'Cause if you were ever late
I don't know what I would do.

Time is really movin'
And I'm watchin' the clock
'Cause I gotta be ready
For the moment you knock.
Gotta iron my dress —
It's ten after four!
(I gotta look good
When I open the door!)

Time for a shower
It's gettin' near five.
Ooh, I'm so excited
Yeah, I'm feelin' alive.
Lord, it's six!: T minus two.
Got my makeup and my hair
and my nails still to do!
It's half past seven
And I'm in heaven!

(repeat chorus)

It's 7:56, You couldn't be far.
It's 7:57, Ooh, there's your car!
It's 7:58, I see you park!
It's 7:59, And here you are!

It's EIGHT
And you're flyin' through the gate
Ooooh, I couldn't wait
Another minute for you.
Exactly EIGHT!
Thank the Lord, you're never late!
'Cause if *you* were ever late,
I don't know what I would do!

▲ Comment

Here's a writer who understands that a song needs only one simple idea—in this case, anticipation. This lyric points up an often ignored fine point of lyricwriting: Make sure every repeat of the initial chorus reflects plot developments. In "Eight," time moves. The third chorus, which is sung after the bridge says it's 7:59; it could no longer say, *"You'll come flyin'* through the gate." He *is* flyin' through the gate! Give your first drafts a critical look to be sure that the statements made by the chorus reflect the developments of your previous verse or bridge.

Although Regine Urbach is a right-dominant intuitive/feeling writer who generally leans toward metaphoric language (see "Oceans of Love," page 88), in this lyric she purposefully accessed her sensing function to produce a more literal and concrete style of writing, something she had challenged herself to do. "Eight" illustrates that, although we have a dominant style, we're capable of great versatility. It's simply a matter of purposefully accessing the qualities in those specific brain areas which we usually tend to bypass.

WrapUp

Remember, if the suggestions for a particular strategy don't produce instant results, that's okay. Never let yourself get stressed with any of those J-produced *oughta/gotta/shoulda* blocks. Trust your process. When the idea is ready to emerge, it will.

A Female Name Title

The Purpose

We're still working on title memorability through specificity. Of all the ways to be specific, using a woman's name in a title seems to be the one songwriters have chosen the most in every genre—pop, rock, country and theater.

Some Female Name Titles

Angie, Baby	Laura
Candy	Sweet Lorraine
Delilah	Lucille
Dinah	Lulu's Back in Town
Dolores	Mimi
Hello, Dolly	Motorcycle Irene
Sweet Georgia Brown	Nola
Gigi	Rosanna
Gloria	When Sunny Gets Blue
Hard-Hearted Hannah	Suzanne
Sweet Caroline	Sweet Sue

The distaff roster points up both sides of the picture—the paeans to femininity, "Sweet Sue," "Candy" and "Laura," and their flip side—the portraits of the *femmes fatales*, "Hard-Hearted Hannah" and "Delilah"—women who do men right and women who do men in. Pick your plot.

Prewriting Suggestions

The straightforward song of praise—in the "Mimi" tradition—might be considered a bit too simplistic for our complex time—unless of course it's done with unusual freshness and style. Laura Branigan's '80s hit "Gloria" had an edge to it—telling off the singee. That's an approach, naming your singee to draw a picture of a particular kind of person.

Consider viewpoint as a design device: You might want to treat your title as the one being addressed (in second-person) as in "Georgy Girl," or the one talked about (in third person) as in "Lulu's Back in Town." Still another approach would be to pick a vogue name that hasn't yet been immortalized—Debbie, Hilary, Wendy—and thus aim for a classic.

Female Name: Example No. 1 (Verse/Chorus)
ANNA

I'm skippin' like a stone some kid has thrown
From the bank of a crystal pond.
I'm rollin' like a breeze as free as you please
Just a happy vagabond.

I'm laughin' like the water in a mountain stream.
Dancin' like a kettle with a head of steam.
And I'm lookin' in the eyes of a perfect dream
Called ANNA.

I'm shinin' like the smile of a happy child
When papa says, "Let's play."
I'm shakin' like the tail of a kite a-sailin'
On a windy April day.
I'm flappin' like a flag on the fourth of July.
I'm floatin' like the scent of a fresh-baked pie.
Fallin' deeper and deeper in love with my
Sweet ANNA.

ANNA,
I wish I could say how I feel.
But the feelings get blurred
Like the spokes on a wheel
As they spin 'round my heart
And they whirl through my brain
Till all I can hear
Is the sound of your name,
ANNA.

I'm blushin' like the dawn when the night has gone
And the rosy day unfolds.
I'm burnin' with desire; it's a friendly fire.
I stay warm when the wind blows cold.
I'm singin' like a bird on a telephone line.
Poppin' like a bubble in sparklin' wine.
And Lord, I'm lovin' the life that's mine
With ANNA.

(repeat chorus)

▲ Comment

The freshness of "Anna" proves that a positive love song needn't be banal. The consistent chime of the inner-rhyme pattern of each verse's first two lines adds to the musicality of the lyric: *stone/thrown*; *breeze/please*; *smile/child*; *tail/sail*; *dawn/gone*; *desire/fire*. It's easy to identify the dominant cognitive style of a writer whose lyric sings and wings and bubbles with sights, smells, tastes, sounds and textures. That's sensate/feeling (SF) writing at its best—touching all our senses in a song.

A Rhyme Exercise

In addition to the major-accent perfect rhymes in "Anna," (stream/steam/dream), Dan Fox also incorporated such minor-accent subtypes as *light rhyme* (pond/vagabond), *augmented rhyme* (smile/child) and *trailing rhyme* (tail/a-sailin').

Whatever your rhyme preferences — perfect or near rhyme — your lyrics will sound fresher and more original if you include some of the less commonly used rhyme types. As you saw from the Rundown on Rhyme, there are eighteen *different kinds of rhyme to draw from.*

By conscious practice of some of the underused forms of rhyme, you'll find that new combinations will spring more readily to mind as you write. Using the examples given on page 5 as role models, exercise your rhyming skills by coming up with rhyme mates for each of these initial rhyme agents:

- Give three *trailing* rhyme mates for:
  ran/ _____; _____; _____
  damp/ _____; _____; _____
- Give three *apocopated* rhyme mates for:
  comfort/ _____; _____; _____
- Give three *light* rhyme mates for:
  him/ _____; _____; _____
- Give two *broken* rhyme mates for:
  cutlery/ _____; _____
- Give two *unstressed* rhyme mates for:
  oven/ _____; _____
- Give three *para* rhyme mates for:
  pressed/ _____; _____; _____
- Give three *feminine para* rhyme mates for:
  beacon/ _____; _____; _____
  (Some possibilities are listed on page 51.)

The following role-model lyric spins a tale of a particular kind of woman we all recognize.

Female Name: Example No. 2 (Verse/Chorus)
TINSEL

She was workin', she was dancin'
'N' her dancin' was the best.
Here 'n' there she wore some spangles,
But her body did the rest.
Oh, she sparkled and she shimmered
And she flickered like a flame,
With a lusty kinda luster
And TINSEL was her name.

TINSEL shines.
TINSEL shimmers.
TINSEL's flashy.
TINSEL's bright.
Always flashin' the reflection
Of somethin' else's light.

TINSEL shines.
TINSEL glimmers
Always pretty to behold.
Always movin'
Always provin'
All that glitters is not gold.

I was blinded by her dazzle
When she lighted up my life.
Though she wanted fame and fortune
She agreed to be my wife.
I spent my money on a diamond
And we set the wedding day.
As I headed for the altar,
TINSEL headed for LA.

(repeat chorus)

She was headed down the freeway
In a chauffeur driven car
And the older man who owned it
Promised her she'd be a star.
Now, I wonder, will her sparkle
Start to tarnish, turn to brown
In the hot light of a spotlight
In the heart of Tinseltown.

(repeat chorus)

© 1981 Words by Jim Morgan/Music by Alan Cove. Used with permission.

▲ Comment

The lyric surprises us in the second verse when we learn the singer's relationship to the singee. The writing points up the distinction between surprising the listener and baffling the listener: we were never baffled because a skilled hand knew how to take us where he wanted to go, always maintaining the third-person reference. Drawing on many writerly devices, Jim interweaves purposeful repetition, alliteration, assonance, consonance and pun (*lusty/luster, tinsel/tinseltown*), making the lyric a pleasure to read aloud because of the musical interplay of vowels and consonants. With originality, he invented a name for his singee, which not only symbolizes her profession and her character, but the town she was headed for—Hollywood.

WrapUp

Those two role-model lyrics suggest that talent and technique can triumph over a seemingly banal device. What's in a name? Well, as the two lyrics suggest— a strategy for successful songwriting.

Some Possible Rhyme Mates for Rhyme Exercise on page 49.

Trailing:	ran/planning/tandem/Stanley
	damp/camper/grandpa/lampshade
Apocopated:	comfort/dumb/numb/some
Light:	him/synonym/paradigm/seraphim
Broken:	cutlery/butler re(entered)/
	subtler rea(son)
Unstressed:	oven/woven/given/enliven
Para:	pressed/priest/Proust/priced
Feminine para:	beacon/beckon/bacon/Bach'n

A Title With a Top-Ten Word: Heart, Night, If

Some Background

A virtual instant cure for the student syndrome "I've got no ideas," results from the assignment to write a title from a "top-ten" keyword—especially when it's *heart,* or *night,* or *if*—three of the most popular in songdom. Innovative writers seem never to run out of fresh ways to treat these ordinary words. Let's start with *heart* and *night.*

Some *Heart* Titles

Heart in Motion	Harden My Heart
Heart of Glass	Bulletproof Heart
Heart of Stone	Hungry Hearts
Heart of the Country	Put a Little Love in Your Heart
Heart of the Night	My Heart Belongs to Daddy
Heartbreak Hotel	Young at Heart
Heartbreaker	Warm Your Heart
I Don't Have the Heart	My Foolish Heart
Heartbreak, Tennessee	I Don't Want Your Body If Your Heart
Look Me in the Heart	Isn't in It

Some *Night* Titles

Blues in the Night	The Night They Drove Old Dixie
The Night We Called It a Day	Down
Night and Day	The Night They Invented
Nights in White Satin	Champagne
Stay the Night	The Night Was Made for Love
Rhythm of the Night	You and the Night and the Music
The Way You Look Tonight	Night Fever
Nighsthift	The Night Has a Thousand Eyes
Right Time of the Night	Last Night When We Were Young
Strangers in the Night	Help Me Make It Through the Night
Night Moves	Teach Me Tonight

Prewriting Suggestion

This is a good time to practice some of the right-brain techniques described in Part II—free writing and other-hand writing. Both can help generate a fresh title or two that'll give birth to a concept complete with viewpoint, voice, time frame and setting. Write the word *heart* on the first line of your page and just keep writing in short phrases rapidly one after another. Let random connections occur. If rhymes pop out, let them. Keep your pen or pencil on the paper—and free write. If you find you're pausing, it's because your left-brain editor is interfering. Try switching your pen or pencil to your nondominant hand. You may be surprised at the ideas that emerge — often a thought closer to your heart than your head. Here are two lyrics that sprang from this strategy. First, an example of the classic theme: "trying to get over you."

Example No. 1: A Heart Title (AABA)
MY HEART HAS A MIND OF ITS OWN

My friends and relations
Say I mustn't think of you.
Well, that's easy to say,
But awful hard to do.
It wouldn't help a bit
If my brain were made of stone
'Cause MY HEART HAS A MIND OF ITS OWN.

I close the windows, pull the shades,
And lock the house up tight
To keep those memories of you
From haunting me at night.
I beg my heart be quiet,
And for once leave me alone.
But MY HEART HAS A MIND OF ITS OWN.

Nobody cries forever.
Sooner or later tears run dry.
I've seen others recover.
Why can't I?

Somewhere there's an answer
That will help me to forget.
I'm struggling for an answer
But I haven't found it yet.
Working free of your memory's
The hardest job I've known
'Cause MY HEART HAS A MIND OF ITS OWN.

© 1990 Don Weill. Used with permission.

▲ Comment

The lyric has all the ingredients of a chart hit — strong colloquial title and a singer in a universal situation with which millions can identify. Don was disappointed to discover that his title was not unique to him: A song with that title had been a No. 1 hit for Connie Francis in 1960. He felt reassured, however, that he was thinking commercially. And, of course, that title could make it again. After all, four songs with the identical title "Heartbreaker," by four different writing teams have made it to the chart! Although we strive for originality, ideas are swimming around in the collective unconscious. And it's simply a matter of who reels them in — and when.

THE ULTIMATE NIGHT

I'll be dressed in gold lamé
Gardenias in my hair.
He'll be partly Schwarzenegger,
Partly Fred Astaire —
Our eyes will meet and wordlessly
We start the big affair.
That's the scene I see —
The way it all will be
THE ULTIMATE NIGHT.

He'll glide across a ballroom floor
And sweep me off my feet
Whisk me to a limousine
And never miss a beat.
A private plane will take us
To his St. Tropez retreat:
There'll be a balcony
That overlooks the sea
THE ULTIMATE NIGHT.

He'll fill me up with Montrachet
(The rarest vintage year).
I'll hear his love words and the surf
Whisp'ring in my ear.
There'll be velvet walls, a canopy,
A crystal chandelier,
And perfumed satin sheets
And chocolate pillow treats
THE ULTIMATE NIGHT.

We'll light the lemon candlesticks
And when I count to ten,
He'll rub me down with jasmine oil —
Won't stop till I say "When!"
I'll give him my best *femme fatale*;
Then we'll do it all again.
We'll be so high on love
That we could fly on love
THE ULTIMATE NIGHT.

But meanwhile there are rooms to dust
And dishes in the sink —
A button off, a cavity —
A TV on the blink.
And meanwhile, there's a fellow
Who'd supply the missing link;

But I'm unconvinced he's it
And unwilling to commit.
'Cause there's still a part of me
That's holding out to see
What may be waiting slightly out of sight
On some magical, glamourous,
Fairytale, amorous,
Starlit ULTIMATE NIGHT.

▲ Comment

"The Ultimate Night" was designed for a character in a revue whose mundane world is sustained by her fantasy life. The revue writer can, of course, sprinkle lyrics with such non-pop words as *Montrachet* (pronounced Mohn-trah-SHAY). I also want to point out the extended final A. Unlike the pop lyricist who generally adheres to the major song formats (outlined in Part I), the revue, cabaret and theater lyricist is concerned about creating a theatrical moment and thus giving the singer something to perform that builds to applause. The writer could have ended the verse: "Cause there's still a part of me/That's holding out to see/The Ultimate Night." It's okay, but flat. Trust your intuition (which the intuitives of course do naturally). Sensates, who tend to adhere closely to traditional forms, may need encouragement to bend the forms when appropriate. So follow any hunch that suggests that you stretch or add or shorten or twist a verse or bridge or chorus. Song forms are not sacred shapes: When you've learned the "rules," you've earned the right to bend them.

The Big Little Word

Since the word *if* has begun almost as many hit song titles as the word *love*, it rates its own category.

Some *If* Titles

If	If He Walked into My Life
If I Had You	If My Friends Could See Me Now
If I Had My Way	If You Could Read My Mind
If I Loved You	If I Only Had a Brain
If I Ruled the World	If You Knew Susie Like I Know Susie
If I Were a Bell	If I Were a Rich Man
If I Were a Carpenter	If I Could Put Time in a Bottle
If I Didn't Care	If Ever You're in My Arms Again
If I Had a Hammer	If Ever I Should Leave You
If I Fell	If Love Were All

Prewriting Suggestions

The foregoing examples illustrate that an "if" concept can express various attitudes—rueful, hopeful, playful, and so on. To connect you with your own significant "if," the brainstorming process will generally do the trick. Or, you could work from specific viewpoints; for example, try three columns headed "Mine," "Yours," "The World's." The first would naturally emphasize personal "ifs," the second, interpersonal, and the third, social/global.

Small Craft Warning

A grammar refresher: The use of *if* or *as though* in contrary-to-fact statements requires the verb *to be* in the subjunctive mood; for example, "You look at me as if I *were* (not *was*) crazy." The subjunctive mood is also required in statements expressing a wish as in "If I *Were* (not *was*) a Rich Man." Be mindful too that in using the conditional, you'll most likely be employing the helping verbs *could*, *would*, *should* rather than *will*, *shall*.

Example No. 3: An If *Title (Verse/Chorus/Bridge)*
IF I'M GONNA BE LONELY, I'D RATHER BE ALONE

The phone is ringing and I know it's you.
You're with some friends having a drink or two.
I'm not worried about when you'll be here
It's how you'll treat me when you appear:
Without emotion you'll kiss me hello.
But tonight is the night
I'm gonna let you know:

IF I'M GONNA BE LONELY,
I'D RATHER BE ALONE
I've never been frightened
Of being on my own.
This place we're sharing,
Doesn't feel like a home
And IF I'M GONNA BE LONELY,
I'D RATHER BE ALONE.

I can remember how I used to turn you on;
We'd make love into the dawn.
But now at night instead of reaching for me,
You're reaching out to turn on TV.
It's an empty feeling living this way.
So tonight is the night
I'm gonna have my say.

(repeat chorus)

© 1991 Noel Cohen. Used with permission.

▲ Comment

Noel Cohen's opening lines thrust us right into the moment. They immediately show that the singer is alone and thinking about the lover/singee. The flashback device of the second verse helps to develop the plot. The lyric written for a woman, would make feminist/songwriter Holly Near cheer: She once said, "If you write love songs . . . write positive . . . as opposed to themes that are not useful to the population. If songwriters begin . . . to make the listener feel some sense of self, of dignity and pride, of hope . . . that can be the beginning to being a conscientious songwriter."

WrapUp

Three little words, three big possibilities. After you've tried these three strategies, you'll have had practice using a conceptual device you can rely on time and again. And you'll undoubtedly discover a few more top-ten keywords to shape into songs.

A Book-Title Title

The Purpose

This strategy aims to sharpen your awareness that song ideas lurk everywhere—
including on book covers. Generally "book-title" songs come from a film made
from the book, such as "Three Coins in the Fountain" or "The Way We Were."
An assignment to write a film title song, however, is given to only a handful of
songwriters—who've usually had previous hits *and* live in L.A. But an assignment
to write a book-title song is something you can give to yourself.

Some Book Title Examples Unrelated to Films

Gone With the Wind	I Never Promised You a Rose Garden
From Here to Eternity	Games People Play
That Goodbye Look	Real Men Don't Eat Quiche
How to Win Friends and Influence	
People	

Prewriting Suggestion

To expand your song title supply, read book reviews and best-seller lists, and
scan the bookstore windows and library shelves. I've personally experienced the
rewards of this strategy when two book titles turned into recordings: "It's Hard
to Leave While the Music's Playing" and "A Walk in the Spring Rain."

Here's a student lyric whose title springs from Betty Rollins' best-selling autobiographical account of her battle with breast cancer, *First You Cry*. The statement
summarizes the singer's initial reaction to the end of a relationship.

Book Title: Example No. 1 (Verse/Chorus/Bridge)
FIRST YOU CRY

What do you do
When the one you love no longer's loving you?
When he proves to be untrue?
When you've said your last goodbye
And you've swallowed so much pride
That you feel like you could die
What do you do?

FIRST YOU CRY.
You release the hurt and anger deep inside.
Tears will ease the pain you feel.
Tears must flow to help you heal, so
FIRST YOU CRY.

What do you do
When the hand you've held has found another hand?
And it's more than you can stand

When there's no one on the phone
And there's no one waiting home
And you're sleeping all alone
What do you do?

(repeat chorus)

For now there are friends to see you through.
And soon the sun will shine
And in time somehow you'll find
Someone new who'll love and cherish you, but

(repeat chorus)

© 1992 Nancy Smith. Used with permission.

▲ Comment

The verses' question motif and a rhyme scheme featuring a three-line purposive linking of sounds (*goodbye/pride/die*; *phone/home/alone*) both help build the tension that pays off with the chorus' title answer. The bridge brings contrasts with a hopeful look ahead to a happier future. Nancy Smith has designed a strong song that sends a helpful message rooted in truth.

The next example turns Thomas Wolfe's memorable book title into a country story.

Book Title: Example No. 2 (Verse/Chorus)
LOOK HOMEWARD, ANGEL

Mamma told me she'd left home
The day she'd turned eighteen—
A small town girl with her Chevrolet
Full of clothes and big city dreams.
Her mother'd cried and handed her
A sampler she had made
With these words to comfort her
Through the lonely city days:

LOOK HOMEWARD, ANGEL
When you need a hand.
LOOK HOMEWARD, ANGEL
Mamma understands.
LOOK HOMEWARD, ANGEL
You'll never be alone:
You can't be a stranger
When you turn your heart toward home.

Mamma cried when I left home
Said I'd grown up too fast.
But baby shoes and Barbie dolls
Were never meant to last.
I knew the love she raised me with
Was meant to set me free.

When she gave me Grandma's sampler
And whispered tenderly:

(repeat chorus)

The angels took my mamma home;
They came for her last fall.
And I've found strength and comfort
In that sampler on the wall.
So when my little girl grows up
and wants to move away,
I know the gift I'll give her
And the words I'm gonna say:

(repeat chorus)

By Dan Knipp and Rick Swiegoda
© 1989 Blue Valentine Music. Used with Permission.

▲ Comment

With its story plot, commercial chorus and traditional homespun values, "Look Homeward, Angel" sounds like a natural contender for country success. Songwriting genres—rock, pop, cabaret, country—reflect a state of mind, rather than a state of residence. Rick Swiegoda, though originally from Long Island, New York, had always felt an affinity for country music. After fortifying his talent with the technique gained from several semesters of my workshops, he headed for Nashville. He's now enjoying life as a professional (recorded) songwriter.

WrapUp

To help put theory in practice, why not give yourself an assignment to expand your song title list with a few book titles. There might even be one lurking on your own bookshelves. . . .

PART FOUR

More Title Strategies: Wordplay

Activating the creative process with a title has staunch supporters: Jimmy Webb admits to being a title-first writer, "If you start out with a *tangible*, then the whole song stays more focused. I almost *have* to do it that way." Veteran lyricist Mitchell Parish asserted, "If you get a good title, that's half the song."

So we'll concentrate here on additional ways to get "half the song" by adding to your repertoire of title techniques. First we'll draw upon such basic devices as *antonyms*, *questions* and *colloquialisms*. Then we'll experiment and get inventive with words.

This may be a good time to take inventory of your basic reference works. If you don't own them already, consider acquiring such standards as *The Handbook of Commonly Used American Idioms*, *The Pocket Dictionary of American Slang*, *The Concise Oxford Dictionary of Proverbs*, and *A Dictionary of Catch Phrases*. Words beget more words.

An Antonym Title

Some Background

An *antonym* is a word opposite in meaning to another: *hot* is an antonym of *cold*. Antonyms make for memorability; that's why they're a favorite device of advertising copywriters. Madison Avenue has produced such memorable slogans as "Tide's *in*, dirt's *out*; Oldsmobile's "This is the *new* generation of *Olds*"; and Motorola's "The way we put things *together* sets us *apart*." Similarly, songwriters have a knack for panning the antonym goldmine—then penning platinum standards.

Some Antonym Titles

Full Moon and Empty Arms	I Got It Bad and That Ain't Good
My Past Is Present	Come Rain or Come Shine
My Future Just Passed	Sleeping Single in a Double Bed
New Looks From an Old Lover	Everybody's Got the Right to be
Another Mr. Right Just Left	Wrong
The High Cost of Low Living	They're Either Too Young or Too Old
Last Thing I Needed First Thing	Been Down So Long It Feels Like Up
This Morning	to Me
The Night We Called It a Day	

Left Hemisphere Vs. Right Hemisphere

Brain lateralization studies confirm that syntax is a left-hemisphere function. So it's not surprising that the lyrics of many left-brain dominant writers tend to be grammatical and to employ balanced structures like antonyms. If you're a sensate/thinker (ST), it's likely you'll find this strategy a snap because antonyms will come naturally. Conversely, if you're a right-brained intuitive-feeler (NF), it may take a little more work. But remember, it's the exercise of bridging the hemispheres that makes for whole-brain thinking and writing.

Prewriting Suggestions

Taking this strategy in step-by-step stages is likely to be more fruitful than demanding of yourself an instant title. To begin, set aside in your idea notebook an Antonym page or two for storing a list of antithetical pairs. List-making can help shift you into the lower left mode of focused thought. Alphabetizing, another left-brain activity, also abets step-by-step thinking. Making an alphabetized antonym list serves to get your brain into a linear, logical furrow as you store ideas for future songs. You could start your list with the antonyms from the song titles above and augment it as new antonyms occur.

Step two entails being playful and imaginative in order to discover a fresh treatment of your antonym. That requires a shift to the right: A little doodling or a walk around the block would get you over to the right side. You might also free associate on paper from a particular set of antonyms. Remember, at this stage, allow yourself to "goof around."

Brainstorming orally into a tape recorder can also get you into a creative flow — an activity especially helpful for extraverts. If you're a car commuter, set a recorder up on your dashboard, or simply have one with you at home while you cook or wash dishes. It's akin to the composer's process of noodling on the piano or guitar. The right-brain starts to make random connections. Random is right for now. (Logic comes later in the structuring process.)

This antonym title evolved from writing to a melody.

Antonym Title: Example No. 1 (Verse/Chorus)
IF I COULD JUST REMEMBER TO FORGET

So you've come back to ask me to forgive you
You're sorry for the pain you brought my way.
And your eyes that lied so many times aren't lying now:
I can tell you mean ev'ry word you say.

But how am I supposed to face the question?
Would I be smart to risk my heart once more?
Even though you say you're home to stay I still recall
The nights I cried after you walked out our door.

If I could only leave the hurt behind,
If I could make believe you'd never left,
If I could drive that mem'ry from my mind
Then I might love you yet.
IF I COULD JUST REMEMBER TO FORGET.

To fly into your arms would be so easy
But do I want to take a second chance?
For each reason I can find why I should try again,
I can find a dozen reasons why I can't.

If I could only wave a magic wand.
If that would bring us back to when we met.
If suddenly these doubts of mine were gone
Then I might love you yet.
IF I COULD JUST REMEMBER TO FORGET.

If I could only leave the hurt behind,
If I could make believe you'd never left,
If I could drive that mem'ry from my mind
Then I might love you yet.
IF I COULD JUST REMEMBER TO FORGET.

© 1990 Lyric by Don Weill/Music by Danny Arena. Used with permission.

▲ Comment

Danny Arena, a country-oriented composer wrote a melody whose title motif clearly landed in the last line of the chorus — a composing style more common to country than to pop songs. In his lyric to the chorus melody, Don carefully led the listener to the title by means of the succession of lines starting with "If I could." This start-of-line repetitive device (*anaphora*—a-NAF-ora) emphasizes the music structure as it unifies the lyrical thought. (Choruses with last-line titles virtually demand such a unifying device.) Don created a strong finale by ending with a double chorus: He wrote new words for the second chorus and then returned to the first chorus for emphasis. Remember, nowhere is it written that the chorus words can't vary. Once you know your song forms, permit your intuition to consider the possibility of variation.

Antonym Subtypes

Antonyms come in two levels of sophistication. Level I comprises a pair of opposites—*remember/forget, up/down, on/off*, both of which are used in a literal way. Level II uses one or both of the pair in colloquial or *figurative* ways that are not literally opposite in meaning, for instance the song titles "The High (expensive) Cost of Low (immoral) Living," and "My Future (years to come) Just Passed (went by)." Such figurative antonyms can be considered a subdivision of the pun.

Here's a lyric that plays on two meanings: the word *thick—heavily built* and the expression *in the thick of*—to be *in the most active part of.* The lyric also features an *introductory verse*—once an integral part of the AABA form (in 1930s' and 1940s' film and theater songs). You'll be seeing more intro verses throughout the book because they're still common in contemporary cabaret and theater songs.

Antonym Title: Example No. 2 (AABABA w/Introductory Verse)
IN THE THICK OF GETTING THIN

Mirrors never lie, that's a well-known fact.
Mirrors tell the truth. (Mirrors have no tact.)
My mirror tells me things I would not repeat.
That's why I'm trying hard to become petite.

So I work out at aerobics,
But much to my despair,
I'm aching now in muscles
That I never knew were there.
I go all out; and then I feel all in.
I'm IN THE THICK OF GETTING THIN.

I've joined a weight-reduction group,
With a diet just for me:
No meat, no milk, no bread, no fruit—
It's pretty much food free!
I go there every week to get weighed in.
I am IN THE THICK OF GETTING THIN.

How I long to be chic and cadavarous,
With complexion intriguingly pale.
Although my wallet has slimmed down a lot,
Not a word have I heard from my scale!

I'm even trying yoga
To think off each flabby pound.
But, after meditating,
I can't get up from the ground.
Oh, what a sad fiasco this has been!
Nothing does the trick.
And I am getting sick
Of being IN THE THICK OF GETTING THIN.

Maybe fat is part of my destiny.
Maybe fat is part of my fate.
Though I'm losing my patience, and losing my mind,
I'm still firmly attached to my weight.

And still I keep on trying,
'Cause who is there to say
That tomorrow's diet craze
May shrink the poundage of today.
So I'm saying, "Let the miracle begin!"
And let it happen quick!
So I can finally kick
This being IN THE THICK OF GETTING THIN.

▲ Comment

Employing antonyms, concrete images, repetitive devices and perfect rhyme all come naturally to Rebecca Holtzman. Being an ESTJ—extroverted, sensate, thinking, judging writer—translates to being an enthusiastic, detailed, logical and rhythmic lyricist. In addition to the antonyms in the title, you may have caught the figurative opposites of *all out/all in* and the pun exploiting the multiple meanings of *losing,* playing off its sound link with *loose*—the opposite of *firmly attached.* As you've already seen in Dr. Joe's "Napkin in Nashville," a satiric outlook often accompanies the sensate/thinking/judgment (STJ) temperament. So it's not surprising that Rebecca playfully jibes at society's preoccupation with slimness.

WrapUp

If the punning aspect of "In the Thick" appeals to you, you may want to fast forward to Strategy No. 17 for an in-depth look at the particulars of the pun. Next, getting the most out of colloquial expressions.

An Idiom, Axiom or Paragram Title

Some Background

Like titles that employ names, dates and places, those built on familiar expressions exert an instant appeal. This strategy comes in two parts. First you'll explore the possibilities inherent in the idioms and axioms of everyday speech. Then you'll be encouraged to be inventive by giving one of those familiar expressions a twist.

Some Definitions

I'd like to make a distinction between idioms and axioms. Under idiomatic, we can group such informal expressions as *beyond belief, take it or leave it, no problem*. An axiom — also called a maxim or proverb — is a self-evident *truth* based on common sense, widely accepted on its intrinsic merit: *finders keepers — losers weepers* or *a stitch in time saves nine*. Although idioms and axioms work equally well as song springboards, the axiom, on occasion, may land you in more interesting waters. (A student role-model lyric you'll see shortly will illustrate what I mean.)

Some Idiomatic Titles

Here and Now	Good Thing Going
The Best Is Yet to Come	A Place in the Sun
Day In, Day Out	For Once in My Life
If Looks Could Kill	Signed, Sealed and Delivered

Some Axiomatic Titles

All That Glitters Isn't Gold	Opposites Attract
Easy Come, Easy Go	Luck of the Draw
Love Will Find a Way	Too Close for Comfort
Fools Rush In (Where Angels Fear to Tread)	When in Rome, Do as the Romans Do

Prewriting Suggestion

To produce idiomatic and axiomatic titles requires an alert ear for natural dialogue, an alert eye for signs and billboards — and a handy pen and paper for saving what you find. Two of my own recorded songs resulted from starting with a colloquial expression: "Living Together" (1972) jumped out at me from the title of a *New York Times* feature article, and "Early Bird Special" (1981) flashed from a parking lot sign.

When a title strikes, mull over the potential plot treatments. Explore all the possibilities, which means, stay in the incubating mode for a while. Lyricists often start writing before they've exhausted the potential of the title. Ask yourself: What might the situation be? Who is thinking it or saying it to whom? And why?

What other possible meanings might it have? Only begin to write when you feel you've considered all the possible angles and have chosen the best.

Here's a common expression used to convey the world-weary wariness of a love skeptic. The song, at this writing, is heading for a Broadway revue.

Example No. 1: An Idiom Title (AABA)
WAIT AND SEE

You and I
We meet, we find
We're so alike
In heart and mind.
It must be love
But love is blind.
We'll have to
WAIT AND SEE.

You and I,
Like Jack and Jill,
We've both been up
And down the hill,
Around the block
And through the mill.
We'll have to
WAIT AND SEE.

Where love's concerned
I've lived, and learned
To keep it cool
And keep my fingers crossed.
I don't begin
By leapin' in,
'Cause s/he who doesn't hesitate is lost.

You and I,
We haven't found
If we're on sand
Or solid ground.
Time will tell.
So stick around
For what's to be—
Or not to be.
It's touch and go.
But soon we'll know.
And so—
We'll WAIT AND SEE.

© 1991 Lyric by Jim Morgan/Music by Paul Trueblood. Used with permission.

▲ Comment

Simple, direct and clear: The art that conceals art with economy of words. The second verse illustrates the principle of unifying a series of similar ideas by making them either consistently literal or consistently figurative. In this case, figurative: *up and down the hill, around the block*, and *through the mill* metaphorically depict the jaded attitude of the singer. Another feature: the twist on the maxim, *he who hesitates is lost.* That's a preview of how you'll be twisting a title — part two of this strategy. But first an example of a maxim/axiom title.

Example No. 2: An Axiom Title (Verse/Chorus/Bridge)
CAN'T JUDGE A BOOK BY ITS COVER

A sharkskin suit is coming up the street
Swinging his attaché to a funky beat.
Looking-fine females stop to see.
Check it out: He looks at me!
As we talk I wonder about us:
Casual dating can be dangerous.
He invites me out. Should I go
With a man that I don't even know?

CAN'T JUDGE A BOOK BY ITS COVER
Not when it comes to picking your lover.
CAN'T JUDGE A BOOK BY ITS COVER
Not when it comes to picking your lover.

Side by side we walk down the street
Both of us swaying to a funky beat.
So far so good: I like this man.
(Especially the way he holds my hand.)
Over a drink he talks about his life.
All through dinner he talks about his strife.
He doesn't care to know about *me*,
All he speaks about is *he, he, he.*

(repeat chorus)

I say "Thanks a lot" and head for the door.
He wants to know what I'm dissing him for —
That he bought me dinner — now I *owe* him.
I say I've no use for an empty sharkskin.

(repeat chorus)

© 1992 Vernetta Cousins. Used with permission.

▲ Comment

"You Can't Judge a Book By Its Cover" was an axiom waiting to happen. Fresh and feisty with a funky beat. Sorry that the page can't play the demo but you can probably tell from just reading the lyric — it dances. That's an example of a *situational* plot — that middle ground between an attitudinal plot and a story song. The writer's use of *sharkskin suit* enlivens the lyric for two reasons. One, it creates a memorable effect by substituting the apparel for the person. (More on that figure of speech called *metonymy* in Part V.) And two, the reappearance of *sharkskin* at the end for emotional closure, a device called the *return*, adds memorability to the lyric. Did your ear notice the two instances of *light rhyme* — *us/dangerous* and *him/ sharkskin*? An occasional touch of minor accent rhyme (heard more in poetry) helps to freshen the pop soundscape which tends to lean heavily on major accent masculine rhymes (*beat/street, life/strife*).

Paragram Time

Now we'll look at the art of giving an old saw a new twist by making a *paragram*. A paragram is a play on words made by altering a word, or sometimes only a letter, in a common expression or literary allusion. I did it earlier in "an axiom waiting to happen" — a play on the colloquialism, "an *accident* waiting to happen."

The majority of the following paragram titles emanate from the Nashville area; it would seem that country writers have virtually cornered the market on twisting the idiom. As you read the examples, see if you can pinpoint the various techniques used to revamp a common expression.

Some Paragram Titles

Friends in Low Places	Love at Second Sight
The High Cost of Loving	What You See Is What You Sweat
Every Heart Should Have One	Fit to Be Tied Down
Two Hearts Are Better Than One	Only In It for the Love
Can't Teach My Old Heart New Tricks	I Meant Every Word He Said
	Above and Beyond the Call of Love
You're Gonna Love Yourself in the Morning	We've Got to Start Meeting Like This

Making Paragrams

What's the technique? Often the colloquialism's key word is replaced by one of those top-ten songtitle words *heart* or *love/loving* as in the expression, "Only in it for the money (love)." Sometimes the twist comes via an antonym — *high/low, good/bad, head/heart, stop/start*. Strategy No. 7 gave you some practice thinking in antonyms so you're likely to be revved up for this exercise. Although making paragrams may come more easily to some writers than to others, everyone can do it with a little practice. Like any form of word*play*, paragrams require a *play*ful attitude — like that evidenced in the next example.

Example No. 3: A Paragram (Twist on an Idiom) Title (AABA)
FLATTERY WILL GET YOU EVERYWHERE

Oh, baby, don't be shy,
I can tell you've got something to say
About the wiggle in my walk
Or the outfit that I'm wearing today.
Tell me how my eyes just light up the room,
Or how you're hypnotized by my natural perfume,

And when we dance I make you feel like Fred Astaire.
FLATTERY WILL GET YOU EVERYWHERE.

Now, I don't wanna hear
That I've got a mind like Margaret Mead.
Something much more superficial
Is the kind of thing I currently need.
So pick a perfect rose and say I'm prettier by half,
Lay it on so thick even my mother'd have to laugh.
It feels so good it's almost more than I can bear.
FLATTERY WILL GET YOU EVERYWHERE.

I'll take you back home
And love you all through the night.
No need to tell me how you want it,
'Cause I always do it thoroughly right.
And 'round about morning,
When the slap and tickle's done,
You'll swear by all that's holy
That you've never had such fun.

'Cause you're a man of taste
And infinite sincerity—
But that's enough about you,
It's time to talk some more about me:
Rhapsodize, exaggerate, glorify and gush,
Kiss me on the nose and say I'm lovely when I blush,
Go on and praise me to the skies. But don't stop there.
FLATTERY WILL GET YOU EVERYWHERE.

© 1986 Maureen Sugden. Used with permission.

▲ Comment

It's not only fresh and fun, it's full of notable literary devices. Notice how alliteration linked related ideas through the repetition of initial consonants— *wiggle/walk/wearing*, *mind/Margaret Mead*, *pick/perfect/prettier*, and how assonance linked *eyes/hypnotized/light*. But neither effect was overdone to call attention to itself. (Like metaphor, alliteration and assonance should *make* a point, not *be* the point.) The writer also employs two more useful devices: *metonymy*—substituting *slap and tickle*, an attribute of lovemaking, for the word itself; and *synonymy*—using successive synonyms (*rhapsodize, exaggerate, glorify* and *gush*) for purposeful exaggeration. (Lots more on metonymy in Part V.)

WrapUp

Keeping your notebook stocked with colloquial expressions that strike your ear and eye will forestall writers block. And an occasional reading of the reference books cited will help pave the way to "paragramming." But the best resource of all is a receptiveness to the accidental: Respect and relish the random.

A Coined Word Title

Some Background

Get ready to suspend traditional thinking and become inventive. The object: To create words no one has yet put into a song. This strategy combines your left brain's flair for word links and your right brain's flair for playfulness.

Defining Some Terms

New words, called *neologisms*, are constantly entering the language. Sometimes new technology and new products create words like *fax*, *Camcorder* and *Nintendo*. Writers and public figures can help the language evolve through new usages of words; for example, General Schwarzkopf in a TV interview turned the noun *caveat* (a warning) into a verb when he remarked that during the Gulf crisis he was constantly being "caveated" by Washington memos. Here are the main ways in which neologisms are formed:

"Verbifying": Turns a noun or proper name into a verb form. The dictionary has recently legitimized some new verbs that started life as nouns; for example, "They *stonewalled* my idea," "We *mothballed* the project." After the now notorious speech by Senator Biden in which he appropriated the words of a British politician as if they were his own, I coined the verb *Bidenize* meaning to plagiarize.

Acronym: Makes a pronounceable formation by combining the initial letters of syllables of a string of words; for example, AIDS (acquired immune deficiency syndrome). One of the newest acronyms is NIMBY (not in my backyard!), an expression derived from an objection commonly raised by a neighborhood group to a proposed service center such as a new drug rehab clinic that they fear would lower the area's quality of life.

Portmanteau Word: Blends two related words into a third one: *smoke* and *fog* formed *smog*; a fusion of *pal* and *alimony* coined *palimony*; a fusion of *cassette* and *single* created *cassingle*.

"Adjectivizing": Turns nouns and proper names into new adjectives. Soon after the publication of Kitty Kelley's sensationalized biography of Nancy Reagan, the media began referring to sleazy journalism as *Kitty Kelley journalism*.

Some Lyricist Tricks

In addition to drawing upon these basic devices by which new words enter the language, lyricists also alter the spelling or pronunciation of words. Generally the coinage is made to either create perfect rhyme or regulate the meter. Such *nonce words* — coined only for the occasion — may occur within the body of the lyric or as the song's title. Here are some lexical inventions by lyrical wordplayers.

- *Portmanteau*: "hobohemia" (Hart); "tinpantithesis" (Porter); "imposeros" (Harburg); "everybaudy" (Sondheim); "Beelzebubble" (Lerner)

- *"Nounify"*: "ungallantry," "evermores" (Lerner)
- *Verbify*: "noblessely obliged" (Lerner); "she's skying" (Chapin); "Lorelei them" (Lerner); "Krup you!" (Sondheim/Bernstein); "I've à la carted" (Gershwin)
- *"Adjectivize"*: "unwinceable," "Gallicly/phallicly" (Lerner); "spoony" (Fields)
- *Clip*: "rigor mort," "Tampa, Fla," "Rhododend," (Lerner); "Saks Fifth Ave" (Rome); "dish/disposish" (Gershwin)
- *Stretch*: "flatterer/Cleopatterer" (Porter); "identical/authentical" (Lerner); "Cartiers/Partiers" (Gershwin); "skinish/giveinish/finish" (Harburg)
- *Mispronounce*: "boy and goil" (Hart); Milton Berle/castor erl" (Porter); "introfaduce me" (Loesser)

Inventiveness lends distinction to a lyric. Here's a unique 16-bar cabaret divertissement in which the writer "adjectivized" a noun:

A Coined Word Title: Example No. 1 (Through Composed)
THE BUTTERFLY

The butterfly (or *papillon*)
Is lepidopterous.
It is neither jet-propelled
Nor "helicopterous."
It floats and flits
In starts and fits
Sublimely fritillary.
Has tiny wits,
Yet somehow it's
Considered literary.
On saccharine flight
From bloom to bloom
(So like the human heart!)
It sups with dainty appetite
But roses make it fart.

© 1976 Lyric June Siegel/Music by Jimmy Roberts. Used with permission.

▲ Comment

Inventive, and impeccably rhymed. The lyricist wisely shunned the three major song forms to provide her collaborator with the structure for a *through composed* melody—one that never returns to its initial melodic phrase. *Helicopterous* is of course the graphically apt adjective. Though June Siegel's neologism is a copyrighted original, her method of creating it is public domain: She fused a noun to the suffix *-ous*, meaning "characterized by." As an aid to inventiveness, we'll soon take a closer look at how new words can be formed. But first, some song titles that feature nonce coinages.

Some Coinage Titles	
Mairzy Doats	How Can I Unlove You?
S'Wonderful	My Wubba Dolly
Edutainment	Yester-me, Yester-you, Yesterday

De-Lovely

Heartquake

Delishious

Wouldn't It be Luverly?

I Got a Code in My "Dose"

Supercalifragilisticexpialidocious

Another Coining Device

In addition to verbifying, stretching, clipping, mispronouncing, "acronyming," "portmanteauing" and adding suffixes, you might also *subtract prefixes* as in this example.

A Coined Word Title: Example No. 2 (AABA Form w/Introductory Verse)
GRUNTLED AND SHEVELED AND COUTH

I know many a man who's disgruntled —
Who is angry, and surly and glum.
I know many a man who's disheveled —
Who looks like a two-legged slum.
And then there are men who are simply uncouth —
Whose mouths should be washed out with soap.
I dream of a man who is different by far.
And I sit. And I wait. And I hope.

The man of my dreams, I can picture him now
Just the way that I have since my youth.
Though we still haven't met
It's a pretty safe bet
He'll be GRUNTLED AND SHEVELED AND COUTH.

I won't care if he's not at all handsome or rich.
I won't mind if he's long in the tooth.
That would not bother me.
All I want him to be
Is GRUNTLED AND SHEVELED AND COUTH.

Disgruntled isn't fun at all.
Disheveled is unaesthetic.
Uncouth I once dated,
(And was none too elated).
The date was, in fact, pathetic.

So whenever my dream guy appears on the scene,
I'll spot him. And that is the truth.
He will need no ID.
I will know that it's he:
For the man I've been seekin'
Will shine like a beacon,
So I won't have to act like a sleuth:
He'll be GRUNTLED AND SHEVELED AND COUTH.

© 1990 Rebecca Holtzman. Used with permission.

▲ Comment

Most words with negative prefixes such as *dis-* and *un-* have a positive form—*disorganized/organized; unnecessary/necessary*. But as this song's title humorously reveals, the three words in question lack that positive form. The lyric's first draft—presuming the audience would immediately get the joke—opened on the line, "The man of my dreams. . . ." The class reaction suggested that an introductory verse was needed to prepare the ear. It did the job well.

Irving Berlin once said, "You can be too clever, you know." I would amplify: Being "too clever" translates to ineffectively setting up the cleverness. Poor communication results from either a *poorly sent* message or a *poorly received* message. As lyric communicators we must send with care—which includes assessing the relative sophistication of our target audience.

Prewriting Suggestion

Perhaps you have a current lyric that could be enlivened with a coined word. Or maybe you want to generate a concept for a new one. The examples and techniques already suggested are enough to warm up the wordplayer in you—when you're ready to call upon it. But being more knowledgeable about how words are formed will give you an even better launch pad for flights of verbal fancy. Here's a list of Greek and Latin prefixes and suffixes that may lead you into minting a gold-record coinage.

Prefixes	Meaning in English
a/im/in	not
ante	before
anti/contra	against
inter	between
magni	great
mal	bad/wrong
oro	mouth
re	again
schizo	split
sy, syl, sym, syn	with
tele	distant

Suffixes	Meaning in English
al	action or process
able	capable of
biosis	life
chrome	color
gram	writing
mania(c)	craving
meter	measure
onym	word
opia	eye/sight
phone	sound
sophy	wisdom

To spur the germinating process, you may want to transfer these lists to your idea notebook. Play around. Cross-pollinate. It's yet another device to help you produce "magnigramic" lyrics.

Getting Sensibly Nonsensical

The discussion of word coining would be incomplete without a mention of the contribution made to lyrics by nonsense syllables. Like most of the strategies, nonsense syllables are used two ways in songs: as a subtle refrain within the lyric or as its title. Open vowel sounds, so expressive of feeling, can serve to underscore and enhance tone whether soulful, baleful or gleeful.

Some Titles With Nonsense Refrains

Three Little Fishes ("boop boop didim dadum wadum choo")
Feelings ("wo, wo, wo")
Lawyers in Love ("ooo sha la la")
Mrs. Robinson ("wo, wo, wo," "hey hey hey," "coo coo ca choo")
Reunited ("hey, hey")
Hey Jude ("na na na na na na")
I Am the Walrus ("goo goo goo g'joob")
If I Were a Rich Man ("daidle deedle daidle")
The Little Things You Do Together ("uhhuh, mm-hm")
If Love Were All ("hayho")
A Bushel and a Peck ("doodle oodle oodle")

Some Nonsense Titles

Diga Diga Do	Heigh-Ho
Ob-la-di, Ob-la-da	Hoop-Dee-Do
De Do Do Do, De Da Da Da	Bibbidi-Bobbidi-Boo
Na Na Hey Hey	Chica Chica Boom Chic
Zip-A-Dee Doo Dah	Do Wah Diddy Diddy
Da-Doo, Ron Ron	Do Wacka-Do
Aba Daba Honeymoon	Dum Dot Song
Chi-Baba Chi-Baba	Chim Chim Cher-ee
Doodle Doo Doo	Sussudio

WrapUp

Inventive ways of thinking that may appear to come readily to some can be made to come to all—if not readily, well, at least eventually—with a little practice. You may want to look ahead to see how one role-model lyric used a nonsense refrain to reinforce emotion—"What Do I Do With the Anger?" (page 129), and another used "portmanteauing" to design a Christmas song (page 214). Or, you may want to save them for later, and head for the next strategy.

Starting With "And . . ."

The Strategy's Advantage

What, you may wonder, is the advantage of starting a title or lyric with a word that lacks meaning. My response: "And . . ." offers a means to thrust your character into the middle of something, into the heat of the action, the debate, the emotion. . . . That single word might also prompt a more personal, or more original lyric that you may yet have written.

Some *And* . . . Examples

And . . . songs are special—not only for their rarity but for their distinctiveness. For example, Paul Simon's "Mrs. Robinson": "And here's to you, Mrs. Robinson,/ Jesus loves you more than you will know . . . ."; is a compelling opening to a memorable song. And . . . songs also frequently introduce uncommon themes. For instance, Joe Raposo's "There Used to Be a Ballpark" draws us into the middle of a wistful recollection of Ebbets Field and lost youth: "And there used to be a ballpark/Where the field was warm and green." Similarly, in "When October Goes," the Johnny Mercer/Barry Manilow ballad, "And" starts the autumnal reverie of a life past its prime, "And when October goes/the snow begins to fly. . . ." And, of course, Paul Anka's English lyric for the French ballad "My Way" thrusts us into that moment in which the singer is coming to terms with his life: "And now the end is near/And so I face that final curtain. . . ."

Prewriting Suggestion

This exercise again calls for spontaneity—but not for wordplay in the sense of play *on* a word, but play *from* a word. Your activating process can be written and/ or verbal. You might start to free associate from the word *and* . . . on an unlined blank paper to give randomness a chance to expand. (The use of some centering music in the background would help your feelings flow and words to emerge.)

Or you could "voice activate" the lyric by verbal brainstorming: Turn on your cassette recorder and pretend you're in conversation with someone. Try out different opening gambits:

"And I don't know why you're telling me this. . . ."
"And I'm not going, that's all there is to it."
"And I don't care what your father said!"
"And what if I should tell you that . . ."

And here's a sample of what might happen:

An And . . . *Opening Line: Example No. 1 (AABA)*
IT HASN'T BEEN THAT WAY AT ALL

And the sun still rises.
And the sun still sets.

Spring turns into summer,
And summer into fall. . . .
When you left, I thought
The world would come to a halt.
But IT HASN'T BEEN THAT WAY AT ALL.

The moon still waxes,
And the moon still wanes.
The stars still twinkle,
And the tides still rise and fall;
I'd have thought they'd notice
When we two split apart.
But IT HASN'T BEEN THAT WAY AT ALL.

Though I've had to make some little changes,
Like cooking for one, instead of two—
Like saying, "I" instead of saying "we,"
Like getting a whole new point of view—
(Which is hard to do),

Still, I go through the motions.
And I say things are fine.
I come out smiling
And I practice standing tall.
In time, I'll get over you,
But somehow, as yet,
IT HASN'T BEEN THAT WAY AT ALL,
No, IT HASN'T BEEN THAT WAY AT ALL.
And the sun still rises . . .

© 1991 Rebecca Holtzman. Used with permission.

▲ Comment

Rebecca Holtzman's earlier lyrics "Thick of Getting Thin" and "Gruntled, Sheveled and Couth" typify her breezy wordplaying style. The spontaneity of the *And* . . . led her to a more reflective place and expanded her emotional spectrum. So here we find references to the sun and moon and stars—not her usual down-to-earth vocabulary. This is an example of what I mean by the possibility of *And* . . . leading you to a more feeling lyric than you may yet have written. The song, introduced at an ASCAP-sponsored showcase at the John Houseman Theatre, brought Rebecca's talents to the attention of New York's cabaret community.

An And . . . *Opening Line: Example No. 2 (AAA)*
AND HE WOULD SAY . . .

AND HE WOULD SAY, "I'm sure that we've met before."
I'd shake my head and smile at the marble floor.
And he would say, "I couldn't forget that face.
I've looked into those eyes some other place."

I'd start to walk away—
He'd somehow make me stay—
Oh, yes—that's when he'd say, "You've haunted me."

Then HE WOULD SAY: "It seems like yesterday—
That woman in the painting by Manet,
Seated on a balcony painted green
Dressed in white, surveying the Paris scene,
Holding in her hand
A folded ivory fan.
Are you that same enchanted beauty?"

I'd laugh and say, "I've never set foot in France!"
A waltz would play and we would begin to dance.
And he'd say, "But I recognize your perfume.
It comes to me at night in my room—
Yes, every single night—
And see—you're wearing white!
I loved you at first sight!
How I've wanted you!"

He'd lead me through a broad brocaded hall
To two of those French windows twelve feet tall.
He'd gaze at me and fling the windows wide.
I'd take his hand and step outside—

(instrumental interlude)

Then high above Paree
On that balcony
He would say to me, "Remember?"

He'd whisper: "I have loved you since time began."
I'd tilt my head and open an ivory fan.
The air so warm, I needn't wear a shawl—
And somehow I would have a parasol
And he would kiss my ivory brow
And I'd say: "I remember it now . . ."
    AND HE WOULD SAY . . .
    And I would say . . .
    AND HE WOULD SAY . . .

© 1991 Francesca Blumenthal. Used with permission.

▲ Comment

And I would say that "And He Would Say" took the writer of "Black and White Movie" and "Acapulco"—to the ultimate in romantic fantasy. Quite coincidentally, the lyric shares elements with "The Ultimate Night"—the marble floors, the French setting and the balcony. But where "Ultimate" presents the wishful thinking of a singer bored with her mundane existence, "And He Would Say" brings us into a surreal world that incorporates features of Edouard Manet's famous painting *The Balcony*. A unique lyric. Mated to the ideal melody, the song had a Town Hall debut at The Second Cabaret Convention and has since charmed its way into the New York cabaret repertoire.

WrapUp

After you've tried the *And*... strategy, you might take a cue from Francesca Blumenthal and seek lyric concepts from the realm of art. It's only rarely been tapped: Jay Livingston and Ray Evans turned the "Mona Lisa" into a Nat King Cole golden oldie. Don McLean's tribute to "Vincent" (van Gogh) has become an unexpected standard. And Georges Seurat's masterpiece "A Sunday Afternoon on the Island of La Grande Jatte," served as the matrix for an entire Broadway musical by Stephen Sondheim. A vast world of art still awaits to be rhymed.

PART FIVE

Design Strategies: Figurative Language

The next seven strategies bring you into the domain of figurative language—that is, into ways of thinking and writing that are nonliteral. For example, the song titles "I Write the Songs," "Don't Rain on My Parade," "Take Me Home, Country Roads" and "Rhinestone Cowboy" all use nonliteral language: Each employs a different figure of speech—*personification*, *metaphor*, *apostrophe* and *metonymy*, respectively. (Detailed definitions coming soon.)

In Aristotle's time, figures of speech were thought to be mere ornaments with which writers decorated their prose and poetry. Since the eighteenth century, we've known that figures of speech are actually figures of *thought*—ways in which we conceptualize reality to make it more comprehensible.

There are four master figures—called *tropes* (pronounced like *ropes*)—to which all others can be reduced: *irony, metaphor, metonymy* (meh-TAHN-a-mee); and *synecdoche* (se-NEK-doh-key). You may wonder why I include the unfamiliar Greek terms metonymy and synecdoche. I guarantee that only their *names* are Greek to you. The devices themselves are ones you hear and read and use everyday as much as you do forms of metaphor. It's a bit like being unfamiliar with the term for the fibrous tissue that connects the right and left hemispheres of your brain—the *corpus callosum*. Although you may not know its name, you certainly use it every day. But as a writer you want to make *purposeful and skilled use* of all four figures to enhance your facility for language: Skilled use of a tool—and these are songwriting tools—requires *conscious* practice. (It's hard to practice something you can't name and define.)

Because the figure metaphor also acts as an umbrella term that includes a number of common subtypes, three separate strategies will be devoted to the diversity of metaphor. Synecdoche, which substitutes the part for the whole, and its related figure, metonymy, which substitutes a symbol for the thing meant, will each get a section. Pun, a subtype of irony, greatly enlivens lyric writing, so of course we'll play with pun in its various forms.

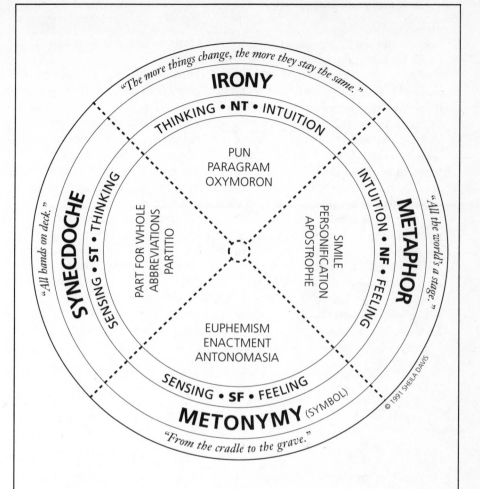

The figure text, reading around the wheel:

"The more things change, the more they stay the same."

IRONY

THINKING • **NT** • INTUITION

PUN
PARAGRAM
OXYMORON

"All hands on deck."

SYNECDOCHE

SENSING • **ST** • THINKING

PART FOR WHOLE
ABBREVIATIONS
PARTITIO

SIMILE
PERSONIFICATION
APOSTROPHE

INTUITION • **NF** • FEELING

METAPHOR

"All the world's a stage."

EUPHEMISM
ENACTMENT
ANTONOMASIA

SENSING • **SF** • FEELING

METONYMY (SYMBOL)

"From the cradle to the grave."

© 1991 SHEILA DAVIS

Personality Type, the Brain and the Four Tropes

Teaching songwriting from the triple perspectives of type, brain lateralization and figurative language has made apparent the interconnectedness of those three realms: Accumulated evidence reveals that each of the four cognitive styles exhibits a preference for one particular trope (and its subtypes) over the other three. I've identified the relationship this way: Intuitive/Thinker (NT)-*Irony*; Intuitive/Feeler (NF)-*Metaphor*; Sensate/Feeler (SF)-*Metonymy*; Sensate/Thinker (ST)-*Synecdoche*.

This symbolic brain model illustrates the affinity between cognitive style and its related master trope. The circle's outer rim gives a well-known example of each trope; the inner wedge gives three of its common subtypes, which we'll be practicing in the coming chapters.

These four wedge-shaped windows of the mind provide four distinct views of reality: the philosophic (NT-irony), the idealistic (NF-metaphor), the symbolic (SF-metonymy), and the realistic (ST-synecdoche). Each of us tends to view the world primarily from one of those windows, yet we all travel around the circle exploring other vantage points to expand our understanding of the whole. For example, although an NT's dominant trope tends to be irony, the writing will also exhibit, from time to time, aspects of metaphor, metonymy and synecdoche—often in support of irony. Similarly, for the other three types—which you will soon see.

You may have been wondering if your writing reflects a preference for the trope that the model suggests would be your favorite. At this stage of the book that may be hard to determine because you are likely to be unfamiliar with the Greek terms for common figurative expressions. But the next section will serve as your "Figurative Language 101," giving you enough examples of the figures encountered daily in conversation, on TV, in advertising, and, of course, in lyrics to enable you to answer that question—and turn you into an expert on the four tropes. We'll start with metaphor.

Metaphor as Design Device

A Definition and Some Background

A metaphor is a figure of comparison that implies some likeness in two disparate realms thus making a verbal equation: "All the world's a stage and all the men and women merely players" (Shakespeare). That statement claims, in effect: Life = a play. This metaphor reflects one of our basic concepts as heard in such common expressions as "my *role* as teacher," "She was *upstaged* by her sister," "The *curtain came down* on our affair."

Thinking metaphorically draws upon the right brain's ability to visualize, note similarities, and synthesize, thus using a thought process natural to the right-brain intuitive/feeling type, the NF.

Simile: A Tentative Metaphor

A simile is the most common subtype of metaphor. It makes a direct comparison using the words *like*, *as* or *than*. I've dubbed a simile a *tentative metaphor* because it lacks the metaphor's assertiveness. For example, compare the relative power of the statement "All the world's a stage" to "All the world is *like* a stage," or "I Am a Rock" to "I Am *Like* a Rock." The essential meaning is the same, but the "like" considerably lessens its impact.

Since similes are by nature metaphoric, all the upcoming theory, exercises and guidelines on the successful use of metaphor pertain equally to the use of simile.

The Verbal Equation

It's been observed that it's virtually impossible for anyone to talk for more than three consecutive minutes without recourse to a metaphor. That's because we envision so many basic aspects of life, quite unconsciously, in terms of something else. As a consequence, when we use certain phrases we're often unaware that we're not being literal. For example, the following phrases may not immediately strike you as metaphoric. Yet each embodies a verbal equation:

This Metaphoric Phrase	Implies	This Verbal Equation
"You won that round"		arguments = prizefights
"Jumpstart the economy"		economy = engine
"That's hard to swallow"		ideas = substances
"What's the bottom line?"		life = a balance sheet

A metaphoric expression states, in essence, "A equals B." Thus, to reflect truth, each attribute given must reflect "B-ness." Shakespeare expanded his concept that the world (A) is a stage (B) by noting further likenesses to the stage — his *semantic field* — the area of comparison: Players have "their *exits* and their *entrances* and one man in his time *plays* many *parts*." Every attribute is an aspect of B-ness (the stage) and thus reflects truth. The clarity, consistency and coherence of the metaphor result from a unified semantic field — in this case, the stage.

Identify and Unify Your Semantic Field

The fresh, inventive or stunning metaphor is a rarity. The majority of metaphors that we read, hear, speak, and write are uninspired, banal—and often muddled. The muddle results from the thinker's feeling state that has blurred or overlapped two or more semantic fields; for example, this student lyric phrase: "I think I'm going under/Trapped in all the games surrounding me." Going under? In what, water? Or quicksand? How is one *trapped* in games? What kind of games *surround*? Card games? Board games? The singer's emotion is obvious—distress. But what is the semantic field? The essence of metaphor is to understand one thing in terms of another—thus enriching meaning. There is no clear "other" here and thus no enriched meaning—only distressed feeling. Making coherent metaphoric statements requires first being conscious of your initial semantic field of comparison—your B ("other")—and then, keeping it consistent.

The Mixed Metaphor

A metaphoric statement that begins by saying A equals B and then adds characteristics unrelated to B results in the infamous "mixed metaphor." Here, for example, is a metaphoric statement that hopes to offer a formula for success: "If you play your cards right, you'll hit the bull's-eye." Attaining success (A) starts out being compared to a card game (B). But the thinker lost sight of his original semantic field, and wandered into a second semantic field: a target range (C). The result, a "mixing" of two fields of comparison (B + C) instead of augmenting one (B + B). There's a simple trick to writing coherent metaphors: *See* what you *feel*.

Unmixing the Metaphor

Let's unmix that mixed metaphor. Visualize on your mind's mental screen an image of a card game and keep it there until you complete the metaphor for success. What does a card game look like? What do you do during a card game? Now, keeping that image in your mind, come up with a new phrase that adds card-game-like attributes ("B-ness") to the introductory statement. Think for a minute. Have an idea yet? Here's one treatment: "If you play your cards right, you'll hold the winning hand." Any variant on that would work fine.

Now, let's do it again, only start from the second half of the statement. Picture a target. What, literally, do you have to do to hit the bull's-eye? Think of an opening phrase to introduce target. Okay, what's your phrase? It might be something like, "If you shoot enough arrows, you'll hit the bull's-eye." Or, "If you aim your darts carefully, you'll hit the bull's-eye." Remember the guideline: *See what you feel*. With a little practice, it becomes automatic.

Keep a Series of Ideas Consistent

When writing a series of related ideas, be sure to keep the series either consistently figurative or consistently literal. For example, William Faulkner once observed, "Hollywood is the only place I know where you can get stabbed in the back while you're climbing a ladder." Faulkner's remark is funny and insightful and the images—stabbed/back/ladder—consistently figurative. Now, here's a blooper that begins with a literal statement that's immediately followed by a figurative one: "While they were out walking the dog (literal), she let the cat out of the bag" (figurative). Because the mental picture is so incongruous, it's inadvertently funny. Humor, however, was not the writer's intention. The statement can easily be fixed by making it either all literal or all figurative. Figurative: "When they were horsing around, he let the cat out of the bag." Literal: "While they were out walking the dog, he inadvertently alluded to the matter."

Oops: A "Malaphor"

It's strange, but seems to be true: A recorded lyric is the only published writing that doesn't pass through an editorial process; that is, it lacks a review by a professional editor to check for proper syntax and semantic accuracy. Perhaps that's why a printed lyric, when exposed to the glare of the bare page, often reveals metaphoric blunders, specifically of the kind that contradict reality in some way. *A metaphor suggests a potential reality.* A metaphor that falsifies reality, I've termed a "malaphor." Here are some recorded malaphors I've noted:

- A female singer wants to open her lover's locked heart and says, "I hold the lock and you hold the key." Nope—if he had locked his heart, *he'd hold the lock as well as the key.*
- A male singer compared himself to a rock—"charging from the gate . . . carrying the weight." Nope—rocks are incapable of either activity.
- A male singer said he was (metaphorically) "sliding on ice" while "caught in a vice." Nope—if you're in a vice, you're immobilized; a case of seduction by rhyme.
- A lyric alluded to "the stepping-stones of life . . . *along the road.*" Nope—stepping-stones are those stones *in water* that allow to you cross from one shore to the other.
- A lyric in which the singer vowed to go metaphorically on strike had her packing and *never coming back.* Nope—*on strike* means "a *temporary* cessation of activities."

To avoid such malaphors, make sure—*before* the demo session—that your left-brain editor gives a reality check to your right-brain images.

The Overstated Malaphor

There's a particular kind of malaphor that results from a lyricist mistaking metaphoric overstatement for "dramatic" writing. The result: A falsehood. For example, in a "goodbye song" with a winter setting, a singer claimed, "my heart *is frozen* in the snow." No, it isn't. That line flunks the reality check. Luckily there's a simple remedy for this type of malaphor. Modify the false metaphor to a true simile: "My heart *feels frozen like* the snow." Now it passes the reality check.

The Murky Metaphor

Besides the mixed metaphor and the malaphor, another major cause of flawed figurative lyrics stems from the writer's unconscious linking of unrelated metaphoric expressions that muddy the intended meaning. For example, a student's chorus contained this (con)fusion of ideas: "Where there's smoke there's fire/ When we met you started a spark/Now there's a fire in my heart." *Started a spark* and *fire in my heart* accord in meaning because they both reflect the basic metaphoric concept: passionate emotions = fires. But the adage "Where there's smoke there's fire" uses fire in a wholly different context. The metaphoric colloquialism suggests a result/cause (smoke/fire) relationship by implying that some concrete evidence (smoke) points to an incriminating cause (fire). The lyricist unwittingly subverted her chorus' intended positive statement by introducing it with an unrelated negative implication.

Learning to Discriminate

As just noted, all figurative uses of a single word, such as *fire*, do not necessarily embody the same meaning and thus, if linked, may convey incoherence. Metaphoric competence requires the ability to discriminate—to make fine distinctions. And as the improvement in students' writing makes clear, it's a learnable skill—and one that's essential to writing coherent lyrics. A lyric's coherence or lack of it depends on a series of good judgments. Good judgments—whether thinking or feeling judgments—require the ability to discriminate between literal and figurative, between identical and similar, between false and true. Here's an exercise to activate your ability to analyze.

Identify These Implied Verbal Equations

Take a few minutes now to identify the metaphoric equation implicit in these common expressions. I'll give you the first one for starters:

That delay cost me an hour	time	=	money
Their affair is on the rocks	_____	=	_____
She turns me on	_____	=	_____
He leaves me cold	_____	=	_____
Her image has frayed	_____	=	_____

(Answers on page 90.)

The Metaphor Strategy

The objective now is to write a lyric whose central design rests on a metaphor that unites two different fields. Challenge yourself to select one semantic field and keep it consistent. Many famous songs draw upon society's most basic metaphoric concepts. Let's look at four:

Titles That Embody Four Basic Metaphoric Concepts

Rain = trouble/hard times	Stormy Weather
	I Made It Through the Rain
	Raindrops Keep Fallin' on My Head
	Rainy Day Woman
	Let a Smile Be Your Umbrella
Sun = happiness/good times	You Are My Sunshine
	Sunny Side of the Street
	When the Sun Comes Out
	You Are the Sunshine of My Life

Music = romantic feelings	With a Song in My Heart
	The Song Is You
	How Do You Keep the Music Playing
	The Song Is Ended, But the Melody
	Lingers On
Life = a road journey	Somewhere Down the Road
	Two for the Road
	Merrily We Roll Along
	Boulevard of Broken Dreams

Those metaphors represent the staples of songdom because they reflect truth. So they're worth emulating—of course with a fresh slant. But the song that really grabs us is the one that makes a comparison that we've never heard before, like these:

Titles That Reflect Fresh Metaphor/Simile Concepts

You Ain't Nothin' But a Hound Dog
(Like a) Bridge Over Troubled Water
Everything's Coming Up Roses
Running on Empty
If You Don't Want My Peaches, You'd Better Stop Shaking My Tree
You Can't Be a Beacon If Your Light Don't Shine
I Don't Mind the Thorns When You're the Rose
You Are the Wind Beneath My Wings

Prewriting Suggestion

Any of the foregoing metaphors may suggest a fresh approach, or you might consider some other mainstream concepts:

Love is magic	Silence is a wall
Feelings are temperatures	Troubles are burdens
Relationships are a gamble	Infidelity is a crime

After you pick one, or come up with an original one, then comes the free associating process. Whatever your favorite mode—paper or PC—let spontaneous phrases tumble out. If, for example, you picked "relationships are a gamble," start out with that phrase, suspend your left-brain's critical judgments and let your right's randomness come out to play. Freely jot down any related words or phrases that spring to mind—*roulette wheel, game of chance, place my bet, stakes are high*. Stay in that "flow" mode for a while letting random thoughts connect, rhymes spill out—*wheel/deal/steal/appeal/conceal....* The longer you sustain the flow, the richer will be the source material from which you begin to write. So keep going and going and going. Suddenly, a phrase may come out that makes you say, "Hey, that's it—a title." Now you've experienced the *activating/associating* phase.

Then you move into phase two—*incubate*. You muse about the title, walk around with it, ask yourself who's saying it to whom, and why. Maybe even sleep on it. As you begin to sift and sort and shape all that rich randomness into the suitable song form, you'll have moved over to the left hemisphere. As you *separate*, you eliminate inappropriate ideas that no longer fit your title.

When you've got a first draft finished, then comes the editing process — *discriminate*. Be sure your title (logically) sums up your main thought. Ask yourself if you've kept to a single semantic field. Does every metaphoric statement have "B-ness"? Does every metaphoric statement pass the reality test? (No hearts frozen in the snow.) Here now is a student lyric that was activated by the strategy and went through every phase in the four-part creative process.

Metaphor: Example No. 1 (Verse/Chorus/Bridge)
OCEANS OF LOVE

If you wanna sail to heaven,
Leave it all and put to sea,
Take a fantasy cruise forever,
Well, you can book your passage with me.

I wanna give you
OCEANS OF LOVE
Waves of pleasure,
Waves of pleasure,
OCEANS OF LOVE.
You gotta feel the rhythm,
The motion,
The oceans and oceans
The rhythm,
The motion,
And the OCEANS OF LOVE.

Or if you are a seasoned sailor,
And the seas hold no surprises for you,
I can take you on a voyage
That will thrill you through and through.

(repeat chorus)

Deeper than the great Pacific,
Wider than the seven seas,
My love is endless as the blue horizon,
And it's only there to please you.

(repeat chorus)

If you wanna sail to heaven
Float away to paradise
Let me navigate the waters
So you can rise and fall with the tides.

(repeat chorus)

▲ Comment

Not only did the writer incorporate consistently appropriate nautical allusions to support her premise that sexual pleasure = an ocean trip—*sail, cruise, book passage, seasoned sailor, seas, voyage, navigate the waters*—she punned on *oceans* and *waves*, playing off the two meanings implicit in each word. In the chorus, by manipulating her rhythm, she also managed to make her love boat "rock." I want to point out the instance of trailing rhyme in *seas/please you*. Had you given any thought to the writer's type?

Well, she's as right-brain dominant as one can be—an ENFP with all four preferences in the right hemisphere. So it's no wonder we get the sexual/loving subject matter, the metaphoric language, and an attitude characteristic of the intuitive/feeling type—aiming to please.

Here's another metaphoric example. Though the subject is love again, you'll hear quite a change in the attitude. Remember, the right-dominant (NF) is not the only type who can think metaphorically.

Metaphor: Example No. 2 (Verse/Chorus/Bridge)
STRANGE, STRANGE POISON

I still don't know how you get in—
How you get underneath my skin.
Must be somethin' in the lovin'
You've been givin' me.
Must be somethin' in your lips—
Some kind of deadly kiss.
I've been hurt before by this.
Still I go down easy.

Hey, ain't love a
STRANGE, STRANGE POISON?
Sometimes sickly sweet,
Sometimes powerful and pure.
Hey, ain't love a
STRANGE, STRANGE POISON?
And though it makes me weak,
I know your poison is a cure—
A STRANGE, STRANGE POISON
That's for sure.

There's really nothin' I can do,
No, not when it comes to you.
It's jus' somethin' I go through
When you're lovin' me.
I feel you running through my veins
Like the river floods in monsoon rains.
You really muddy up my brain;
Still I go down easy.

(repeat chorus)

Gotta keep this lovin' feelin' goin'
Even though it's changin' me.
So I let you pry me open
Knowin' your love is rearrangin' me.

(repeat chorus)

© 1990 Kevin Dowling. Used with permission.

▲ Comment

A central design metaphor, yes, and a fresh one, yet totally unlike the ENFP's playful, romantic tone and style. Here we get the questioning, analytical, paradoxical viewpoint so characteristic of the intuitive/*thinker*. The writer, an EN*T*P, uses metaphor in service to his ironic view of life. I'm sure you noticed the fresh metaphoric concept "pry me open" implying the singer is a sealed container.

WrapUp

Each lyric example reflects an aspect of its writer's essential view of life. It is perhaps this very integrity—integrated whole-brainedness—that contributes to the clarity and effectiveness of both lyrics.

Writing coherent metaphoric lyrics requires mastering two skills: 1) Becoming conscious of your initial semantic field; and 2) Learning to *see what you feel*. Till then, first drafts may require some metaphoric revisions. Of course all initial lyric outpourings need a cool, objective look from your left-brain critic whose gift is to detect discrepancies. But quite naturally, it is the feeling types who may especially need to develop that critical ability—in both senses of the word. (Ts of course do it automatically because thinking is a dominant function.) But without a conscious effort to access the left-brain editor, a feeling type may read over a first draft more in appreciation of its wordplay than in appraisal of possible flaws. But by purposefully accessing the left brain's analytical skills, every type can acquire the ability to produce coherent metaphors. One last editorial guideline: Beware of your favorite lines; they're usually the ones that require the sharpest blue pencil. Now to a special metaphoric subtype: The Compact Simile.

Answers to the Exercise on Page 86

Their affair is on the rocks:	relationships = a sea voyage
She turns me on:	people = machines
He leaves me cold:	emotions = temperatures
Her image has frayed:	reputations = fabrics

The Compact Simile as Design Device

Some Background

As we noted in the last strategy, simile, a direct comparison, is subject to all the guidelines and craft warnings of the indirect comparison of metaphor. In other words, whether you're saying "A Pretty Girl Is *Like* a Melody" or "The Song *Is* You," the same caveat applies to stay in the semantic field of music and take care not to waltz into a related field—like dance.

The Compact Simile

Many common similes—*white as snow, sweet as cherries, sharp as a tack*—are so visually, orally, tactilely apt that they're hard to improve upon. As a consequence, these little truths, which come in so handy to express our thoughts, become clichés. In fact, they often attain a reduced form I've termed the *compact simile*: For example, *snow white, arrow straight, hairpin curve*, and so on.

One of the newest compact similes taken up by the media is "the glass-ceiling syndrome" referring to the non-existence of executive positions for women due to a covert policy that top-level jobs are reserved for men—*as if* there were a glass ceiling at the top of the metaphoric ladder of success. In songwriting, the goal of course is to think as freshly as did the anonymous originator of that expression.

The Compact Simile as Song Title

The form of the compact simile obviously lends itself to constructing fresh and memorable song titles. Yet, ironically—as I am unable to offer you a string of hit examples—it appears to be a virtually untapped vein in the gold mine of title strategies. (The only one that I've been able to turn up is "Ebony Eyes," the title of two different songs which both made it to the charts.) But as class assignments and the upcoming examples attest, the strategy produces fresh results.

Creating Compact Similes: The Process

The process of creating original compact similes engages both the similarity-finding function of the right brain and the contracting function of the left brain—a true whole-brain exercise.

In creating a compact-simile title, the first objective is to choose a subject for comparison (like *eyes*) and then find an appropriate image that's reducible to a single word (like *ebony*) which acts as an adjective to compactly convey your comparison.

I suggest that you start your title search by taking out a lined notebook or sheet of paper. Make two parallel lists: On the left side of your paper head a column "Subject for comparison." That's the A of your verbal equation. It might include such popular (abstract) song subjects as *smile, heart, lover, night, life, memory, promise, dream*, and so on.

Then on the right, under the heading "Potential Semantic Fields," (your B), list vivid sensate images that convey distinct properties — such as *lemon, lace, velcro, velvet, glass, plastic, peppermint,* etc. With your pencil, connect a subject word from the left list to a modifying word on the right until you get that "Aha!" If nothing turns up from your initial try, add to both the left-hand and right-hand lists when you come across sensate images that strike you. The important thing is you've started a mental process, called *entrainment*: you've laid down a kind of mental track on which you have hooked up an abstract concept with a concrete image; you can now travel that track again with more ease. Trust your creative process. Eventually, a song title will emerge. Here's a lyric that evolved from this exercise:

Compact Simile: Example No. 1 (AABA)
RAWHIDE HEART

You almost fooled me, baby,
Till I heard you on the phone,
Promising to meet him
As soon as he got home.
I never would have guessed it,
But I guess I should have known
You're a woman with a RAWHIDE HEART.

A heart that can't be trusted
Is an easy thing to hide
Underneath your satin skin
And steamy bedroom eyes.
I'd thought your tender touch
Came from tenderness inside
But it covered up your RAWHIDE HEART.

Before I trust another woman
You can bet I'll find out whether
Her heart is made of muscle and blood
Or untanned leather.

I'm glad I got the message
Before it got too late.
Go ahead and meet him.
I'm in no mood to debate.
You showed me what you're made of
And saved me from the fate
Of a woman with a RAWHIDE HEART.

© 1991 Jan Tranen. Used with permission.

▲ Comment

It's old "hard-hearted Hannah" revamped with a country-fresh memorable title. The paradox of the satin exterior covering the leather interior was, of course, noted by an intuitive/thinker (NT) whose metaphors are usually less-than-romantic (as we noted in "Strange Poison").

LIGHTNING LOVE

I had been wandering—
Drifting from man to man
Staying if things were simple
Leaving if he made demands.
No interest in becoming
Part of a pair
But suddenly I turned
And you were there—
It was

LIGHTNING LOVE
You struck me like a flash
LIGHTNING LOVE
Like a bolt out of the blue
LIGHTNING LOVE
You flared up such a passion
Now all I want is you.

How did you do it—
Dazzle me with your eyes—
Break through my defenses
Taking me by surprise?
Thought I'd built a fortress
No one could penetrate,
But somehow you have
Gotten through the gate
With your

(repeat chorus)

Sparks fly when we're together
Lighting up the dark
Sparks fly when we're together
Warming up my heart

(repeat chorus)

© 1991 Marie Stewart. Used with permission.

▲ Comment

Another inventive title—this time to underscore a positive emotion. The writer amplified her simple metaphor with allied words like *stuck/flash/bolt/dazzle/spark*, but was careful not to overdo a good thing. I also want to point out the chorus' fresh sound of trailing rhyme (*flash/passion*) instead of a commonplace masculine rhyme pairing of, for example, *flash/clash*—a result of the writer's practice of minor rhyme (see page 50). This is the kind of improvement you'll start to see in your own writing as you expand your range of possibilities through the mastery of technique.

WrapUp

The next time you're stuck on a long supermarket line, you might try exercising your ability to make compact similes. Not only is it guaranteed to make the time pass faster, it may even generate a new song title before you reach the checkout counter. Now on to a popular metaphoric subtype, personification.

Personification as Design Device

Some Background

Personification, a subtype of metaphor, is a figure of speech attributing human characteristics to abstractions or inanimate objects: "The sun *smiled* on the Memorial Day parade"; "Illiteracy is *robbing us* of future leaders"; "Inflation *is eating up* the profits."

Some Lyric Line Examples

Personification is most frequently heard in lyrics in one-liners such as these by Oscar Hammerstein—for whom the device was a favorite: "The wind got confidential and *whispered* through a tree"; "The world will *open its arms* to me"; "The soft mist of England was *sleeping* on a hill."

Some Song Examples

As a design strategy, personification takes two forms. The basic form is one in which an abstraction/place/thing is referred to in third person as if human. For example, in "The Summer Knows" (Bergmans/Legrand) summer is personified as a woman who "*smiles/knows/dresses/sheds her clothes.*" Similarly, in "The Last Time I Saw Paris" (Kern/Hammerstein), Paris was a "lady . . . romantic and charming" whose "laughter" was "heard in every street café." And then, there is perhaps the grandaddy of all personification songs, "Ol' Man River" (Kern/Hammerstein).

The second and more dramatic form takes personification to the ultimate: *the singer becomes the thing personified.*

In the C-section of "Bali Ha'i," Oscar Hammerstein makes an intriguing transition from having the singer talk about the special island to having the singer *become* the island, ". . . Someday you'll hear me call you . . . come to me, come to me."

Two distinguished songs that take the strategy all the way are "(I'm the train they call) The City of New Orleans" (Goodman) and "(I am music and) I Write the Songs" (Johnston). It is this form of the device that I encourage you to try.

The Strategy's Advantage

When you choose to transform your singer into an inanimate object or abstraction, you give yourself an ability to treat nonhuman entities in terms of human characteristics, activities and motivations. Personification thus expands your lyric themes by providing an oblique approach to subjects—as you will shortly see in two student examples.

Narrowing Your Focus

There are, of course, a limitless number of abstractions or objects which can be personified. Narrowing the range of options will make your choice easier. I suggest, for your initial experience in becoming something nonhuman, that you personify some category of building—or a particular famous building or edifice. This aspect of personification usually sparks a uniquely individual statement from a writer.

Prewriting Suggestion

As you know, making lists is a productive way to activate certain kinds of lyric concepts. This kind of list will get you into a realistic, factual focused left-brain frame of mind. In your idea notebook write down as many categories of buildings or particular names of famous buildings/edifices that spring to mind—*supermarket, jail, courthouse, silo, school, the Pentagon, the Golden Gate Bridge, the Sphinx*, and so on. To get one *good* idea requires getting a lot of ideas, so try to fill the whole page. This process generally yields a word that links you to a theme that excites you.

When you've got your theme—let the concept incubate. Walk around with it, sleep on it. Ask yourself key questions using the first person: What am I made of? Where am I located? How old am I? Who lives or works in me—or visits me? Am I open during the day, at night, on weekends? Try to *feel* the answers. *Experience* the building. *Become* the building.

Then ask yourself, "What *one* emotion do I want my audience to feel?" When you know the answer, you are ready to begin the lyric. Here's a little trick to help you stay focused: Write at the top of your lyric sheet a short sentence summarizing the single point you want to make. Looking up at it occasionally will keep you on the subject.

Small Craft Warning

When personifying an abstraction/place/thing, it is, of course, appropriate to attribute any of the many human emotions to your subject—elation, envy, conflict, pride, and so on. But it is not appropriate to attribute characteristics or properties to your subject that it does not possess—as some first drafts by students have done. For example, an office building does not wear a red brick vest; a heartache does not own luggage. Make sure your personification passes that reality check I spoke about—that it makes no metaphoric claim for its subject that does not check with reality.

A second important caveat: Your audience's enjoyment of the song requires that they know, right from the beginning, who is doing the talking. So be very sure to make the singer's identity clear by the second line of the first verse. Here are two student examples that do the job well.

Personification: Example No. 1 (Verse/Climb/Chorus)
ONLY LOVE CAN MAKE THIS HOUSE A HOME

I've been cold, dark and empty
Since my old owners divorced
But I used to be the house of their dreams
With my modern country kitchen
And sunken living room
And my ornamental plants and evergreens.

Then you brightened up my morning
With an orange moving van.
I'm glad you and your wife are here to stay.
'Cause I'd almost forgotten
The warmth of family.
You gave me a new lease on life today.

Now our first night together's full of unfamiliar sounds
But I'm really looking forward to having you around

To share the joy of loving laughter
As it echoes off the walls
And to keep love's fire burning
In the bedroom down the hall.
Without love I've been a prison
Made of plasterboard and stone, 'cause
ONLY LOVE CAN MAKE THIS HOUSE A HOME.
Yes, ONLY LOVE CAN MAKE THIS HOUSE A HOME.

I heard you tell the neighbors
'Bout your renovation plans
To tear out all my crystal chandeliers,
And change the color of the kitchen,
And enclose the swimming pool
With a six-foot cedar fence across the rear.

But these so-called home improvements are meaningless to me.
All this house ever needed was a caring family

(repeat chorus)

© 1988 Rick Swiegoda. Used with permission.

▲ Comment

That's what I mean by *become the building*. Concrete images, colors, sounds and textures animate the lyric: *evergreens, orange van, crystal chandelier, laughter, cedar, stone*. By drawing on the device of personification, Rick Swiegoda was able to express his personal values and deliver an anti-materialistic message in a fresh and original manner.

Personification: Example No. 2 (Verse/Bridge/Chorus)
DON'T THREATEN LIBERTY

I've been standin' out here
In New York harbor,
Shinin' with joy
For a hundred years,
Holdin' my torch
High to light the world.
Now what do I find
The military mind proposin'?:

To slip a nuclear fleet
In at my feet.

DON'T THREATEN LIBERTY,
Don't close in on me.
Keep these waters free.
DON'T THREATEN LIBERTY,
Don't threaten me.

For I'm puttin' my trust in life,
In the voices of the earth.
Know that freedom is the way.

I want to stand out here
In New York harbor,
A beacon of hope
For ages to come,
Beamin' my light
On the children,
Dreamers of ev'ry land.
So don't harbor death,
Don't harbor death for a moment.
To this fleet I say, "No!"
This fleet's got to go.

DON'T THREATEN LIBERTY
Don't close in on me
Keep these waters free.
DON'T THREATEN LIBERTY
Don't threaten me.
Keep these waters free.

© 1985 Sue Stater. Used with permission.

▲ Comment

The passionate anti-nuke statement was Sue Stater's response to a current event. Her message was rendered more effective coming from the voice of the Statue of Liberty than through her own. The song, performed by the writer/artist, won first place in a contest sponsored by the Coalition for a Nuclear-Free Harbor.

WrapUp

I hope these examples of personification will serve to suggest a way to approach subjects that you might not otherwise tackle. As you can see, the device can be especially useful in handling serious themes and social statements. Whenever a subject seems to defy treatment, consider becoming a lawyer's yellow pad, the judge's gavel, a taxi meter, a fly on the wall. . . .

Apostrophe as Design Device

Some Background

Apostrophe (A-POS-tro-fee) is a figure of speech in which a place, thing, or absent (often dead) person is addressed as if alive and will presumably answer. It is a subtype of metaphor related to personification. This strategy employs the second-person viewpoint in a figurative, rather than a literal, way.

Some Apostrophe Examples

Apostrophe as a design device comes in four discrete categories: The singer addresses a place, absent person, aspect of nature, or an abstraction or inanimate object:

Place	Absent (or Imaginary) Person
Swanee	Blow, Gabriel, Blow
California, Here I Come	Amelia
Galveston	Please, Mr. Postman
April in Paris	Mr. Sandman
San Francisco	Vincent
Don't Cry for Me, Argentina	Papa, Can You Hear Me?

Aspect of Nature	Abstraction or Inanimate Object
Willow, Weep for Me	Mona Lisa
Moon River	Time, Don't Run Out on Me
Skylark	Luck, Be a Lady Tonight
Snowbird	Good Morning, Heartache
Evening Star	Happy Birthday, Dear Heartache
Green Finch and Linnet Bird	Goodbye, Yellow Brick Road
Glow Worm	Take Me Home, Country Roads

The Strategy's Advantage

Like personification, apostrophe offers the lyricist two advantages: First, a means to approach familiar subjects from a fresh angle. For example, instead of having the singer conventionally describe an emotional state, the lyric has the singer hold a conversation about it with the moon ("Blue Moon") or with an abstraction like heartache ("Happy Birthday, Dear Heartache"), as if talking to a person. Perhaps more important, apostrophe provides a means to treat themes not easily treatable by the literal approach of the first-, second-, or third-person viewpoints. (More about unusual subjects in a minute.)

Here's an example of how apostrophe can give a face lift to an old feeling—regret; it's a lyric I wrote many years ago to a jazz-tinged piano piece by Walter Gross, composer of "Tenderly."

CLARINET

Make the song sad and slow
CLARINET
Cause I feel awf'ly low
CLARINET
Fill the room with blue tune
While I light up one more cigarette.

When love was new
I called for gay songs
Now love is through
Play those cliché songs
Love-is-passé songs.

As I sip on my third
Anisette.
Sinking deep in my corner
Banquette
Fill the room with a blue tune
One that matches my mood of regret.

Where was my mind?
Where were my senses?
Deaf, dumb and blind
Without defenses
For his pretenses.

Faded dreams, foolish dreams
Haunt me yet.
Guess it's time that I learn
To forget.
Till I do, play a blue tune
Keep the song sad and slow
CLARINET

Lyric by Sheila Davis/Music by Walter Gross
© *1965 Solar Systems Music. Used with permission.*

Talking to a clarinet makes the blues more interesting than talking to yourself. But, it is the more unusual theme that I encourage you to explore with this device. Songs like "Vincent," "Amelia" and "Don't Cry for Me, Argentina," illustrate how apostrophe can lead you to fresher subject matter.

Prewriting Suggestion

You can best tap the possibilities of apostrophe through a kind of structured free association. In your brainstorming notebook you might head four columns with the words, "Places," "Aspects of Nature," "Abstractions/Inanimate Objects" and "Absent/Imaginary People." In each column write down—in an uncensored manner—any person, place or thing that springs to mind with whom, or which, you might dialogue. Then consider the various attributes you could hold toward a given subject: praising, critical, disappointed, outraged, and so on. Consider, too, the possibility of starting with a particular emotion. Then pick a place, object or absent person to whom you can convey the emotion you are feeling. Cynthia Weil, whose chart successes span three decades, sometimes activates the lyric process with that approach. She told me, "I'll think of concepts instead of titles and the title comes out of it." Like personification, apostrophe lends itself to making a strong political statement. Here's an example of what I mean.

Apostrophe: Example No. 2 (AAA)
FOX

O, I am fierce in my love for you, FOX
Wolf, lynx and coyote,
Bobcat and beaver, opossum, raccoon,
You lift me with your wild beauty.

Then beware where you step in the wood.
Beware the means of the trapper:
When those steel jaws close over your leg,
You'll bleed through my dreams forever.

So I imagine a possible world
Where no woman would ever consider
Wrapping her vanity up in skins
Wrenched from a fellow creature.

And here in my possible world
No FOX will ever be harrowed
Or hung on a peg, but left to roam free
To sniff out his own tomorrow.

O, I am fierce in my love for you, FOX
Wolf, lynx and coyote,
Bobcat and beaver, opossum, raccoon—
You lift the world with your wild beauty.

© 1991 Words and Music by Sue Stater. Used with permission.

▲ Comment

When a writer feels as passionately about a subject as Sue Stater does about animal rights, apostrophe provides a means by which to express the passion yet avoid the pitfall of preachiness: The listener, instead of being directly reproached by the singer, is delivered the message obliquely in an overheard conversation. I'd also like to point out the writer's sensitive choice of unstressed rhyme, (*trapper/forever, coyote/beauty, harrowed/tomorrow, consider/creature*), to match the seriousness of the subject; the slickness of perfect rhyme might easily have undermined the desired effect. The line "Wrapping her vanity up in skins/Wrenched from a fellow creature" deserves mention for three writerly devices: Alliteration in the repeated *wr* of *wrapping/wrenched*; metonymy (*vanity*, the attribute substitutes for the possessor) and synecdoche, (*skins*, the part substitutes for the whole). The latter two figures of speech will be treated fully in the next two strategies.

Now, in a lighter vein, Mr. Murphy, the designer of the law which asserts that "if anything can go wrong, it will," gets a complaint.

Apostrophe: Example No. 3 (Verse/Chorus w/Intro Verse)
HEY, MR. MURPHY

As a law-abiding citizen, I can't be beat:
I pay my taxes promptly (and I never cheat).
I don't litter, I don't jaywalk — so I would stand and cheer
If the law that's known as Murphy's Law would disappear.

HEY, MR. MURPHY, why did you write that law?
As laws go, Mr. Murphy, it's the worst I ever saw.
It's appalling, disgraceful, an outright crime.
For what *can* go wrong always does
At the very worst possible time.

You programmed each appliance that I ever bought
So that none of them would operate the way they ought
What's more, my radio, my stereo, and color TV
Each expired one day after their warranty.

And once some exotic virus came and knocked me flat,
And you made sure that my insurance wouldn't cover that.
And you saw that it would happen at the very time
When I'd used up all my sick leave — so I didn't get a dime.

HEY, MR. MURPHY, why did you write that law?
As laws go Mr. Murphy, it's the worst I ever saw!
At messing up my daily life, I'd say you've been the tops,
And you still keep thinking up new ways to bust my chops —

Like when I look for romance (as I often do),
I know somehow I'll end up looking straight at you.
'Cause every time a dreamboat sails into my life
I find that he is anchored to a very stubborn wife!

HEY, MR. MURPHY, why did you write that law?
As laws go Mr. Murphy, it's the worst I ever saw!
And that is why I'm begging you on bended knee
Wipe out that lousy law before it wipes out me!
Why, MR. MURPHY, why did you write that law?

© 1990 Rebecca Holtzman. Used with permission.

▲ Comment

Had the writer expressed her complaints in a more conventional first-person manner, the song would have lacked the charm that apostrophe made possible. In the realm of rhyme, Rebecca Holtzman, like Sue Stater, made the appropriate choice; in this case, frequent and perfect rhyme in service to the lyric's lighthearted tone. As a left-brain dominant (ESTJ), Rebecca rarely uses metaphor. When it did appear—remarking that her *dreamboats* are *anchored* to their wives—the tone was resentful rather than romantic: No *waves of pleasure* here as in "Oceans of Love" written by a feeling dominant (page 88).

Small Craft Warning

When using apostrophe, bear in mind two important caveats. As early in the lyric as possible make clear to the ear who is being (or about to be) addressed; all three role-model lyrics carefully prepared the listener. Be mindful too that the addressed place/object/abstraction becomes the lyric's "you"—for the entire lyric. So be careful not to let another "you" sneak in there. Sometimes that glitch gets vinylized: As *SLW* pointed out, no one caught the inconsistency in "Time, Don't Run Out on Me" in which the writers, after establishing "Time" as the *you* of the lyric, followed the title line with "gotta make *you* love me the way *you* used to." Logic required that the line be, "Gotta make *him* love me the way *he* used to." Nowhere during the joint creative effort—writing, producing, arranging, performing—did the lyric pass through the fourth step in the creative process—*discriminate*. The result—less than a whole-brain lyric.

WrapUp

On occasion, a student, when given this assignment, may come to class empty handed. But several weeks later, presumably out of nowhere pops an "apostrophe lyric" in which the writer unconsciously employed the device. The muse works in mysterious ways. So if the prewriting guideline doesn't immediately generate an idea that excites you, don't feel discouraged. The creative process simply may require more time. Bracket it. And go on to something else, confident that your unconscious has stored away some valuable information which it's incubating. When the time is ripe, the lyric will emerge.

Synecdoche as Design Device

Some Background

Synecdoche (Se-NEK-doh-KEY), one of the four master tropes, is a figure of reduction that substitutes the part for the whole or the whole for the part. It acts as a kind of verbal shorthand: The sportscaster reports, "The Dodgers need a *strong arm* in center"—*arm*, in this instance, the most significant *part* of the outfielder, substitutes for the *whole* person. A newspaper headline announces, "*America* is collapsing and buckling." Well, not exactly. Its *bridges* are collapsing and its *highways* are buckling. *America* substitutes the whole for its parts—bridges and highways. Synecdoche can produce an eye-catching headline. It can also produce an ear-catching song title.

The Left-Brain Trope

Synecdochic (SYN-ek-DOCK-ic) thinking draws on left-brain functions: being specific, detailed, concrete, and separating into parts. It's the dominant trope of the ST and is readily used by J-types who like brevity. After getting the hang of how it works, substituting the part for the whole can come easily to all.

The Types of Synecdoche

Here are some major categories of part for the whole and whole for the part.

- *The species for the genus*: Her favorite shopping is Cartier and Tiffany
- *The raw material for the finished product*: You look great in velvet
- *The trade name/producer for generic product*: Got a Kleenex?
- *The nickname for person/thing*: I like Ike
- *An abbreviation/acronym for the whole term*: I got your R.S.V.P.
- *The place for event*: The 25th anniversary of Woodstock

The Compact Synecdoche

Like simile, synecdoche has a compact form. One of the most common forms of synecdoche is the reduction of the *place for the event* which turns the place into a modifying adjective. This is most observable in the media's rapid "titling" of news stories: *The Gettysburg Address*, the *Boston Strangler*, the *Persian Gulf Crisis*, and so on. It often gets compacted even further: *Watergate*. A synecdoche, because it abstracts an integral part of the thing for which it substitutes, always forms a whole. Here are some song titles that feature types of synecdoche.

Some Synecdochic Song Titles

Abraham, Martin and John	part for whole
Love Me, Love My Pekinese	species for genus
Take Back Your Mink	species for genus

Woodstock	place for event
Rum and Coca Cola	trade name for product
Goodbye, Norma Jean	part for whole
G. I. Jive	abbreviation
Tschaikowsky	part for whole
Orbach's, Bloomingdale's & Saks	species for genus
Does the Spearmint Lose Its Flavor on the Bedpost Overnight	trade name for product

Synecdoche in One-Liners: An Exercise

In addition to its use both as a title device and an occasional design strategy, synecdoche abounds in one-liners. Read the following examples of lyric lines, enjoying the wordplay. Then, purposefully switch to your analytical thinking function to pinpoint the particular category from those just cited which the lyricist used:

"Your girlish *glands* revive there" (Gershwin)
"Where the crowds at El Morocco punish the *parquet*" (Porter)
"With a *Schlitz* in her mitts" (Sondheim)
"There's oil all over your *address*" (Loesser)
"Diamond bracelets *Woolworth's* doesn't sell" (Fields)
"The *canvas* can do miracles" (Cross)
"Trading *golddust* in for *mushrooms*" (Davis)
"Bottles full of *bubbles* for your troubles" (Gershwin)
"Clicking *heels* on *steel* and *cement*" (Sondheim)
"Tell him to *Hollanderize* it for some other dame" (Loesser)
"One day when I was *twelve and three*." (Lerner)
"The *M.P.* makes you *K.P.* on the *Q.T.*" (Mercer)
(Answers on page 109.)

Perhaps that exercise made you aware that you've unconsciously used synecdoche in some form in your own lyrics. Perhaps it's even your favorite figure.

Ira Gershwin and Synecdoche

A reading of Ira Gershwin's memoirs *Lyrics On Several Occasions* suggests he was an ISTJ—an introverted/sensate/thinking/judgment type. A close analysis of his lyrics confirms that he favored synecdoche in its many forms over the other three master tropes.

As synecdoche functions to reduce a thing to some inherent part, a contraction is considered a subtype of synecdoche. Gershwin's typewriter keyboard must've had a busy apostrophe key. Hardly a lyric went by without a contraction or two. Sometimes he'd playfully shrink a word—*sassafrass* to "sass," *governor* to "gov," *emotion* to "emosh." Often he used contraction to even out the meter—*heav'nly, awf'ly, 'round, shriv'ling*, or in service to rhyme—*bewild'rin/children; a-struttin'/nuttin', gospel/pos'ple, hapless/Minneap'lis, country/effront'ry.* Naturally his song titles featured contractions: " 'S Wonderful," (which included " 's marvelous . . . 's awful nice . . . 's paradise"), "I'm Bidin' My Time," and "I Got Plenty o' Nuthin'."

Synecdoche and Song Design

Because of its inherent emphasis on *the part*, this trope lends itself more to partial use within a lyric than to total song design. That's probably why, to my knowledge, only one song exists that's entirely structured on synecdoche—"Tschaikowsky." The lyric, comprised solely of a rhymed list of the last names of forty-nine Russian composers (!), was written by, you guessed it—Ira Gershwin. With music by Kurt Weill, "Tschaikowsky" became a show-stopping tour de force for performer Danny Kaye in the 1941 Broadway musical *Lady in the Dark*.

Partitio: Using a Series of Parts for the Whole

A modified type of synecdochic song design features *partitio* (par-TEESCH-io)—substituting a series of parts for the name of the whole. Two of the most striking examples of the technique are "The Physician" (Cole Porter) and "Bobby and Jackie and Jack" (Stephen Sondheim):

- The female singer of "The Physician" complains—tongue in cheek—that though her doctor, on his house calls, would give high praise to each of her anatomical parts—*larynx, lymphatics, medulla oblongata, umbilicus*, etc.—"He never said he loved *me*."
- "Bobby and Jackie and Jack," sung by a trio in Sondheim's *Merrily We Roll Along*, chats about the various members of the extensive Kennedy clan using their first-name monikers only—from Eunice and Peter and Jean and Joan to Joe and Rose—without even a recourse to the surname.

In this student lyric, partitio emphasizes the singer's case of terminal inertia.

Synecdochic: Example No. 1 (AABABA)
BUT NOT JUST YET

I'm planning to go on a diet
To acquire a slim silhouette
I'll forgo chocolate bars,
Ice cream cones, Mallomars—
BUT NOT JUST YET.

I'm thinking of joining a health club,
To work up a nice, healthy sweat—
Doing weightlifts, and rowing,
And stretching, and throwing—
BUT NOT JUST YET.

Some remodeling
Would be helpful.
(This is certainly open-and-shut.)
But improvement
Calls for movement—
And I'd have to get out of my nice, cozy rut.

Signing up for assertiveness training
Is something I'd never regret.
When I gain all that clout,
Everybody, look out!
BUT NOT JUST YET.

Though my options
Lie before me,
And go on and on without end,
I'm half-hearted
Getting started,
When I think of the effort I'd have to expend.

Well, one of these days I'll get to it.
I'll relinquish my snug safety net.
I'll be radiant and trim,
Full of vigor and vim,
And I'll know what to say
Anytime — night or day.
Yes, the world will then see
A resplendent new me —
A me it will not soon forget!
BUT, please, NOT JUST YET.

▲ Comment

In both the first and second A sections, Rebecca replaced a general category — *sweets* and *exercise* respectively — with a series of particular kinds. Introducing the partitio device in the first two verses establishes a style for the song. It's not required to impose "a series of parts" throughout subsequent verses. The writer, trusting her instinct to know when enough was enough, let go of the device to write a perhaps more fully realized, feeling song. You'll note that her two series of related ideas were kept consistently literal. Rebecca, a left-brain dominant (ST), is a writer for whom consistency and synecdoche come naturally.

Employing the Strategy

Now that you've seen some of the ways synecdoche can contribute to both the design and content of your lyrics, why not look over some works-in-progress to see if there's a spot where the substitution of a significant part for the whole — perhaps a brand name — would enliven a line. Consider too if there's a subject you've been wanting to tackle that would lend itself to a series of parts, especially if the theme suggests a lighthearted or playful attitude like "But Not Just Yet."

Here's another form of synecdoche — abbreviation — the device that Johnny Mercer employed to such effect in "G.I. Jive."

Synecdoche: Example No. 2 (Verse/Chorus/Bridge)
LFS

He: Do you believe in UFOs?
She: No, I don't think so.
He: How do you feel 'bout ESP?
She: Well, it's a possibility.
He: Baby, I'm hooked on LFS
She: LFS, I gotta confess I don't know what that means.

He: LFS is AKA
    Love at first sight.
    It's easy to give in to
    'Cause it feels so right.
    With no warning sign
    There isn't time
    To put up a fight.
    So I fell — LFS
    Love at first sight.

She: Do you believe in romantic bliss?
He: That's what started when we kissed.
She: You got it darlin', PDQ
    The speed is magic with me and you
He: So how do ya feel 'bout LFS?
She: LFS, it's the best
    Now I know what it means.

She: LFS is AKA
    Love at first sight.
    It's easy to give in to
    'Cause it feels so right.
    With no warning sign
    There isn't time
    To put up a fight.
Both: So I fell — LFS
    Love at first sight

She: Don't need to send out an SOS
    For someone to rescue me.
He: We'll save each other with our love
    And do it all, ASAP
Both: (repeat chorus)

▲ Comment

A fresh and original lyric that sprang from the concept of initials. The writer, who obviously did some prewriting SJ-mode list-making, developed his plot by associating the title with other common three- and four-letter abbreviations. This lyric is also notable for its duet feature—another underutilized device we take up in Strategy No. 23.

WrapUp

I encourage you to get over whatever hesitancy you may be experiencing in pronouncing synecdoche and synecdochic. They're both easier than "Supercalifragilisticexpialidocious," and that was a hit! Repeat Se-NEK-doh-KEY and SYN-ek-DOCK-ic a few times so that they roll off your tongue as easily as *metaphor* and *metaphoric*. There's a Latin axiom *nomen est numen*—to name is to know. I add: To pronounce is to master. Now to metonym and symbol.

Answers to Exercise on Page 105

Substitution	*Type of Synecdoche*
glands	part for whole
parquet	part for whole
Schlitz	trade name for generic product
address	part for whole
Woolworth's	genus for species
canvas	raw material for finished product
golddust/mushrooms	nicknames
bubbles	part for whole
heels/steel/cement	parts for whole
Hollanderize	trade name for generic process
twelve and three	parts for whole
M.P./K.P./Q.T.	abbreviations

Metonymy and Symbol as Design Devices

Metonymy: A Definition

Metonymy (meh-TAHN-a-mee), one of the four master tropes, is a figure of symbolic substitution, related to (and often confused with) synecdoche, in which we replace the thing meant with an attribute of it. For example, "from the cradle to the grave" is a metonymic expression that substitutes two concrete associated images for the two abstract terms meant—birth and death. I want to emphasize the distinction between the two tropes: Synecdoche substitutes an *integral part* of the thing (a strong arm) for the thing itself (the outfielder), and thus always makes a whole with it; metonymy substitutes an *attribute* or *associated aspect* of the thing (*cradle/grave*) for the thing itself (*birth/death*) and thus creates a *symbol* of it.

Metonymic thinking requires a combination of left- and right-hemisphere functions. If you look back at the brain model on page 81, you'll see how metonymy "resides" between metaphor to the right and synecdoche to the left. Thinking metonymically thus requires the right's imagistic, spatial perceptions and the left's ability to match by function and separate into parts. It's clear then why sensate-feeling types—with a dominant function in each lower hemisphere—tend to think in symbolic terms and hence employ metonymy in its various forms in their writing.

Common Categories of Metonymy

The most common metonyms embody one of two basic kinds of substitutions: 1) *Cause for the effect/effect for the cause*; and 2) *Attribute for subject/subject for attribute*. For example, the advertising slogan for Retin A—"The face cream that erases the years (wrinkles)"—substitutes the cause (years) for its effect (wrinkles). The proverb, "The pen is mightier than the sword" substitutes two *attributes* (pen and sword) for the two *subjects* (literature and combat) represented. Other common metonymic substitutions include:

- *The possession for the possessor*:
  "A *sharkskin* suit [person in it] is coming up the street."
- *The controller for the controlled*:
  "*Bernstein* [the orchestra] gave a great concert."
- *The place for the administration/industry*:
  "*Detroit* [the automobile industry] claims profits."
- *The container for the contained*:
  "Let's have a *brown bag* [food contained in it] lunch."
- *The creator for the creation*:
  "You're never alone with a *poet* [a book of poetry] in your pocket."

Examples of these types of metonym abound in lyrics. Read the following lines for enjoyment; then reread to try to identify the type of substitution (cited above) that each line expresses.

"I have my *Emily Dickinson* and you your *Robert Frost*" (Simon)

"Evenings of the Budapest playing *Vivaldi*" (Sondheim)

"To trade the *handshake* for the *fist*" (Mitchell)

"To the *paunch*, and the *pouch*, and the *pension*" (Sondheim)

"I could plainly see her *vitamin D*" (Porter)

"I'm just a *dirt man* from the North Dakota Plains" (Chapin)

"Finding solace in a *chalice*" (Davis)

"I pour myself a cup of *ambition*" (Parton)

"I'll try my utmost to see you never *frown*" (Sondheim)

(Answers on page 119.)

Subtypes of Metonymy

Metonymy, like every master trope, has its subtypes: *Euphemism, The Enactment, Antonomasia* and *Symbol.*

Euphemism: Being Oblique

A euphemism, according to my Random House dictionary is "the substitution of a mild, indirect, or vague expression for one thought to be offensive, harsh, or blunt." In the expression "he passed away," for example, the speaker has substituted a kinder, gentler way to express the blunt truth, "he died." You may remember in the role-model lyric "Look Homeward, Angel," the subject of death is treated euphemistically in the line, "The angels took my mamma home. . . ." Harry Chapin used an "indirect" word to show that a victim of "The Sniper" was bleeding: "*Reality* pouring from her face, staining the floor." In the final line of "Officer Krupke," a vulgarity is amusingly suggested with "Krup you!" (Sondheim/Bernstein). Matters sexual in pop songs can be handled obliquely through the "vague" metonymic substitution.

The Enactment: Showing the Effect for the Cause

I'd bet that in reading how-to books or articles on creative writing you've come across the advice to "Show, don't tell." What that means is: Replace a literal statement with a symbol of it—or a metonymic *enactment*. For example, instead of flatly stating the word "shy," Rupert Holmes *showed* the effect for the cause: "You take a sudden interest in your shoes." Again employing the effect for the cause, Janis Ian *showed* "lonely in bed": "And in the winter, extra blankets for the cold." Thom Schuyler in his saga of struggling songwriters, "16th Avenue," *shows* the effect of being broke: "They all phone collect to home . . ." The more you let your characters *enact* their emotional and physical states through behavior, the more metonymic—visual, vivid and original—your songs will be.

An Enactment Exercise:

Try it now with a commonly expressed lyrical emotion—suspicion of infidelity. Picture the attributes of suspicion. Close your eyes and draw upon some visual memory from either real life, or a novel or TV. How does suspicion manifest itself? What does a suspicious person do? What might a suspicious person say? What are the *effects for the cause*? When you *see* an image, translate it into a short phrase using the third person.

She _____ .

Antonomasia: Metonymic/Symbolic People

There are famous people and characters in fiction so associated with a particular attribute that they become symbols of it. We say, for example, that Fred Astaire was the epitome of grace. And in a remark like, "Well, he's no Astaire," the late dancer goes into the language as a symbol. The Greeks (who had a name for everything) called the substitution of a proper name for a general class or type *antonomasia*. Some celebrated "antonomasians" whose names immediately conjure up a dominant trait include: Delilah, Midas, Svengali, Tarzan, or more contemporarily, Schwarzenegger. "Ultimate Night" (pages 54-55) invoked antonomasia to characterize her fantasy man, "partly Schwarzenegger/partly Fred Astaire." Using this subtype of metonymy will enliven your lyrics as in these lines:

"I'm a Hannibal at scheming" (Porter)

"Faced with these Loreleis/What man can moralize" (Sondheim)

"You're not a Robinson Crusoe" (Holmes)

"Sometimes in a clerk/You find a Hercules" (Sondheim)

"Little chaps will wish they were Atlas" (Lerner)

"Sidewalk Cezannes" (Sondheim)

Antonomasia Antics

Those were straightforward usages of antonomasia. But there's an easy way to be still more inventive. You could create neologisms stemming from famous names—the way that many have evolved. For instance, *Herculean task*, derives from Hercules, the mythic hero who possessed great strength. Similarly fictional characters have spun off such derivations as *quixotic* (extravagantly chivalrous) from *Don Quixote*, the fervent idealist created by Cervantes, and *Walter Mittyish* (fancifully impractical) from the daydreaming hero in a James Thurber short story.

Why not start an Antonomasia page in your idea notebook: Make three columns. On the left-hand side of the page, head Column A, "Attribute/Characteristic" and list, for starters, such archetypes as *magician, temptress, womanizer, traitor, faithful friend, spy*—adding to your list as you think of more. Next, in the middle of the page, head Column B, "Famous Person." Then for each characteristic in A write in B the names of a famous person from life or literature (which includes fiction/poetry/cartoon's/comics/radio/TV sitcoms) who embodies it. For example, *Magician-Houdini, Temptress-Lorelei, Womanizer-Casanova*, and so on. That's activating the process with left-brain list-making.

Now comes the right-brain fun: Head the C column, "Neologism." This part requires your being playful. The goal: See how many names from your B list you can transform into new words by using such techniques as verbifying, "adjectivizing," "portmanteauing" and, of course, making compact metonyms. Here's a free one to get you started: "Casanotable reputation"—a compact metonym made by "adjectivizing" a proper name and using it as a modifier. (For a refresher on nonce coinages, check back to pages 71-73.) Then play a while. As an added resource, you'll find the *Dictionary of Classical, Biblical, & Literary Allusions* published by Facts on File to be a useful addition to your reference shelf. Now let's look at the way metonyms can appear in song titles.

Some Metonymic Song Titles

He Wears a Pair of Silver Wings	symbol
Golden Ring	symbol
Ebony and Ivory	symbol
Nine to Five	symbol
I Still Love the Red, White and Blue	symbol
These Boots are Made for Walkin'	possession for possessor
Love for Sale	euphemism
(She's Got a Perfect) Personality	euphemism
Can That Boy Foxtrot!	euphemism

Designing a Metonymic Lyric

Sometimes we want to be literal and direct — maybe even blunt. Other times we seek subtlety and obliqueness — we want to couch some word, phrase, or concept in a less direct, yet instantly comprehensible way. For example, Cole Porter's use of "*Love* for Sale," a prostitute's euphemistic way of describing her product. Here's a student example that employs a metonym to good advantage.

Metonym Example No. 1: The Euphemism (Verse/Chorus)
FRIEND IN MY POCKET

Looking back to the good old days
Times have made us change our ways.
But we still can have the same old fun —
It all depends on how it's done.
Oh, let me introduce you to a

FRIEND IN MY POCKET
FRIEND IN MY POCKET
I never leave home without a
FRIEND IN MY POCKET
It never lets me down.
That's why I carry it around.
If I need it, I've got it.

So if you'd like some fun tonight
I promise that we'll do it right.
I play safely when I do
'Cause I care for me and I care for you.
That's why I have brought along a

(repeat chorus)

© 1988 Joe Bracco. Used with permission.

▲ Comment

The title's metonym enables the writer to send a cautionary message in this era of AIDS in a non-preaching way—avoiding the bluntness of the prophylactic term. "Friend" here can be interpreted as either a euphemism, a "vaguer" way to suggest the intended meaning, or indeed, the effect (friend) for the cause (protection).

Here's a song written for the Christian market that employs a metonymic title replacing the subject meant with its attributes:

Metonym Example No. 2: The Symbolic Title (Verse/Chorus)
GOLDEN CIRCLES
(Verse/Chorus)
In just a few moments, a woman, a man
Will place golden circles on each others' hands
And promise to love as long as they live.
More precious than gold is the promise they'll give.

In just a few moments, a groom and a bride
Will promise to walk hand in hand, side by side
Through all of the joy and the pain life may hold
They'll seal their sweet promise with circles of gold.

These GOLDEN CIRCLES, so brightly gleaming
Are signs of a greater treasure.
The love of Jesus, from His heart streaming
Will bind these two hearts together, forever.

In just a few moments, the words will be said
The vow will be spoken, these two will be wed.
Oh, Father, the author of love ever true
Let these GOLDEN CIRCLES remind them
Their strength is in You.

(repeat chorus)
© 1988 Daniel Fox. Used with permission.

▲ Comment

In this song Dan Fox, a sensate/feeling (SF) type, has expressed his dominant trope, the metonym, through the symbol of the wedding band—an attribute of the marriage ceremony. Did you notice the use of apostrophe in the third verse, "Oh, Father . . . " How appropriate to the moment. It was easy for a sensate/feeler to "slide up" to employ a form of metaphor which was just around the bend, so to speak.

The Compact Metonym

A Definition

Like simile and synecdoche, metonymy also comes in a concise form which I've termed the *compact metonym*. The compact simile, you'll remember, creates a comparison (*arrow straight*) by using the compared word as an adjective; a compact metonym creates a symbol by using an associated attribute as an adjective; for example, *coffee-table book*: a (usually expensive) large-format book that is too big to fit on a bookshelf, thus it's displayed on a table — effect for the cause. A compact metonym — usually two or three words — can be readily distinguished from a compact simile by a definition that always begins *one that*, *one who*, *those which*, and is followed by a significant quality or attribute. For instance, a *Frisbee dog* is *one that* has been trained to catch *Frisbees* (an attribute). One of the most memorable lyrical compact metonyms is Lennon and McCartney's "kaleidoscope eyes" *those which*, after taking a hallucinogen, see the world in refracted images ("Lucy in the Sky With Diamonds"). Examining some of our most common phrases, we begin to see the prevalence of metonymy in its compact form. As I pointed out earlier, only the *term* was Greek to you. Here are some common compact metonyms identified by their category:

fire sale	effect for cause
money review	effect for cause
sticker shock	effect for cause
briefcase flight	effect for cause
returning bodybags	container for contained
Sunday painter	attribute for subject
white-collar crime	possession for possessor
bifocal set	possession for possessor

A Compact Metonym Exercise

The advertising slogan, "Maalox moment," attests to the effectiveness of cause/effect thinking: "I need a Maalox (effect) because my husband just asked for a divorce" (cause). Stop for a minute to see how you might adapt that slogan by linking the word *moment* with a happier time — one to celebrate or capture. Think of a commercial product (trade name) that we use to send a congratulatory message and/or preserve a significant event. Got an idea yet? You might have come up with *Hallmark moment, Mailgram moment, Kodak moment* or *Camcorder moment*. With a little practice, you'll entrain a metonym track across your lower cerebral cortex for devising future song titles.

Making Fresh Titles

Reducing the compact metonym even further offers a way to quickly identify groups of people by a habitual attribute; for example *straphanger*. Again, it's *one who* rides the subway, holding on to an overhead strap. We daily use such slang terms: *bag lady, hash slinger, wino*, etc. Turning the compact metonym into an adjective offers a means of devising fresh song titles; for example, "The Clock-puncher Blues," or "Number Cruncher Day."

Some Compact Metonym Song Titles

Mail Order Annie	Rocky Mountain High
Material Girl	Radio Heart
Poetry Man	Motorcycle Irene
Second-Hand Rose	Society's Child
Mississippi Man	Earth Angel
Pac Man Fever	Chelsea Morning

Heartbreak Hotel   Pillow Talk
Barefoot Boy   Sunday Morning Sunshine

You've already read two role-model examples of the compact metonym title, "Black and White Movie," and "Sunday Morning Love." Here's a lyric whose title symbolizes the object of the subject—interracial romance.

Metonym Example No. 3: The Compact Metonym (Verse/Chorus/Bridge)
MY AFRICAN MAN

I've savored all the colors of love
In my travels 'cross the continents—
Lost my heart to an Irish boy
Left home for a Spanish prince.
But of all the lovers
From the islands to the Orient
None is sweeter or feels more heaven sent

Oh, I'm in love with an AFRICAN MAN
A solid rainbow of brown and tan
With chocolate kisses
That melt in my mouth
I'm in love with my man
I'm in love with MY AFRICAN MAN.

He spins his story 'round my heart
And ties it with a golden thread.
He turns me upside down to see
The choices in my head.
He loves the blueness in my eyes
Says my hair's like lemonade
He laughs and swears forever
That vanilla is his favorite shade.

(repeat chorus)

And we're high, so high
It feels like flying
And the moment we touch the sky
Colors that were real
Softly disappear

I want to live a hundred lives
With that coffee skin and the cocoa eyes
We'd be in paradise
Just me and my man
My sweet African.

(repeat chorus)

Ashana amplifies her metonymic title (one who) with metaphoric uses of color to vivify the interracial relationship: *black and tan rainbow, hair like lemonade*, and the compact similes, *coffee skin, cocoa eyes*. A subtle treatment of a rare lyric theme.

The Symbolic Lyric: An Extended Metonym

The Symbolic Lyric: A Definition

A symbolic lyric is a form of extended metonym in which an image is used to mean not only what it says but to imply a larger meaning. One of the classic symbolic lyrics is "April Showers" (1921). While it literally invokes the axiom that "April showers bring May flowers," it symbolically suggests that bad times will be followed by good times. *Showers (rain)*, here, acts as a *symbol* for troubles — not a *metaphor* for them.

Distinguishing Metonym From Metaphor

Metaphors are different from symbols. This is an important distinction to grasp. When used as a metaphor, a word — let's stay with *rain* — always means *something other than its literal meaning* as in "I Made It Through the Rain"; *rain* here means solely *trouble*, not at all literal rain. When rain is used symbolically, however, it means real rain *plus* something more significant that's only implied. Such is the case with all the symbolic images in the following song titles: They mean literally what they say *plus* something more that they symbolically imply by the lyric's central image:

Some Symbolic Titles

This Image	*Symbolizes*	*This Larger Meaning*
My Old Yellow Car		lost youth
Anyone Can Whistle		inability to let go
It's Not Easy Being Green		being different is hard
When October Goes		aging
September Song		aging
I Like to Lead When I Dance		I want control
Stop and Smell the Roses		enjoy life's little things
Let's Face the Music and Dance		face life with courage
Don't Sit Under the Apple Tree With Anyone Else But Me		be faithful to me

Metonym Example No. 4: A Symbolic Lyric (Augmented AABA)
BAREFOOT IN THE RAIN

I've never run
BAREFOOT IN THE RAIN
Or even gone hatless in the snow.
I've lived by the safest and the san-
Est axioms I know.

I've never thrown
Caution to the winds,
Awakened with something to regret.
'Cause when an impulsive urge begins
I lose my nerve. And yet

There is much I've missed
Your touch proves that so well.
Down with this dull exist-
Ance. I'm bursting from my shell!

Wanna be reckless,
And heedless,
Impetuous,
Headstrong—
Deciding without thinking twice.
And if I am feckless,
Imprudent,
Or foolish,
Or dead wrong,
I'll gladly pay the price—
All because

You have released
My yen to play,
To overindulge, be led astray,
I'm breaking loose,
So don't say "Whoa!"
Down with the rules and *comme il faut*!

I'm ready to run
BAREFOOT IN THE RAIN
Whenever you say, "Let's go."
Let's go!
Let's gooooooooooooo!

Words by Sheila Davis/Music by Ben Allen
© *1966 Solar Systems Music. Used with permission.*

▲ Comment

Yes, the singer is ready to literally run barefoot in the rain—or more precisely *waltz* as the lyric's meter suggests. But the image implies that she's finally ready to shake off a more profound inhibition. As you can tell, this is a cabaret song that permits a non-pop vocabulary—with the confidence that words like *feckless* and *comme il faut* will be appreciated by the audience.

In over a decade of teaching lyricwriting not once has a student spontaneously presented a symbolic lyric! As a consequence, I have never dared give an assignment to write one for fear that an entire class would come in empty-handed. Writing a symbolic lyric seems to be a bit like falling in love—it's not something we do by design or on demand, but rather something that simply happens to us when we least expect it.

WrapUp

This theory on metonym and symbol is meaty and rich, so it may take a while to completely digest. Give it all the time it requires. Read over the definitions and examples. Play with the exercises. Internalize an understanding of making metonyms. Then when you least expect it, it'll happen. You'll look up from a new lyric and exclaim: "Look what I did: I made a compact metonym!" Or even more exciting, "I wrote a symbolic lyric!"

I hope that this basic course in metonymy will help alert you to the trendy, voguish misuse by the media of the term metaphor: It's now common to hear major events such as the Alaskan oil spill referred to as "a *metaphor* for larger problems." No, it's not a *metaphor* for anything; there's no comparison being made between two different realms. The Alaskan oil spill is a horrific *fact*, one that can be considered a representative enactment of our gross mistreatment of the planet, and thus a *symbol* of it.

Now that you've begun to differentiate metaphor from metonym and symbol, I hope you'll enjoy correctly identifying the daily *symbolic* news events — despite an anchorman (or statesman) mislabelling them "a metaphor for . . . ."

Answers to Exercise on Page 111

Image	Type of metonym
Emily Dickinson/Robert Frost	creator for creation
Vivaldi	creator for creation
handshake/fist	effect for cause
paunch/pouch/pension	effect for cause
vitamin D	cause for effect
dirt man	attribute for subject
chalice	attribute for subject
ambition	effect for cause
frown	effect for cause

Pun as Design Device

Some Definitions

Pun is a subtype of irony, one of the four master tropes. A pun playfully exploits *homophones*, words pronounced the same but differing in meaning from one another—whether spelled the same way or not. Puns, though frequently funny, are often used for serious effect. A pun's irony resides in the incongruity inherent in one sound resounding with multiple meanings; for example *stare/stair*, *Rome/roam*.

Many homophones are *homonyms*—words spelled alike though different in meaning as in the multiple definitions of *train*: 1) To teach; 2) A vehicle that runs on a track; 3) A succession of connected ideas; 4) The trailing part of a skirt, etc.

Puns come in two major forms, each having its own subtypes. All have multisyllabic and difficult-to-pronounce (and remember) Greek names. In the interests of simplicity, I've termed the two major forms the *instant pun* and the *sequential pun*.

The Instant Pun

The instant pun employs a word or phrase that *simultaneously* expresses two dissimilar ideas. For example the slogan for the no-cholesterol cooking spray Pam: "Don't make a big *fat* mistake" simultaneously exploits two meanings of fat (*grease*) and the slang usage meaning *enormous*. In Jimmy Webb's hit, "Wichita Lineman," the phrase "and the Wichita lineman is still *on the line*" suggests that the singer has maintained both the same lineman job and the same loving feeling. As you've already seen in the antonymic pun title "In the Thick of Getting Thin," some puns consist of contrasting a literal meaning against the figurative meaning.

The Sequential Pun

The sequential pun requires a delayed use of the initial word or phrase to express the second idea: In an ad campaign, *Time* magazine, for example, exploits the two meanings implicit in its name, "Make *time* for *Time*." The lyrics of Stephen Sondheim abound with all manner of sequential puns: "*Weighty* affairs will just have to *wait*"; "for a *sense* of *sens*uality; *raptures* that are still un*wrapped*"; "while *withers wither with her*." (More on the sequential pun later.)

The Strategy's Advantage

An occasional pun within a lyric adds zest to a song as you saw in "Tinsel" (*lusty/luster*). Here we'll focus on pun as a design device. Pun-designed lyrics produce memorable songs because, by their very nature, they're unique. The strategy comes in three styles: the *Instant Pun Title*, the *Sequential Pun Title* and the *Sequential Pun Plot*.

Examples of Instant Pun Titles

In "If I Said You Had a Beautiful Body Would You Hold It Against Me?" both the literal and colloquial (figurative) meanings of the phrase *hold it against me* are instantly apparent. In the country hit "On the Other Hand," the singer recounts the ways in which, on one hand (way) he is attracted to the singee, but regrets that on the other hand (literally his left hand), he wears a wedding ring.

Prewriting Suggestion

For a pun warm-up exercise, we'll go to the source: sound-alike words. I recommend starting a section in your notebook headed: "Homophones." To begin, make a list of open vowel sounds— ah/ay/aw/ow, etc. The noted impresario and songwriter Billy Rose learned—in research done many years ago—that the vowel -oo- was the sound most commonly found in the titles of hit songs. Acting on his discovery, Rose "designed" the (1923) hit song, "Barney Google (With the Goo Goo Googily Eyes)." There's a thought process that went from the part to the whole!

Taking a tip from Mr. Rose, you might begin your first list with the simple -oo- sound. Think alphabetically. And encourage yourself to make connections with those words that are spelled differently; also include proper names and foreign words. And add two-syllable words that spring to mind in which the vowel sound -oo- is only the first syllable. By that method, you might arrive at such homophones as: *blue/blew/blue*; *coup/coo/coocoo*; *do/dew/due/Dewey*; *hew/hue/Hugh/human*; *loo/lieu/Lew/lucid/loony*, and so on. When a word spelled the same way has multiple meanings, write it twice (*blue/blue*).

That was a left-brain listing way to activate the creative process by producing concrete material. Step two takes you over to the right brain to play with the material. The objective now is to expand a set of your homophones into a phrase— not a phrase to be turned into a lyric—just a fun phrase. Let yourself be playful— even silly: "The *dew*, when it's *due*, will *do* its thing." Try to extend your "vowel thought" as far as you can; for example, "When *Lou*ise went to the *loo*, *Lew*, in *lieu* of *Lou*ise went *loo*ny over *Lulu*."

The practical reward from exercising your inherent ability to discover multiplicity in sameness comes in developing a more agile and imaginative mind. Pun exercises engage both sides of the brain and thus create another entrainment you can travel again more readily. Like doing crossword puzzles, pun making is a stimulating whole-brain activity.

Guideline

When writing a pun title or pun phrase, there's one main caveat: Be sure that your meanings—whether instant or sequential, funny or serious—are always apparent to the ear *and* appropriate to the context. Be wary of attempting to be clever at the expense of truth. The result may be a *pseudo pun* such as a Dupont Carpet slogan: "Save a pile on Dupont Carpet." Though obviously aspiring to be an instant pun—expressing two facts simultaneously—*save a pile* works only on its slang level *to save money*. The word *pile* has indeed two meanings; but the phrase *save a pile*, only one: Because the only way to *save a (carpet) pile* is by not walking on the carpet! Just as a coherent metaphor suggests a potential reality, a coherent pun conveys truth.

Pun Example No. 1: The Instant Pun Title (AABA)
HEART OVER HEELS

Romance is a game that I'd love to be winning
But I seem to attract impossible deals:
Dapper Dan looks my way and my head begins spinning,
And there I go — HEART OVER HEELS.

He tells me I'm special, he smiles at me sweetly
But, oh, what deception a sweet smile conceals!
Soon he's standing me up, or he drops me completely.
Doesn't care that I'm HEART OVER HEELS.

I meet another Don Juan and the story repeats
Right down to my last bitter tear.
Liars, Lotharios, lechers and cheats —
Why do they all have to gravitate here?

Mr. Right, when will *you* be the one I am choosing?
For once, I would like to find out how *that* feels.
To win would be nice, 'cause I'm tired of losing,
Losing my heart over all of those heels
Losing my HEART OVER HEELS.

© 1990 Rebecca Holtzman. Used with permission.

▲ Comment
The title "Heart Over Heels" embodies two literary devices: first it's a para-gram on the colloquialism *head over heels*, but more significantly here, it's the play on the word *heel*—meaning simultaneously *part of a foot* and a *cad*. The writer set up the "heel" pun clearly with "Dapper Dan" so that we knew the singer had a habit of choosing surface over substance.

Double Entendre — A Risqué Instant Pun
This subtype of instant pun goes by the French term *double entendre* (DOOBla ahnTAHNdra) which means *double meaning*. In this particular form of pun, one of its two meanings has a crude or vulgar connotation—usually either sexual or scatalogical. As a result, *double entendres* are more commonly heard in cabaret com-edy songs and old blues lyrics than in pop. One of the most amusing and flawlessly executed lyrics in this genre is "If I Can't Sell It, I'll Keep Sittin' On It," (Rasaf/ Hill). The singer is ostensibly trying to sell a valuable chair from her furniture shop to a male customer; yet, it's evident that she's in fact discussing the value of her sexual wares. And *sittin' on it* is immediately perceived both in its literal sense and in its colloquial sense, *to refrain from acting*. Each of the lyric's many *double-entendre* lines clearly works on both levels of meaning. The blues artist Ruth Brown, with her hilarious performances of the classic, has made the song her own. ("Sittin' " is part of the *Blues on Broadway* album on the Fantasy label.)

If, the first time you read "Eight" (pages 44-46), you didn't catch the *double entendre* in its second verse, you might want to identify it now: It plays off two meanings of the verb *to come*.

Examples of Sequential Pun Titles

In a sequential pun title, the pivot word (or part of it) is repeated with a shift in meaning. "A *Ring* Where a *Ring* Used to Be," "I *Like* the *Likes* of You," "What's *Good* About *Good*bye?" Then there's the potential of structuring a chorus on the different meanings inherent in a single phrase or word, as in this student lyric.

Pun Example No. 2: The Sequential Pun Chorus (Verse/Chorus/Bridge)
GETAWAY

It's Friday night at five o'clock
For half an hour I haven't moved a block.
My gas is low and my temper's hot.
Just another day in the old gridlock.

A week of this is sure a grind.
Wanna leave the rat race far behind.
Been workin' hard all week at what I do
Now I'm on my way to pick up you and

GET AWAY
We're gonna GET AWAY:
Miami GETAWAY
Hawaii GETAWAY
Some kind of GETAWAY.
We gotta GET AWAY.

Now here we are in our private suite
With chilled champagne and lots to eat.
The view is great and the music's low.
It's only my apartment, but someday we'll go and

GET AWAY
We're gonna GET AWAY:
Bermuda GETAWAY
Aruba GETAWAY
Some kind of GETAWAY.
We gotta GET AWAY.

A few more hours. Make the weekend last.
'Cause Monday mornin' 's comin' fast. Then it's
See those clients! Check those yields!
Sign those contracts! Make those deals!

But I will persevere and make it through
To Friday evening. Then it's me and you and

GET AWAY
That's when we'll GET AWAY:
Bahama GETAWAY
Jamaica GETAWAY
Some kind of GETAWAY

We gotta get a way
To GET AWAY
GET AWAY

© 1991 Nancy Smith. Used with permission.

▲ Comment

This pun sneaks up on us a bit; it's not as obvious as "Heart over Heels" nor as funny, illustrating that every pun doesn't aim at the laugh meter. Nonetheless, the chorus plays on two meanings of the title phrase—*get away* (to leave) and *getaway* (a vacation place); the final chorus puns *twice*, adding the third inherent meaning, *get a way* (find a method). It's worth noting that the writer did a good job in making clear her two shifts in time frame and setting. This lyric also draws upon the universal need "to escape" which we'll be taking up in Strategy No. 33.

Examples of Sequential Pun Plots

This is a use of puns in which the second meaning of the homophone is usually delayed until the lyric's final line where the pivot word (or phrase) is used in another sense. In the standard "Mean to Me," its first use of *mean* denotes *cruel* (in the question "Why are you so mean to me?"); in the song's concluding line, "Don't you know what you mean to me?" *mean* denotes *matter*. In the country hit "Way Back," the first use of the title means *a long time ago* (when we were happy) and the second use means the path, as in the thought "we have to find the way (path) *back*." In "Class Reunion" the literal meaning of the term is later played against a second meaning of *class*—*elegance of style*; in the final chorus, the title becomes an exclamation, "What a Class Reunion!"

Spelling Counts—More

In all the foregoing pun examples, the pivot word was spelled the same in both its instant and sequential uses. Memorable puns often draw on homophones with different spellings. In the lyric of the hit country song "Macon Love," for example, we simultaneously appreciate the meanings of Macon (Georgia) and *makin'*. In the sequential pun plot "But Not for Me," the punch line charms with "there's no *knot* (marriage) for me." The country song "Sowin' Love" exploited the different meanings inherent in the identical sound, *sowin' love/sewin' love*. The trick here is to be sure that your lyric sets up the pun so that it works for the *ear*—as did all the foregoing examples.

Being Playful

Since the playful state is a requisite of creativity, I encourage being playful—even if you have to work on it! Here for example is a lyric that playfully incorporates the names of thirty-two flowers, ferns, grasses and vines to tell the folktale of a love affair gone to seed.

Pun Example No. 3 (AAA)
FORGET ME NOT

O morning glory, sunflower so fine,
When sweet William met his columbine.

She said, "You dandelion," He said, "My sweet pea."
She said, "Tiger lily"; He said, "Peony,"

.They moved in clover, saw how the world glows.
When she said, "You foxglove," he said, "My wild rose."
She said, "You're so jonquil, my wild bergamot."
He said, "Lily of the valley, FORGET ME NOT."

"Tulips are for kissin'," he said, "and tonight."
She said, "Can a shooting star ever stick tight?"
She called him, "Narcissus." He said, "Let's take stock,"
And then he aster if she loved him or not.

They fell on nettles. They lost the gold thread.
When he said, "Snapdragon!" She said, "Fiddlehead!"
He began to dahlia with hot Marguerite.
He was feelin' chilly, kind of bittersweet.

"O, will she crocus," he thought, "when she knows?"
And saw the snow drop on his wild rose.
"Can a false hellebore," she thought, "ever be true?
O bleeding heart, O meadow rue."

No more romps in the clover, no more shooting star.
Just thorn and thistle, that's where they are.
And as the sunflower turns to night shade,
The morning glory begins to fade.

She said, "You're so jonquil, my wild bergamot."
He said, "Lily of the valley, FORGET ME NOT."

© 1991 Sue Stater. Used with permission.

▲ Comment

You may recall from "The Fox," Sue Stater's reverence for all living things. Her writing, of course, mirrors her passions — sometimes seriously, sometimes playfully. "Forget Me Not," doesn't pretend to meet the strict requirements of the instant pun, but with botanical bravado insinuates a love story through the implications of some flower names — *narcissus, clover, rue, bittersweet, stock* — and connotations resonating in others — *crocus* (croak us), *aster* (asked her), *dandelion* (dandy lion), *jonquil* (jolly/tranquil), *dahlia* (dally). "Forget Me Not" creates a floral tour de force that charms folk club audiences.

A Few Words on Oxymorons

Before leaving the pun, let's take a brief look at another subtype of irony, the *oxymoron*. This figure of speech combines incongruous or contradictory words/meanings for effect. The term, from the Greek, meaning *sharp dullness*, is itself an oxymoron. Common oxymoronic expressions include *make haste slowly, cruel kindness* and *serious fun*. Although the oxymoron, a compact irony, is less evident in lyrics than the compact forms of simile, metonym and synecdoche, it does exist in both one-liners and titles. For example, Stephen Sondheim's songs often amuse with such terse paradoxes as "my happiest mistake," "impossible possibilities" and "lovely debris." The provocative pop titles "The Sounds of Silence," "The Tender Trap," and "Killing Me Softly" employ the oxymoron. When you're ready to be earnestly playful, practice its foolish wisdom.

Gaining Pun Competence

Being asked to write a pun-design lyric might feel as threatening as being given the command: "Say something funny." You also may think, "I'm not the funny type." But resist putting any self-limiting label on your creative potential — because it will tend to be self-fulfilling. Being punny, like being metaphoric and metonymic is a thinking style available to every writer — although it's practiced only by a few. Becoming adept at discerning the diversity in sameness and the truth in paradox will enrich your lyrics. (It'll also make life more fun.)

You now know how to initiate the punning process. To gain pun competence requires becoming more pun conscious. Begin to think about the puns you encounter daily on radio and TV, in print advertising and greeting cards. As already noted, all puns are not created equal: They range from inventive to inept.

When you're watching TV commercials or reading a newspaper, stop to analyze the puns. Get your left-brain editor working to identify the type — instant or sequential. If it aspires to be an instant pun, then decide if it *simultaneously conveys two meanings that are both appropriate*. Sometimes it doesn't. As a case in point, not long ago a Bayer aspirin TV slogan suggested to headache sufferers to "Bayer it," a phrase (unintentionally) suggesting that after taking Bayer, the pain still must be borne. Hardly the sponsor's intended message. (Obviously, the ad agency's creative department had bypassed the *discriminate* step.) Shortly after its initial campaign, the punning slogan was revised to "There's no pain you can't Bayer." Perfect. (Lyricists, unlike copywriters, don't get a chance to edit their recorded blunders).

To write a competent pun depends to a large degree on the ability to discriminate between a word/phrase that expresses two levels of meaning, and one that doesn't — *and* to be able to pinpoint *how* it does, or *why* it doesn't. Becoming an armchair pundit will sharpen your ability to make fine distinctions and thus to write better lyrics.

WrapUp

This ends the basic theory of the four master tropes. Throughout the upcoming role-model lyrics however you'll be encountering more examples of paragram, apostrophe, metonym, symbol and pun. As you do, I'm sure you'll be better able to identify the various forms of wordplay. Now, on to a whole new kind of strategy — the framing device.

PART SIX

More Design Strategies: The Framing Device

O ften lyricists just begin to write without doing much in the way of advance planning. The impetus may be a strong emotion, or a new title, or an overheard remark that stirs the imagination. They may plunge right into the writing/shaping mode without going through the associating/incubating modes that might have yielded a far richer treatment of the idea.

The next strategies offer a group of literary techniques that can give your lyric more style. I call them *framing devices*: Just as the ideal frame sets off a painting, so, too, does the ideal frame set off a lyric. Coming up are six types of frames to consider for your future song concepts: *The Question Plot, The Phone Call, The Letter, The Setting, The Third-Person Vignette*, and the *Conversational Debate*.

The Question Title and Question Plot as Framing Devices

Questions and Answers

Second only to the word *sex* as an attention-getting device, comes the question. From my morning *New York Times*, here are a few of the questions that caught my eye: "Enjoy faraway places?"; "Is *Time* the most radioactive magazine in America?"; "Stumped? Call 1-900-994-Clue"; "What's Doing in San Francisco?"; "Want help in choosing the right camp for your child?"

Questions, of course, serve equally well to catch the ear. Questions make for strong opening lines, strong song titles, and they can supply a strong framing device for your plot.

Some Question Titles

Do Ya Think I'm Sexy?	How Am I Supposed to Live Without You?
Is That All There Is?	
What Is This Thing Called Love?	Who's Zoomin' Who?
What Kind of Fool Am I?	Why Was I Born?
Where Have All the Flowers Gone?	Where Is the Love?
Do You Know the Way to San Jose?	Why Did I Choose You?
Who Put the Bomp (In the Bomp, Bomp, Bomp?)	How About You?
	What Did I Have That I Don't Have?
Who Can I Turn To?	

Most lyrical questions are rhetorical — they neither supply nor expect an answer. The majority of titles start with one of the five *W*'s — *Who, What, When, Where* or *Why*; many begin with such interrogations as *Do, How, Have, Will, Can* and *Would* . . . .

Prewriting Suggestion

If you have a personal question on your mind pressing for expression, you're all set. Or if you happen to be a thinking/intuitive type, it's quite possible that your idea notebook has stored away a supply of who/what/when titles, because asking questions is an NT trait. On the other hand, if you're a sensate type who tends to prefer making statements, the exercise of questioning may be more of a challenge for you.

But whichever your favored perceptive mode, intuition or sensation, brainstorming from the five W's should turn up something. Then comes the process of working out a scenario: Who's asking the question? And of whom? What's the best form? And what's the ideal viewpoint? The following role-model situational lyric clearly springs from the writer's personal experience.

Example No. 1: The Question Title (Verse/Chorus)
WHAT DO I DO WITH THE ANGER?

It's rough, tough,
Hard to adjust.
WHAT DO I DO WITH THE ANGER?
This rage each day
Won't go away.
WHAT DO I DO WITH THE ANGER?
Whoa ohh ohh Whoa ohh
Whoa ohh ohh ohh ohh ohh ohh.

I'm minding my own business walking down the street
When a man says to me words I can't repeat
I keep on walking. He waits for my reply.
Then he calls me 'bitch' as I avert my eyes.
I hurry to the corner. (No way I'm looking back!)
He screams he's gonna get me. And his friends start to laugh.
Now there're three men deciding I'm their prey.
And all I can think of is: Get out of their way!

(repeat chorus)

I want my freedom to walk and dress how I please.
Being out on the street doesn't make me public property.
Looking over my shoulder doesn't make me feel good:
I want to feel safe in my own neighborhood!

[Men's Voices Speaking]:
"Hey baby, lookin' for some *action?*
Lookin' good, babe.
Come 'ere, come 'ere, sweetheart:
I got somethin' for ya."

What makes them think they can treat me this way?
Where's the respect? Where's equality?
I can turn off violence when it's on the TV
But what do I do when it's aimed at me!

(repeat chorus)

© 1990 Carrie Starner/Kim Starner/Jay Ward. Used with permission.

▲ Comment

This assertive straight-talking song always evokes an enthusiastic response from audiences (especially women) at Carrie's popular New York shows. Her choosing to start with the chorus, rather than the more traditional verse opening, effectively sets up the situation. Notice how the writer/singer—a rising young artist—underscores her distress by means of a mournful refrain of vowel sounds: *Whoa ohh ohh Whoa ohh/Whoa ohh ohh ohh ohh ohh ohh.* The street scene, the conversational style, the integration of the male voices, the use of the nonsense syllables contribute to a strong pop entry for the Top 40.

What's a Question *Plot*?

In a question *title*, like "What Do I Do With the Anger," the question is clarified, amplified and then reinforced with repetition. In a question *plot*, the question asked in the opening of the lyric is finally answered at its end. Although a common literary strategy—it continues to be an uncommon lyrical strategy.

Some Question Plot Examples

"Who?," the 1925 classic by Oscar Hammerstein and Jerome Kern from the musical *Sunny*, may be the shortest and simplest of question plots: the opening line asks "Who stole my heart away? . . . ." and 30-bars (of cut-time) later comes the answer, "No one but you."

In Stephen Sondheim's Broadway show *Follies*, a long-suffering wife's diatribe to her bore of a husband opens with the sarcastic query "Could I Leave You?" and closes with the penultimate answer, "Yes." Then, in a tag ending the singer appends the question "*Will* I leave you?" and responds, "Guess!"

The most fully developed question plot has got to be the classic from the revue *New Faces of 1952*, "Guess Who I Saw Today?" (Boyd/Grand). This story song begins with a wife asking her husband the song's title. She then recounts the details of her day of shopping in the city. We expect that she will say she ran into an old friend in a restaurant, but in the surprise ending, it turns out she discovered her husband in a tryst with another woman hence, the denouement, "I saw *you*."

Another example, reprinted in *CLW* is my cabaret song "She Knows" (pages 57-58) in which the singer has just been told by her married lover that his wife guessed he was having an affair. In the song's opening line, she asks, "Tell me how she got suspicious/When we've both been so discreet?" As the song unfolds she realizes how the wife had guessed: "You love me so much, it shows./Funny, that's how she knows."

Here's another lyric of my own. This one came music first. The ruminative melody seemed to be asking a question, so that's what the lyric had to do. The answer to the song's title evolved without conscious planning.

Example No. 2: The Question Plot (AABA)
WHAT DO I NEED?

WHAT DO I NEED
To make it sink in?
To show me it's over
With no way to win?
WHAT DO I NEED
To prove that you're gone—
The thunder to roar?
The roof to cave in before
I stop hanging on?

Am I a child,
Unwilling to see
That when a kite's stranded
High in a tree
You've got to walk away
And leave it behind?
Don't stand there and cry!
At least there were all those times
You got it to fly.

But here I go having myself
Another fantasy.
Seems I'm living on love-scene reruns
More and more—
Finding a way of believing
You'll be back with me—
Just like before.

WHAT DO I NEED
To make me let go?
To take up my life again
And face what I know?
I need more than a prayer
Or new affair could ever do:
I need a miracle
To get me over you.

By Sheila Davis
© 1979 Carlyle Music Publishing Corp. Used with permission.

▲ Comment

The lyric illustrates the development technique of stretching the thought by examples; that is, to give the listener a "for instance"—either literal or figurative: Likening the end of a relationship to an inaccessible kite acts to vivify the abstract idea of loss. The bridge offers a contrast to the questions of the A's by making statements—having the singer analyze how she spends her time—reliving the past and giving herself false hopes for the future. The successive related lines, "to make it sink in/to show me its over/to make me let go," illustrate both the value of parallel constructions and the principle of putting ideas in ascending order of importance. "I need a miracle," of course, is the answer to the title's question.

Because it's a melody I'm particularly fond of, I'm pleased that Muzak includes "What Do I Need" in their catalog. Muzak gets a lot of kidding by the public, but never by songwriters! In an interview in the *Boston Phoenix*, Paul Simon expressed my sentiments: "I really get off on getting in an elevator and hearing one of my things on Muzak . . . I feel like I succeeded: This tune made it—it made it into people's ears."

WrapUp

Many lyric questions titles are not asking for an answer, like "What Do I Do With the Anger?" Others, like "What Do I Need," seem to want to be resolved. There are a few well-known recorded question-title songs that I personally find unsatisfactory in that the lyric promises at the beginning more than it delivers at the end. The next time you get a question title, consider the possibility that it may be a *question plot*, a question begging for some emotional closure—especially if it asks something like, "When Do I Start to Get Over You?" Instead of merely repeating the title throughout a chorus, a stronger approach would be to use the AABA form so you can have the singer answer the question in the last A—"Maybe tomorrow . . ."

The Phone Call as Framing Device

The Strategy's Advantage

If there's some subject at the back of your mind nagging to be written and so far you haven't found the right handle — could be it's the phone. Letting the audience act as eavesdropper on one end of a conversation offers a unique opportunity to both move a plot forward and reveal aspects of character.

Some Phone Call Titles

W*O*L*D	Sarah Jackman
I Just Called to Say I Love You	Hello Again
Pennsylvania 6-5000	Operator
Beechwood 4-5789	The Telephone Song
Operator, Long Distance Please	Hello, It's Me

Of all the foregoing titles, "W*O*L*D," Harry Chapin's vignette of an aging deejay, stands out for its exploitation of the phone call device. In four minutes a believable real-life character is brought to life through a conversation that chronicles his failed marriage. You'll find Chapin's treatment of the strategy enriching. (His *Short Stories* album contains "W*O*L*D" along with other inventive story songs).

Prewriting Suggestion

If you're feeling plotless, priming the imagination with a list of caller-callee relationships could generate some ideas. For example: *secretary-wife, doctor-patient, lawyer-client*, etc. Such pairings might also suggest a potential plot. If one rings a bell, then consider whose end of the conversation we'll hear, the caller's or the callee's.

Small Craft Warning

Some small caveats come with the phone call. One, let your audience know at the opening of the first verse that it's overhearing a phone conversation. Chapin started "W*O*L*D" with a direct, "Hello, honey, it's me." That enables the listener to *experience* the song, rather than have to *decode* it. There's a big difference between surprising your audience and baffling them; the phone call device should not be treated as a means to "surprise." Point two — in a real phone conversation one wouldn't repeat later on in the call several sentences (lyric lines) that had already been said; consider then, that if you choose the verse/chorus form, the second and third choruses might need some variation to reflect the nature of a conversation. Remember too that every word should sound as if it's *being spoken now*, rather than *being thought later*.

Phone Call: Example No. 1 (Verse/Climb/Chorus/Tag)
SAY IT LIKE A MAN

You haven't been around much,
Blaming it on overtime.
Now you call again to break our plans.
Should I read between the lines?
When I ask, "Am I losing you?,"
You reply in monotone,
"Baby, you know I love you,
But I gotta get off the phone."
   If you plan to disappear,
    Make it clear.

SAY IT LIKE A MAN,
If it's over, say we're through.
Your white lies are driving me mad.
I wanna know the truth.
SAY IT LIKE A MAN
If you're gonna go.
SAY IT LIKE A MAN
So I'm not the last to know.

You dance around the issue.
You must think that I'm naive.
But it's in your voice as clear as day:
You've got leaving up your sleeve.
So I can't ignore the signs,
But I want to hear it from the source.
Have respect. Be direct.
Then let nature take its course.

SAY IT LIKE A MAN
Your kindness isn't kind.
'Cause you're keeping me from moving on
And leaving you behind.
SAY IT LIKE A MAN
Give honesty a try.
SAY IT LIKE A MAN
If you're going, say goodbye.
   And when you say it,
     SAY IT LIKE A MAN.

© 1991 Valerie Ciptak. Used with permission.

▲ Comment

That does the job: By immediately announcing it's a phone call, we experience the song right from the beginning. The chorus varies enough the second time around so as not to violate the style of a phone call, and the tag advances the emotion expressed in the first chorus. The crisp rhythm supports the consistently feisty tone and they both enhance the lyric's conversational dialogue. That's a call from the callee's perspective, now it's the caller's quarter.

Phone Call: Example No. 2 (Verse/Chorus/Climb)
THANK YOU, MAMA

Hello, Mom, no nothin's wrong,
Just called to see what's new.
How are your roses comin' along?
Have you heard from Uncle Lou?
Yes, Bill had a great time in Boston—
They loved the report he gave.
And Robby's decided he won't eat string beans;
He's really a handful some days!

By the by, that little guy
Had quite an adventure last night.
How he got lost at the mall, I don't know;
It gave me quite a fright!
But when I heard the announcement
And reached the lost and found
Robby said, "I did just what you told me"—
Then he hugged away my frown.

And in that moment I thought of all
The lovin' care you gave me.
I'm not sure why I called;
I guess I just wanted to say—

THANK YOU, MAMA
For everything you've done.
The lessons that you taught me
I'm teaching to my son.
I know it might sound silly,
But yet I know it's true:
Every day you play a part
In everything I do.

Are you okay? Your voice is strange—
Yes, colds are going 'round.
Robby's come to say goodnight;
I'll have to leave you now.
Tomorrow he's off to the playground
To spend some time with his friends;
But now he's off to dream awhile,
And so our visit must end.

Although I have to say goodbye,
I'll feel you're still beside me

And when I watch my little one,
I know your love will guide me.

THANK YOU, MAMA,
For showin' that you cared.
You proved that love grows greater
Whenever love is shared.
If I can give half the love
You've always given me,
My son will grow up wise and strong—
And what a man he'll be!

▲ Comment

Here Diane exploits a potential inherent in the phone call device; that is, to suggest, by the singer's reaction, what the callee has said or is feeling: For example, the daughter's opening line "no, nothin's wrong," and her response to the mother's audible appreciation that prompted, "Are you okay?"

In addition to the metonymic line "hugged away my *frown*" (the effect for the cause), three symbolic images help to dimensionalize the characters: the Mother's rose garden implies she's a nature-loving type; Bill's well-received report suggests he's the aspiring junior executive; and Robby's sudden distaste for string beans signals the arrival of a difficult stage. It would appear that sensate/feeling (SF) writers tend to write symbolically because they see life symbolically.

WrapUp

The next time you're brimming over with an emotion to tell off someone, or thank someone (or entreat or challenge someone), consider picking up the phone. Then again, maybe the next framing device will prove even more suitable.

The Letter as Framing Device

The Function

Like the framing device of the phone call, the letter (or note left behind) serves to make the message both more effective and the song more memorable. The two strategies, though similar in function, have attributes which may make one preferable to the other—depending on your plot. As always, content dictates form.

Phone Call Vs. Letter: Some Subtleties

As you saw in the previous section, phone calls are generally made to those we know and thus tend to frame lyric plots of an intimate nature. Another potential plus for a phone call over a letter is the ability that exists to show, through the singer's responses, what the person on the other end may have said. (It's this feature of the phone call that Harry Chapin developed so effectively in "W*O*L*D".) In a letter device the listener can get only the singer's feeling, not the recipient's reaction. The letter device, on the other hand, vastly expands the possible plot lines.

Some Letter Titles

Paperback Writer	Dear Abby
Hello Mudduh, Hello Faddah!	Dear Doctor
P.S., I Love You	Dear Friend
Dear Landlord	Dear Mr. Jesus
Take a Letter, Maria	Dear John
Beatrice Fairfax, Tell Me What to Do	

The wide-ranging subject matter, style and tone of the letter frame are exemplified by two of the fresher treatments of the device, "Dear Mr. Jesus," an abused child's plaintive letter to God, and "Hello Mudduh, Hello Faddah!" a camper's comic letter home.

Prewriting Suggestion

If you haven't a plot idea ready to go, run down in your mind the roster of people in your life, past or present: family members, employers, co-workers, lovers, neighbors, etc. to whom you might like to express some thoughts or feelings. You could use the letter strategy to frame your concern about a social issue on which you'd like to be heard. For example, you might write to your mayor, your congressman, the Governor, and so on.

Small Craft Warning

Just as a phone call has one "hello" and one "goodbye," a letter has but one salutation, "Dear So and So," one closing, and maybe a P.S. The best-crafted lyrics reflect that reality. Though recorded songs exist that repeat the unrepeated, construct your lyric so as to avoid such lapses in logic.

Letter: Example No. 1 (AABA/Tag)
DEAR ABBY

DEAR ABBY, please help me.
By now I'm getting frantic!
I'm what you would call
An incurable romantic:
I've been seeking Mr. Right.
Now, is that so very wrong?
And I wonder if he'll ever come along?

I was always so sure
He'd be suave and debonairish,
His chin would have a dimple
And his shoulders would be squarish.
He'd be charming, he'd be dashing,
He'd be muscular and strong. . . .
But I wonder if he'll ever come along.

Now there's this guy named Joe
I've known a year or so,
Who's not at all the type I had in mind:
His hairline has receded
And his waistline has expanded.
A Greek god he's not,
Not by a long shot,
(To be absolutely candid).

Still, he's always around
To be warm and reassuring.
He's gentle, he's funny,
He's solid and enduring.
Being with him is like listening
To some sweet, familiar song,
'Cause that's the way that Joe is.
So, what I'd like to know is,
Have I been blind somehow
To have missed what I see now?

Has Mr. Right been right here right along?
Signed, Puzzled.
Has Mr. Right been right here right along?

© 1988 Rebecca Holtzman. Used with permission.

▲ Comment

Rebecca's lyric makes evident how a series of appropriate devices unite to convey a playful tone: antonyms (*right/wrong, receded/expanded*); multisyllabic rhyme (*frantic/romantic, expanded/candid, reassuring/enduring*); stretching (*squarish/*

debonairish); and a closing pun (*right* here/*right* along). Another small point worth *pointing* out: When naming your characters, streets, towns, etc., make sure your name *sounds* like the quality you want to convey: *Joe*, for example, appropriately suggests a simple "good guy." Using the frame of a "Dear Abby" letter enabled the writer to draw upon a universal truth of the human condition: In asking a question, we sometimes find our own answer.

Here's a letter in a more serious vein. To fully experience the lyric you need to know that each verse is sung by a different person—first a man, then two different women; the refrain is sung by a mixed group.

Letter: Example No. 2 (AAA w/Outside Refrain)
DEAR MR. TAYLOR

DEAR MR. TAYLOR,
We've left this note unsigned:
But there are times when neighbors
Have to speak what's on their mind.
The walls are thin; We often hear
The angry things you say.
And we won't stand aside and let you
Treat your child that way.

Someone noticed. Someone listened.
Someone found the time to care—
Took a step to touch a life
And make a difference there.

DEAR MR. TAYLOR,
I thought you should know
Maria's not the student
That she was a month ago.
When she turns her homework in,
I see her arms are bruised.
Will you come to school next week
To talk the matter through.

(repeat refrain)

DEAR MR. TAYLOR,
I plan to pay a call.
The hospital informed me
Of Maria's second fall.
When I hear your explanation
I'll tell you what I see;
I think that we can work things out
If you will work with me.

(repeat refrain)

© 1991 Diane B. Engle. Used with permission.

▲ Comment

Creating discrete characters—a neighbor, a teacher, and a social worker—and shaping her letter into the AAA form, enabled Diane Engel to treat the difficult subject of child abuse. With metonymic subtlety, each verse *shows the effects* (anger, bruises, a "fall") *for the cause*. And perhaps most significant of all, without judgments or preachiness, the refrain sends the message that with caring concern one person can make a difference.

WrapUp

These role-model lyrics illustrate that, by choosing the ideal approach, any subject is treatable. As you weigh the appropriateness of a framing device for a particular concept, you'll want to factor in another plot feature—the setting—coming up next.

The Setting as Framing Device

The Purpose

Placing a plot in a place lends distinction to a lyric. The majority of songs takes place, not in a place, but in the singer's thoughts. They're attitudinal songs. Settings lead to situational plots and story songs. Lyrics with settings break down into present-tense plots—with the action *happening* in a particular setting right now—and past-tense plots, where the action *happened* in a particular setting. A place that's merely *referred* to ("Sunny Side of the Street") is not a setting that frames the action.

Present-Tense Titles	The Setting
Last Dance	a dance floor
One for My Baby	a bar
Heaven on the Seventh Floor	an elevator
I Will Survive	inside the singer's door
Sniper	a campus clock tower
Luka	an apartment lobby
Lucille	a barroom and hotel room
Knock Three Times	the apartment below
Piano Man	piano bar

Past-Tense Titles	The Setting
Taxi	taxi
The Gambler	train
Same Old Lang Syne	grocery store and car
Class Reunion	school gym
Harper Valley PTA	PTA meeting
You Could've Heard a Heart Break	bar

Prewriting Suggestion

A setting is a specific, concrete reality. So thinking up possible plot settings may require getting into a left-brain mode. As you know, one quick way to access your left narrow-focus side is to make a list. To prime your imagination, list all the potential settings that spring to mind. Here are a few to get your S function to kick in: *courtroom, hotel lobby, health club, lawyer's office* . . .

Then of course you'll need a plot: What's going on in the courtroom? Will the story be told from the angle of the judge, or a juror, or the plaintiff, or the DA, or the prosecutor? Consider all the angles. Go through the same process with each setting. And stay in that incubating mode until a gut feeling says, "Aha! That's the one I want to write."

Small Craft Warning

Remember that your listeners can know only what you tell them. It's the writer's job to transfer the scene in the head into details on the paper. To help your listener experience your song right from the start, make your opening line identify who, what and where; for example, "On a train bound for nowhere I met up with a gambler." ("The Gambler"—Schlitz)

Scene and Variations

The setting of your song's action can do one of three things: Stay put for the whole song, change from one place to another, or—because it takes place in a vehicle—it can keep moving. Whichever of the three you pick, be definite and be clear.

Setting up Example No. 1: The Stationary Setting

The first of the three role-model lyrics is part of a revue in progress. It was designed for an older woman who is attracted to younger men, rather like the character in the Broadway show (and film) *Pal Joey*. The woman is seated at a table in a café. She sometimes addresses (talking voice) the (unseen) bartender about an (unseen) young man at the bar. She sometimes muses to herself. The distinction between talking and thinking is made evident on stage by the singer's gestures and interpretation; it's made evident here by italics (talking).

Example No. 1: The Stationary Setting (AABA Variant)
THE BOY AT THE BAR

Who is that boy at the bar?
Send him another on me.
What is he drinking?
And what is he thinking of?
Maybe I'll ask him and see.

Look at him smiling my way.
Ask him to join me, okay?
Now that he's rising,
And probably sizing me up.
What am I gonna say?

I should have let him make the first move.
Now I'm on the spot.
Coming on strong was sure the worst move
I could have made. But then, maybe not.

(musical interlude indicates passage of time)

Hands have been shaken; we smile.
Bull will be tossed for a while.
Slowly defenses have lowered;
He senses my need.
Beautiful boy from the bar.
Follow my lead!

Last call's about to descend.
No time for us to pretend.

What will it be?
How does he think of me—as a friend?
Time for a romance to start—
Or else—to end.

▲ Comment

The frame of the bar setting permits the writer to reveal the woman's character through her actions (picking up a young man): Writing that *shows* affects us more than writing that *tells*. Having a singer alternate from thinking to talking is virtually unheard of in pop songs since making the distinction to the ear would be difficult. But Paul Mendenhall appears to have pulled it off. The song could even work as a record if the singer clearly "italicizes" her spoken lines to differentiate them from the thought lines. You might want to add this challenge of combining the thinking and talking voices to your roster of lyricwriting techniques.

In case you were wondering about the writer's type, a number of lyric characteristics point to it: his inventive rhyme pattern with inner and perfect rhyme, the questioning, the thoughtful analysis, the abstract language, and the (paradoxical) May/December attraction of the older woman for the young man: He's an intuitive/thinker (NT)—to whom all those attributes come naturally. The lyric, however, is uniquely his own.

The Changing Setting: A Caveat

If you write a plot that shifts from one setting to another, take special care to make that shift obvious to the ear in a transitional line. (Don't assume the video will do the job!) In "Lucille" when the song's narrator tells how he took his pickup from a bar to a bed, the transition was made clear: "From the lights of the barroom to a rented hotel room we walked without talkin' at all." (Roger Bowling)

Example No. 2: The Changing Setting (Verse/Chorus/Bridge)
HAVE A NICE DAY ?!?

"HAVE A NICE DAY, HAVE A NICE DAY,"
Wherever you go these days that's all you hear.
"HAVE A NICE DAY, HAVE A NICE DAY,"
I've a story 'bout it if you'll just lend an ear.

I left my car at the *reepair* shop
And before I picked it up I stopped
At the diner next door to start the day off right
With a strong cup of coffee and a plate of eggs up.
And as the waitress set up my cup
I said "Please add an order of white toast—light."

We shared a smile while we waited
And when she fin'ly brought my plate, it
Had toast so burnt, if it was white I could only guess.
The eggs were over instead of up
And Lord knows *what* was in that cup!
Then she looks right in my eye as she says:

"HAVE A NICE DAY, HAVE A NICE DAY,"
In that sort of waitressy way.
HAVE A *NICE DAY*, HAVE A *NICE DAY!*
With a breakfast like this, there ain't no way!

Well, that coffee somehow couldn't sweeten,
And I left both them eggs uneaten,
And headed next door to get my car and go.
The guy there says, "$300 bucks."
And I'm thinkin' that the day ain't brought no luck
And it's early yet! It's still got far to go!

Then I reach my car and see the same scratch
('Cause the paint they used was a lousy match)
And I'm sorry I went ahead and paid the bill.
The engine made this clinking sound,
'N' I swear the steerin' wheel used to be round —
Then as I drive past him, he yells:

"HAVE A NICE DAY, HAVE A NICE DAY."
I couldn't believe what he had the nerve to say!
HAVE A *NICE DAY!* HAVE A *NICE DAY!*
I wheeled that mother 'round and headed his way.

When he saw me turn he lost that smile
As I raced to close that quarter mile.
I was only gonna give him a little bump.
But Lord, that man made quite a jump
And I went through the diner window and into my eggs.

Well, they hauled me down to the local court
Where the judge said, "Son, drivin' ain't no sport,
If I had my way you'd be feathered and tarred.
But we can't do that anymore.
So judgin' ain't the fun that it was before —
Still, where you're goin', it's gonna be hard to

HAVE A NICE DAY. So HAVE A NICE DAY."
When he got finished I heard the bailiff say,
"HAVE A NICE DAY, Have *ninety* nice days.
Boy, it's a pleasure to send you away!"

Folks, a man sure gets mighty pale
Spendin' 90 days in the county jail.
Life is really weird b'hind prison walls.
It's the worstest time I've ever had.
But the truth is it ain't all that bad:
No one in here says "HAVE A NICE DAY" at all!

© 1986 Dr. Joe Waldbaum. Used with permission.

▲ Comment

The four settings of this first-person narrative—diner, repair shop, court, jail—shift clearly from one scene to another, making the narrative easy to follow. "Dr. Joe," an (ISTJ) writer/performer, savors every sensate *particular: two eggs, 300 bucks, 90 days, quarter mile* as he happily satirizes an expression favored by his polar-opposite type—ENFP's. This song acted as a catalyst for Dr. Joe's recording career by being banned on a radio station in Clayton, New Mexico! As Joe later commented in a newspaper interview, "In Clayton, they're pretty serious about having a nice day."

The Moving Setting

Of all the thousands of successful popular songs, it seems that only a handful have plots framed by a moving setting. This device entails placing your singer in a moving vehicle. The distinctive quality of all the songs cited below stems from the plot unfolding as the singer is traveling.

Some Titles With Moving Settings

Tie a Yellow Ribbon	on a bus
99 Miles From LA	in a car
By the Time I Get to Phoenix	an unidentified vehicle
Heart in New York	on a plane
Full Circle	on a plane

Although the vehicle in "Phoenix," is never identified (as a car, train or bus), somehow it doesn't matter because the plot is more centered on what the singer imagines the singee, his former lover, to be doing. (The lyric is reprinted and analyzed in *CLW*, pages 36-37.) Sometimes the vehicle is an inherent part of the lyric plot as in "Yellow Ribbon" and "99 Miles From LA."

Prewriting Suggestion

The plots of the foregoing examples of moving settings break down into two scenarios: 1) Singer reluctantly or wistfully or gladly leaves the past situation behind; 2) Singer anxiously or eagerly heads toward a future destination. For a lyric to create a strong effect it must establish and maintain a consistent emotional tone. Here's an example of plot no. 1—leaving.

Example No. 3: The Moving Setting (Verse/Chorus)
80, 90, 100 MILES AN HOUR

The road's so foggy up ahead
I should be going back instead of driving on.
But nothing's back there anymore.
Nothin' that's worth living for now that you're gone.

The windshield's blurred in front of me,
The highway signs, the lights and trees all flying by.
And I don't care where I'm bound.
I lost the one sweet thing I found, and so that's why

I'm driving 80 Miles an Hour
Through the neon rain,
Hearing how you cried, "I'm dying,"
Pounding in my brain.
Driving 80 Miles an Hour
Blinded by my tears,
Wond'ring why your life is over
And mine so full of fears.

I'd found someone that you could trust
To do the thing I felt you must do right away.
I said, "Girl, there's nothin' to it—
Don't worry, you'll come through it."
'N' it went okay.

But suddenly at 2 A.M.
You woke in pain, your body trembling like a leaf.
And then you slipped away from me
And I just stood there helplessly in disbelief.

Now I'm driving 90 Miles an Hour
Racing from my shame.
If only I hadn't made you do it,
I wouldn't be to blame.
Driving 90 Miles an Hour
Going God knows where—
Running, crying, scared and cursing
That life is so unfair.

My hand is shaking on the wheel
The pavement's slippery and I feel my mind explode.
My palms are wet with sweat and fear.
O God, what am I doing here on this road

Driving 100 Miles an Hour
Longing to see you.
Praying heaven will forgive me
For what I had you do.
Driving 100 miles an hour
Much too fast to see
Headlights coming out of nowhere
Bearing down on me.
Driving 100 Miles an Hour
Through the neon rain . . .

[sound of crash]

English lyric by Sheila Davis/Spanish by Roberto/Erasmo Carlos

▲ Comment

This lyric resulted from an assignment from CBS Records to write an English lyric to a song by the Spanish writer/artist Roberto Carlos entitled "120,130,150 Kilometers Per Hora." The publisher made the request that I maintain the title idea. Usually a lyricist is given conceptual free rein with the English lyric (as in my lyric "Who Will Answer," which bore no lyrical resemblance to the original Spanish hit "Aleluya No. 1"). So the car *and* the crash were given me.

Because the Spanish lyric offered no clear reason for its suicide-bent driver, I had to supply a motivation. I hit upon the idea of a young man who wouldn't marry the girl he'd made pregnant, insisting that she have a secret abortion: As a result of a bolixed job, she later dies. I chose to avoid the A-word, and to convey it in an oblique way. The lyric generated a lot of excitement at CBS but the subsequent two single records never "happened" — as they say.

I wanted to show a rainy night through a car window: "The road's so foggy up ahead. . . ." The effect-for-the-cause continues, "the windshield's blurred . . . the lights and trees all flying by. . . ." Once my mind got on that metonymic track, phrases like "neon rain" (compact metonym) and "palms are wet with sweat and fear" (effect for the cause) kept popping onto the page. I'd been given a sensate start by the car and crash, and that entrainment was enough to keep the metonyms coming. But I believe there's another reason that my NT mind was able to get down to the polar opposite area of my brain and leave behind my more usual abstract ("What Do I Need?") style: The shift was aided by writing to a melody. We now know that music can access the deep (emotional) limbic system beneath the cerebral cortex, mediated by the right hemisphere — the area where metonyms are produced. This lyric seems to be evidence that we're all capable of moving around that circle of cognitive styles — regardless of our dominance.

WrapUp

If your primary thinking style is other than sensate/feeling and you'd like to write more metonymically, the single most effective way to access that part of yourself that makes images is to listen to imagistic music. Earlier I referred to Georgi Lozanov, the pioneer researcher in accelerated learning. His studies suggest that particular compositions act as an agent to evoke visual images and feelings — the two requirements of writing symbolically.

Impressionist music, with its dreamlike style and fluidity of movement, has been cited as conducive to stimulating the ability to image, thus enhancing the creative process. Here are some particular works by popular Impressionists you might want to add to your music library:

- Debussy: *Prelude to the Afternoon of a Faun*; *The Girl With the Flaxen Hair*
- Delius: *The Walk to the Paradise Garden*
- D'Indy: *Symphony on a French Mountain Air* (1st movement)
- Ravel: *Daphnis and Chloé, Suite #2 — Beginning Pavanne pour une infante défunte*
- Respighi: *The Pines of Rome*; *The Birds*

After deciding on a place for your setting, why not relax with one of those selections in the background, close your eyes, and image.

The Third-Person Vignette as Framing Device

The Vignette: The Situational Plot

The majority of pop songs feature attitudinal plots in either first person ("I Still Get Jealous") or in second person with the singer making a complaint or request ("Why Don't You Do Right?" or "Let's Fall in Love"). A less common and thus more interesting song is a situational plot set in third-person viewpoint. It's not quite a full-blown story song, but more of an intimate character sketch—a vignette.

Broadening the Plot Base

Tom T. Hall, writer of "Harper Valley PTA" once remarked that "There aren't enough songs about enough subjects. Most songs seem to be written only for commercial success." I second the motion. Harry Chapin, the master teller of story songs, has echoed the sentiment: "There's never been a century that's had more major themes—more things to talk about than the one we have now—not necessarily easy ones, but that's the task for an artist." That's the challenge here: to address the less treated themes through the device of the third-person vignette.

Purpose

By creating a character either with a particular occupation or in a particular circumstance, you give yourself a special vantage point from which to make a statement about the human condition, which would be difficult, if not impossible, to do in first person.

Some Titles Featuring Third-Person Vignettes

She Works Hard for the Money: (The hard times of a waitress.)
Arthur and Alice: (Two retirees tough out the golden years.)
Eleanor Rigby: (A closeup of two of life's lonelies.)
Jack and Diane: (Two teenagers are reluctant to grow up.)
Bad, Bad, Leroy Brown: (A womanizer gets what's coming.)
She's Leaving Home: (Parents are confounded by their runaway.)
Old Hippie: (A holdout from the '60s finds it hard to adjust.)

The Impersonal Onlooker

In all the foregoing examples, the singer of the third-person vignette lacks a personal relationship to the singee. The vantage point is that of the third-person camera eye that's permitted to penetrate the character's heart and mind.

Prewriting Suggestion

To help generate potential plot material, you might begin by asking yourself, "What touches me, concerns me, upsets me, outrages me? What matter of personal importance would I like to arouse interest in or empathy for in others? Your "cause," might be one of our many contemporary problems: the failing health care system, illiteracy, violence, the troubled environment and so on. Then switching from your wide-angle lens that considers the *whole* problem to your narrow-focus lens that singles out an individual who's been *particularly* victimized by the problem will get you into the vignette mode. Your daily paper and nightly news offer a rich supply of potential plots. For example, a human interest story in the *New York Times* about one Georgia farmer's dilemma struck a responsive chord in a student who wrote this lyric.

Third-Person Vignette: Example No. 1 (AAA)
HE BELONGS TO THE LAND

Rising in the dark he pulls on his clothes
And like his grandaddy before him
Walks out through a Georgia dawn
To let the fields restore him.
He worked these fields for forty years
And it's the Good Book he's followed.
"Keep from debt," the scriptures say,
Yet for ten years now he's borrowed.
And though his debts are crushing him,
When he holds earth in his hand,
He holds the sweetness of his life:
HE BELONGS TO THE LAND.

Use to be he could pay his way
With the wheat and corn and barley.
Pay his way and carry on
When the rain stopped falling.
As he stood and watched the sky
He knew the costs were rising
Then the crops began to fail
And he's left agonizing.
To save the land he tries everything
But it's slipping from his hand.
How can he lose what he loves most?
HE BELONGS TO THE LAND

Rising in the dark he pulls on his clothes
Today he woke with a new solution
Before the sun hits the courthouse steps
And his lands are sold at auction.
He lays his insurance papers out,
Writes his wife a note saying
"Here's enough to save the farm."
And his face wears a look of praying.

He goes to the bedroom, sits on the bed
Takes his rifle in his hand.
His account is closed forever.
HE BELONGS TO THE LAND

© 1986 Sue Stater. Used with permission.

▲ Comment

The lyric dramatizes the wrenching decision of one American farmer whose desire to cling to land owned by his family for generations surpassed his desire to cling to life. Sue Stater's sensitivity to the serious theme produced the appropriate subtle sound linkings of unstressed rhyme (*borrowed/followed, barley/falling*). Notice how two synecdoches balance each other: *earth in his hand* (whole for part), and *wheat and corn and barley* (part for the whole). The device of the return—restating the lyric's first line as the opening of the third verse serves to strengthen the song's design. Without making a judgment about the rightness or wrongness of the farmer's final action, the writer allows the audience to make that determination.

Third-Person Vignette: Example No. 2 (Verse/Climb/Chorus)
WORKING GIRL

She leans in the window of a passing car
She says, "Hello, handsome, ya goin' far?
Or can I take ya 'round the world
Sittin' right where you are?"
She's a WORKING GIRL.

She knows a clean hotel, charges by the hour,
Got an ice machine, but you share the shower.
You don't have to buy her candy
Or bring her pretty flowers,
She's a WORKING GIRL.

She got the satin skirt,
She got the sequin shirt,
She got the snakeskin shoes.
She's doin' what she chooses to.

She's a WORKING GIRL,
Gettin' what she can while she's young and ripe.
Just a WORKING GIRL,
Doesn't need to know how to file or type.

She's got the skills
That'll pay her bills.
Business is brisk
So it's worth the risk,
She's a WORKING GIRL.

She's not the kind that you'd bring home to your folks
Or take out with friends for burgers and Cokes.

But whip out your ego and
She'll give it some strokes,
She's a WORKING GIRL.

Don't need help from Freud,
This lady's self-employed.
We're born and die alone,
Ya gotta watch your own rear end.

(repeat chorus)

© 1988 Maureen Sugden. Used with permission.

▲ Comment

The filmic opening line with its lens trained on one individual hooker immediately hooks our attention more than would a wide-angle "they" approach. The breezy style suggests to the listener that the oldest profession is simply another way to make a living. No moral judgment passed. The writer employs a range of literary devices that you can now probably identify: The show-don't-tell *enactment*, introduces the opening verses and climb; we find *metonym* in the memorable line "whip out your *ego* and she'll give it some strokes," substituting the symbolic attribute for the literal object. Did you note the two examples of trailing rhyme: *shoes/choose(s to)* and *alone/own (rear end)* — another underused device that delivers freshness. The writer, an intuitive/thinker (NT), points up the irony inherent in involvement with the kind of working girl "you can't bring home to your folks."

Third-Person Vignette: Example No. 3 (AABA)
SHE TOOK THE BLAME

She was born in times of fury
Into a broken home
Where tears were stopped by the crack of a hand.
Concern was rarely shown.
She could not understand the chaos
Or trust the tenderness when it came.
She brought the world down on herself.
SHE TOOK THE BLAME. SHE TOOK THE BLAME.

It was more than just affection
In her bedroom late one night
When her mother's boyfriend crept in
And whispered, "It's all right."
She was too young to grasp the meaning,
But not too young to feel the shame.
She dared not tell a soul.
SHE TOOK THE BLAME. SHE TOOK THE BLAME.

But she grew up with a dream
That one day she would find
Release from the secret
That ravaged her inside.

And it took an act of courage
And all her strength to tell;
And then she found the others
Who took the blame as well.

Now sometimes in a crowd
She thinks she sees his face
And the feelings come flooding back—
The anguish and disgrace.
But she lets it pass right through her
No more need to relive all the pain
The way she did those silent years
SHE TOOK THE BLAME. SHE TOOK THE BLAME.

© 1991 Carrie Starner/Kim Starner. Used with permission.

▲ Comment

Not an easy subject to treat. But by choosing the third-person viewpoint, it's more easily treatable. And by treating it artfully, the writer brings the subject out of the fearful darkness and into the hopeful light. When Carrie Starner performs the song in her one-woman show in New York clubs, the reaction is intense. The lyric's implicit message "to tell" draws gratitude by men and women alike who've lived the story and found that sharing their long-held secret to be the greatest act of healing.

WrapUp

Suicide, prostitution, child abuse—themes somewhat off the lyrical beaten path. But given the craft evident in these three writers, eminently singable. No theme is taboo. So whenever you picture a difficult subject, consider the third-person vignette as a potential frame.

The Duet as Framing Device

Some Background

Duets come in two distinct categories: 1) In which the singers are in accord; and 2) In which the singers are in conflict.

I want to distinguish between lyrics *designed* as duets by writers, and records *arranged* as duets by record producers. Sometimes songs have successful duet records—for example, "On My Own" and "You Don't Bring Me Flowers"—without their lyrics reflecting any inherent duet quality. The objective here is *to design* a duet. Purposefully designed duets are uncommon—another of those underutilized strategies.

Titles of "Accord" Duets

Somewhere	Up Where We Belong
Reunited	Ebony and Ivory
Friends and Lovers	Thanks for the Memory
Separate Lives	We're a Couple of Swells
Bosom Buddies	Two Sleepy People

Titles of "Conflict" Duets

Baby, It's Cold Outside	I Remember It Well
Let's Call the Whole Thing Off	The Girl is Mine
What Are We Doin' in Love?	Old-Fashioned Marriage
Barcelona	Sue Me
All Er Nuthin'	Anything You Can Do, I Can Do
You Must Meet My Wife	Better
You're Just in Love	You're Nothing Without Me

Prewriting Guidelines

As you may have noted, the majority of the foregoing titles were written for Broadway or Hollywood musicals. But imaginative lyricists can easily create a scenario giving two singers a motivation for a conversation: You can draw upon those moments of accord or conflict built into your own life's script. You might begin by recalling some significant relationship and its memorable emotional milestones—attraction, commitment, disagreement, and so on. That might be enough to generate a lyrical concept.

The Accord Duet

After choosing a subject or an emotion with which two can be in accord, try to "title" it; then decide the song form. As you begin to write, consciously assign lines to the two singers—deciding which will be sung separately and which together. (You've already had a role-model duet example in "LFS" on page 108.) Here's an example that evolved from concept, to title, to lyric, to music.

STAYING IN LOVE (CAN'T BE ALL THAT HARD TO DO)

He: We're sharing a closet — sharing a bed,
She: Planning a future, pulling together,
      Moving ahead.
He: Learning when to bend
      And when to be strong.
She: Not calling it winning or losing —
      Only getting along.

Both: STAYING IN LOVE CAN'T BE ALL THAT HARD TO DO
      Not for you and me.
      STAYING IN LOVE CAN'T BE ALL THAT HARD TO DO
      'Spite of what we see.
      We were made for each other and
      Baby, we'll come through.
      STAYING IN LOVE CAN'T BE ALL THAT HARD TO DO.

She: You're working on your dream; I've one of my own.
He: We're separate and equal, but stronger together
      Than each is alone.
She: Learning how much space is too little,
      How much truth is enough.
He: Holding on through the changes
      When the going gets rough . . . but

Both: STAYING IN LOVE CAN'T BE ALL THAT HARD TO DO
      Not for you and me.
      STAYING IN LOVE CAN'T BE ALL THAT HARD TO DO
      'Spite of what we see.
      Some people have made it, so
      Baby, we can too.
      STAYING IN LOVE CAN'T BE ALL THAT HARD TO DO.

She: If we keep on talking things over
      Really heart to heart,
He: And each of us keeps on growing
      Without growing apart . . .

Both: STAYING IN LOVE CAN'T BE ALL THAT HARD TO DO
      Not for you and me.
      STAYING IN LOVE CAN'T BE ALL THAT HARD TO DO
      'N spite of what we see
      Falling in love was so easy
      Staying should be too
      With a love like ours
      IT CAN'T BE ALL THAT HARD TO DO.

Words by Sheila Davis/Music by Doug James
© 1981 Solar Systems Music/Sumac Music. Used with permission.

▲ Comment

A simple, straightforward lyric that stemmed from wanting to send out a positive message. A literary device worth noting is the lyric's use of parallel constructions. Parallelism consists of arranging phrases of related (parallel) meaning in similar grammatical constructions. For example, *sharing a closet/sharing a bed*; *when to bend/when to be strong*; *how much space/how much truth*; *keep on talking/keeps on growing*. Giving coordinate ideas a similar grammatical form adds clarity, emphasis and memorability to your lyric. This device appears more often in the writing of thinking types, probably because such syntactic constructions are mediated in the left brain. But experience shows that feeling types, when made conscious of the polish that parallelism adds to a lyric, can find places in first drafts that can be strengthened by rephrasing ideas into parallel constructions.

The Conflict Duet

In writing a conversational debate, be playful — take chances. Let your characters criticize each other, interrupt each other, contradict each other, correct each other. And remember, there is no subject you can't tackle.

The next role-model example is from *So Many Ladies*, a musicalized treatment of Georges Feydeau's *Un Fil a la Patte*. In this scene a wealthy aristocratic woman in her thirties, Lucette, has just been told by her long-term lover, Bois, that he plans to marry a younger woman but maintain his weekly liaison with her (Lucette). In the duet, Lucette confronts her lover.

Example No. 2: A Conversational Debate Duet (Verse/Chorus/Coda)
IF I UNDERSTAND YOU RIGHTLY ...

Lucette: IF I UNDERSTAND YOU RIGHTLY,
You're approaching matrimony
As a way to keep a mistress
Whom you call on once a week.
Well, I find that very shabby.
And I find you very phony
If you're looking on your marriage
As a game of hide-and-seek.

Bois: IF I UNDERSTAND YOU RIGHTLY,
You indulge in indignation
At a modern way of living
That's as old as ancient Rome.
If a marriage is a business,
A romance is a vacation
And the love that's most delicious
Is the love that's not at home.

Both: Though you're talking rather strongly,
I shall try to speak politely,
But I think you're acting wrongly
IF I UNDERSTAND YOU RIGHTLY.

Lucette:	I've adored your adoration
	From the Left Bank to the Lido,
	And you never had to worry
	When you never had the francs.
	But I won't play second fiddle
	To your second-rate libido
	And I'll wave you to that altar
	With farewell and final thanks.

Lucette: I've adored your adoration
From the Left Bank to the Lido,
And you never had to worry
When you never had the francs.
But I won't play second fiddle
To your second-rate libido
And I'll wave you to that altar
With farewell and final thanks.

Bois: I'm perturbed and most disturbed
That you can toss away our passion:
In a wedlock there's a deadlock,
But in love there's only joy.
Our affair will still be there
(In just a slightly different fashion)
Or have you a new liaison
With some callow, shallow boy?

Both: Though you're talking rather strongly,
I shall try to speak politely,
But I think you're acting wrongly
IF I UNDERSTAND YOU RIGHTLY.

Lucette: You must understand me rightly,
For I've fully made my mind up
To give up our little love nest
And to seek a fresh rapport.
You've a new wife, I've a new life,
And our playtime we must wind up.
It's a step I may regret,
But *you'll* regret it more.

Now our revels all are over,
And I'll find a new amour.
So, my cast-off Casanova,
May I show you the door.

© 1979 Words by Eben Keyes II/Music by Blair Weille. Used with permission.

▲ Comment

The musical garnered enthusiastic reviews from its initial production by the High Tor Repertory Company of Falmouth, Massachusetts. Using an appropriately playful and sophisticated tone, Eben Keyes employs a virtual style book of literary devices that add polish and panache to this lyric. Before you read the following list of figures of speech Eben used, look at the lyric again to see how many you can pick out—even if you don't recall the terms:

- *Antonomasia*: cast-off Casanova
- *Antonyms*: rightly/wrongly
- *Anaphora*: I find/I find, the love/the love, you never/you never
- *Alliteration*: matrimony/mistress, farewell/final

- *Assonance*: give/little
- *Continguous rhyme*: callow/shallow
- *Interior rhyme*: wedlock/deadlock
- *Metaphor*: marriage is a business/romance is a vacation
- *Metonym*: a fresh rapport (*relationship*: cause for effect); that altar (*marriage*: place for event)
- *Parallelism*: You've a new wife/I've a new life; marriage is a business/romance is a vacation
- *Polyptoton**: adored your adoration
- *Simile*: marriage as a game of hide and seek
- *Synecdoche*: the francs (*money*: genus for species); Left Bank/Lido (*Paris/Venice*: part for whole)

*Polyptoton (po-LYP-toe-ton) is yet another Greek term for a useful device: to repeat the same word or root in different grammatical forms. Practicing it will add polish to your lyrics: (For more examples, see *SLW*, page 83.)

It's possible that Eben Keyes may not be able to identify the term for each device he used so well. That's all right: Naming is not the objective, but rather using. His polished literary style was developed by studying the most illustrious theater lyricists — W.S. Gilbert, Noel Coward, Cole Porter, Stephen Sondheim — to see how they got their effects. Through concentrated reading and listening, the inflections, rhythms, rhyme patterns and literary devices used by the most highly regarded craftsmen become internalized. It is this rich resource from which we can create our own desired effects. Writers can draw upon only those devices with which they're familiar. So read and listen to the best of the genre to which you aspire and analyze how the writers attained the results that you admire most.

WrapUp

This brings us to the end of the framing device as strategy. Perhaps you've read through this section without putting any of the devices into practice because you lacked a theme to frame. Well, Part VII, with its focus on interpersonal relationships, may supply just what you need.

PART SEVEN

Plot Strategies: The Romantic Relationship

P arts III through VI covered ways to generate plots, cap them with memorable titles, enliven them with wordplay, and outline them in the ideal frame. This section addresses songdom's favorite subject—the five main stages of that four-letter word—without which there would be no Top 40: *Love*—sought, found, lost, strayed, stolen, regretted, revived, regained.

You might think that the subject of love needs no prewriting suggestions or small craft warnings. But ironically, the road to love lyrics is perilous—fraught with unseen potholes and hairpin curves—to say nothing of stalled motors. If we consider that love songs are often written in the heat of longing or passion or pain, it's easy to understand why they may need to be rewritten in the cool of logic and clarity and reason. Of course we're talking about the limbic brain versus the cerebral cortex.

So, yes, there'll be some guidelines and caveats to help prevent detours and to keep your creative motor purring. So ready or not, here comes love, or to be precise, its three-letter relation, *Sex.*

Sex as Plot Device

Clarifying the Subject

Earlier I made the point that the best-crafted lyrics result from the writer's having made good judgments based on fine discriminations: for example, between the voices of talking and thinking, between the figures of metaphor and metonym, and now I add—between the subjects of love and sex.

In the pursuit of successful songwriting, let's discriminate between *love*—as in the feelings of caring, concern and commitment, and *sex*—as in physical attraction, desire and copulation. Although in life and song they often bear an effect/cause or cause/effect relationship, the point here is to decide which subject you want to write about in a single lyric. Making that distinction at the outset will help you write a song that can become symbolic of one subject or the other. (*CLW*, pages 305-307, illustrates the pitfall inherent in seesawing between the two meanings suggested by the word love—within one lyric.) Here are some examples that stick to one subject.

Titles on the Subject of Sex

Makin' Whoopee	Just a Little Lovin'
Sexual Healing	Afternoon Delight
Sugar Walls	Feel Like Making Love
Nobody Does It Better	Do That to Me One More Time
O.P.P.	Love for Sale
Do It in the Road	Make Love to Me
Push in the Bush	I Want Your Sex
Teach Me Tonight	What's Love Got to Do With It?
What Do They Do on a Rainy Night in Rio?	

Prewriting Suggestion

As you see, the attitude and tone vary—playful, artful, subtle, blunt and vulgar. Whatever your chosen attitude and tone, make them both clear and keep them consistent. Two earlier role-model lyrics—"Eight" and "Oceans of Love"—had sex on their minds. Here's another one.

Sex as Subject: Example No. 1 (Verse/Climb/Chorus)
2 HOT 2 HANDLE

You are so hot
You can start a fire
Just by walkin' down the street.
Hearts melt on the spot
Burnt up by desire
But, baby, I can take the heat.

Your animal attraction
Makes us a perfect match.
Loving you is not for the tame.
If you need satisfaction
Let's get down to action
'Cause, baby, only I can
Hold a candle to your flame.

You're 2 HOT 2 HANDLE
And that's just how I like it!
Too hot's just right, can't you see?
You're 2 HOT 2 HANDLE
You burn both ends of the candle,
And that's too hot for anyone but me.

You get your kicks
Living for each moment
No heart is safe when you're around.
But, I got a few tricks
That'll start you smokin'
And burn you right down to the ground.

Our physical reaction
Makes us a perfect match,
And now that I'm on to your game,
Who knows what might happen
In the heat of passion
Baby, maybe you'll find
You're the moth and *I'm* the flame!

(repeat chorus)

© 1991 Lyric by Arline Udis and Peter Drake/Music by Hec Stevens. Used with permission.

▲ Comment

This uptempo dance number came music first. Arline Udis, with her taste for idioms and flair for wordplay, picked a title to spark a winning lyric collaboration. The team pulled off a daredevil stunt by incorporating four (!) colloquialisms built on fire metaphors and making each work *appropriately* with the title: *I can take the heat* (the pressure to satisfy); *I can hold a candle* (I can be compared with); *you burn both ends of the candle* (You overdo playing); and *you're the moth and I'm the flame* (you'll be drawn to me!). Wouldn't surprise me if, by the time you read this, "2 Hot" will be sizzling on the Hot 100.

The subject again is sexual activity, but here it's linked to feelings of love.

Sex as Subject: Example No. 2 (AABABA Variant)
EARLY BIRD SPECIAL

Nothing starts the day
Really smiles us on our way
Like an EARLY BIRD SPECIAL.

Nothing satisfies
Really opens up our eyes
Like an EARLY BIRD SPECIAL.

You wrapped up in me
Warm as can be
Heading for love
Before the alarm reminds us
There's an outside world to start thinking of.

No passion in the night
No afternoon delight
Beats an EARLY BIRD SPECIAL.

And though ev'ry time with you
Becomes one of a kind, it's true.
There is something extra appealing
In that waking-up-and-there-you-are feeling
Of an EARLY BIRD SPECIAL
An EARLY BIRD SPECIAL with you.

Headlines never rate a look
And the phone stays off the hook
On an EARLY BIRD SPECIAL.

If the mailman's at the door
Well, the mailman we ignore
On an EARLY BIRD SPECIAL.

You wrapped up in me
Warm as can be
Heading for love.
Before the alarm reminds us
There's an outside world to start thinking of.

No passion in the night
No afternoon delight
Beats an EARLY BIRD SPECIAL.

And though ev'ry time with you
Becomes one of a kind, it's true.
There is something extra appealing
In that waking-up-and-there-you-are feeling
Of an EARLY BIRD SPECIAL
An EARLY BIRD SPECIAL with you.

By Sheila Davis
© *1981 Solar Systems Music. Used with permission.*

▲ Comment

This is the song that a parking lot sign begat and which virtually wrote itself—
words and music—while I was walking along the street. In its initial AABA, 32-
bar form, it felt short, hence the second bridge with a repeat of the final extended

A. Did you catch the allusion to the song title "Afternoon Delight" on the same subject? That's another time-honored device that adds the ring of the familiar to your lyrics.

The Muzak orchestra gave the melody of "Early Bird" a lively treatment and royalty statements attest to its performances in the far-flung elevators of Germany, France and Spain. So never underestimate the value of starting with a colloquial title. And remember, titles are everywhere—if you just keep your eyes open.

WrapUp

Engaging our left brain's ability to discriminate among the right brain's often multiple emotions, got us off to a clear sexy start. Now, on to the real thing.

Love as Plot Device

This time the subject is love, with or without allusions to its three-letter counterpart. In contrast to the song titles in the previous strategy, the following ones speak of commitment.

Titles on the Subject of Love

Always	You'd Be So Nice to Come Home To
Evergreen	You Are the Sunshine of My Life
I Love You	Love Is a Many Splendored Thing
Love Is the Reason	Our Love Is Here to Stay
Love and Marriage	Just the Way You Are
Precious Love	All the Things You Are
Endless Love	We've Only Just Begun
More Than You Know	Through the Years

Approach to the Treatment

Writing about commitment is rather like serving vanilla ice cream—in itself it's bland. It virtually demands an added ingredient or topping to give it some texture, some crunch. You may find it helpful to run your eye down the table of contents (Parts III-VI) as a refresher for treatment strategies. The two songs on the subject of sex ("Early Bird Special" and "2 Hot 2 Handle") each applied a colloquialism as a fresh topping. So give some thought to how a title might garnish your subject.

Two earlier lyrics, "The Strength of Our Love" (pages 9-10) and "Staying in Love" (page 154) both embody the subject of commitment. Here come two more.

Love as Subject: Example No. 1 (Verse/Chorus)
WITHOUT YOU

If it wasn't for your body
If it wasn't for your brain
If it wasn't for your rainbow smile
That eases all my pain,
If it wasn't for your patience
And your understanding too,
I'd get along real nicely
WITHOUT YOU.

If it wasn't for the comfort
If it wasn't for the doubt
If it wasn't for the troubles
And the way we work them out,
If it wasn't for the million
Daily miracles you do,
I'd get along real nicely
WITHOUT YOU.

WITHOUT YOU
I wouldn't be worth a damn.
WITHOUT YOU
I wouldn't be who I am.
I wouldn't know where I'm goin',
Where I've been
Or what to do.
I'd be without within me
WITHOUT YOU.

If it wasn't for your laughter
If it wasn't for your tears
If it wasn't for your carin'
And your sharin' all these years
If it wasn't for your open arms
That say you need me too
I'd get along real nicely
WITHOUT YOU.

(repeat chorus)

© 1980 Words by Jim Morgan/Music by Alan Cove. Used with permission.

▲ Comment

The repetitive device of anaphora (in the phrase *If it wasn't*) scaffolds the lyric by beginning successive lines in each verse. This structural tool appeals more to thinkers—NTs and STs—than to feelers—NFs and SFs. Perhaps it's because syntax functions in the left brain. I encourage all Fs, however, to value the power of purposeful repetition and add an occasional touch of anaphora for emphasis.

To support the country tone, the lyric takes liberty with grammar; hence such phrases as, *if it wasn't* (for *weren't*), *where I been* (for *I've*) and the (substandard English) colloquialism *real nicely*. With irony typical of the intuitive/thinker (NT), Jim Morgan chose a title phrase to celebrate commitment that's associated with the aftermath of breakup. He wraps up the chorus with a subtle pun: the line "be *without* within me" uses *without* as an adverb meaning *lacking something* which plays against the title's use of *without* as a preposition meaning *with the absence*.

Although pop tradition holds that titles of verse/chorus songs restrict themselves to the chorus, we find many successful country V/C songs that also place the title at the end of the initial verse and sometimes every verse—as in "Without You." Be alerted, however, to the danger of boring your listener by too many little references and/or blurring the distinction between the verse and the chorus. As always, there are no "rules," only useful guidelines.

Love as Subject: Example No. 2 (AABA)
A PERMANENT THING

Sunlight may fade into moonlight,
And winter may melt into spring,
As the wise men have found
What goes up must come down.

But our love, baby, our love is
A PERMANENT THING
Our love, baby, our love is
A PERMANENT THING.

No one can count on tomorrow.
Who knows what the future will bring?
Iron may rust,
Diamonds crumble to dust,
But our, love, baby, our love is
A PERMANENT THING
Our love, baby, our love is
A PERMANENT THING.

When we kiss in soft surrender
Time goes drifting away.
Feeling like this is what keeps us together
Day after day 'til the end of our days
You and me, forever.

Flowers may lose all their sweetness
And birds may forget how to sing.
Honey, we'll still be here
'Cause it's perfectly clear that
Our love, baby, our love is
A PERMANENT THING
Our love, baby, our love is
A PERMANENT THING.

© 1988 Words by Maureen Sugden/Music by Barry Wittenstein. Used with permission.

▲ Comment

Although the bridge includes satisfactory sex as a major component in their 'permanent thing,' the subject under discussion is clearly the total relationship. So there is no confusion as to what the term *love* here refers.

It's worth pointing out the way that well-crafted lyrics organize ideas into logical groupings and place them in ascending order of importance: Here, nature references begin with two polar-opposite abstractions *spring/winter, sunlight/moonlight*; develop in the second A to two concrete references *iron* and *diamonds*; and in the third A, to living aspects, *flowers* and *birds*. Perhaps it was Maureen's intuitive perception (NP) that gave her the freedom to stretch her AABA lyric to an added line, immediately repeating her title line, making it almost a refrain. It's unusual, but a very useful device to give the AABA form a "hookiness" equal to the verse/chorus form. Note to S and J writers who tend to stick closely to conventional practice: Once you've mastered your forms, it's okay to loosen them up a bit.

WrapUp

Relative to type and writing style, it seems worth noting that both examples of this strategy happen to have been written by intuitive/thinkers who share a quality common to NTs: an optimistic outlook. In the next section, some of the optimism may fade as infidelity rears its ubiquitous head.

Infidelity as Plot Device

Infidelity and Conflict

The subject of infidelity comes with built-in drama because inherent in the situation is the conflict felt by the two involved parties and the suspicion and anguish felt by the injured third. So in a real sense, it's both a more interesting and a challenging subject than "love." More on the challenge aspect in a moment. First some examples.

Some Infidelity Titles

Torn Between Two Lovers	Me and Mrs. Jones
Talkin' in Your Sleep	Other Lady
Married, But Not to Each Other	Lyin' Eyes
You Could've Heard a Heart Break	Stranger in My House
What She Don't Know Won't Hurt	The Cheater
Her (But It's Tearin' Me Apart)	Cheatin' On Me

Consider the Treatment Options

Infidelity can be treated from a variety of perspectives, voices and tones; for example, from that of the remorseful wife apologizing to her husband ("Torn Between Two Lovers"); the guilty husband breaking off his liaisons with his mistress ("Me and Mrs. Jones"); the anguished wife addressing the mistress in her mind ("Other Lady"); a bartender surveying the pickup scene in ("You Could've Heard a Heart Break"); the third-person camera eye telling the tale of infidelity ("Lying Eyes").

The Challenge: Small Craft Warning

From years of listening to first drafts of cheatin' songs that'll never make it to the cassingle rack, I offer two guidelines: If you write your song in first person from the perspective of the "cheater," be sure to make the singer likable and sympathetic. I've heard so many lyrics where the cheater was characterized as self-indulgent, callous or mean spirited. It's unlikely that a recording artist of either gender would want to identify with an unsympathetically drawn character.

The second guideline: If you write from the third-person viewpoint, guard against taking a morally superior or preachy tone. (This has caused the downfall of many first drafts). Professional singers know that their careers depend on mass-audience empathy. So bear those two caveats in mind. Sometimes a revision of only a line or two can transform a wobbly first draft into a surefooted commercial contender. A small point on *cheatin'* versus *cheating*: When you conceive your song, let the *feel* of it direct you to either consistently drop the -*g* endings of -*ing* verbs or to consistently maintain them throughout. As always, that's a general guideline: Occasionally, a writer wants to emphasize by pronouncing a word impeccably.

LIVIN' ON BORROWED LOVE

I can't believe I've fallen in love
With somebody else's man.
That sure wasn't the plan,
Oh-oh-oh, no-oh.
I can't believe I've lost my heart
That lookin' at you can tear me apart,
That I'd feel like cryin' everytime you go.
   But because it's terribly true,
    I find I'm doin' something that I
   Never dreamed I'd do:

LIVIN' ON BORROWED LOVE
Lovin' on stolen time
Hidin' away from the light of day
Pretendin' you're all mine.
LIVIN' ON BORROWED LOVE
Open to guilt and blame
Hatin' the lies and alibis
That come with the cheatin' game.

I can't believe I've let my feelin's
Get so outta control
Sure is takin' a toll
On my sanity.
And though I know each time we meet
I'm headin' down a dead-end street
My feet keep takin' me where I shouldn't be:
   But because I am hooked on you
    I keep on doin' something that I
   Never dreamed I'd do:

(repeat chorus)

I've heard it said that the
Only way out is through.
So until I see what destiny
Has in mind for me and you, I'll be

(repeat chorus)

© 1986 May Caffrey. Used with permission.

▲ Comment

Topping the subject with a fresh paragram title that sums up the story gets the writer off to a good start. Then she rose to the challenge to render the first-person cheater—an essentially "bad-guy" role—as an essentially decent human being by having her admit to feelings of conflict and guilt. Some writerly fine points worth noting: the *consistently* dropped -*g* endings; the anaphora outlining each verse, (*I can't believe/I can't believe*); and a strongly defined climb that arrives after an 8-bar verse and makes a statement that ideally sets up the title as if to suggest, "So this is why I say: "Livin' on Borrowed Love." A verse/chorus/climb role model.

Here's a lyric designed to let us eavesdrop on the final scene between a woman and her married lover:

Infidelity: Example No. 2 (Verse/Chorus)
WHERE NO ONE'S EVER BEEN

You don't have to say a word,
I can see it in your eyes.
She wants to have you back
And you've come to say goodbye.
I'm trying to fight the panic —
I'm not ready for this yet.
I don't want to be without you
And what about you — can you forget that

You told me that I'd touched a place
WHERE NO ONE'S EVER BEEN.
And that no one else could ever
Get that close again.
You said I'd ruined any chance
That she could tempt you back, when
I'm so deep inside your heart
WHERE NO ONE'S EVER BEEN.

What'll happen when morning breaks,
And quiet fills the air —
And in a dream-illusion
You think *I'm* lying there?
Will you be whispering my name,
Reaching for me across the bed,
Then feel your heart go crashing
When you rest your hand on her instead?

Will you masquerade the pain
When she looks you in the eye
And wants to hear how much you'll love her
Until the day you die?
I'll get through the hurting,
But there's something I need to know:
Are you being true to yourself?
Please be sure before you go.

(repeat chorus)

© 1991 June J. Donovan. Used with permission.

▲ Comment

June's workshop reading of her first draft was met with audible emotion and a few moist eyes. The lyric was essentially in place except that the opening verse left ambiguous whether the singer was alone and thinking, talking on the phone, or actually confronting her lover. In the rewrite (above), the line "I can see it in your eyes," makes clear to the ear that it's a face-to-face farewell, giving the lyric even more power. By showing the singer's devastation at her eminent loss, the writer rendered her character sympathetic.

Finding the Right Viewpoint

Now we'll hear from the "cheatee's" sector. The writer of the next role-model example had previously tackled the subject of infidelity but had directly addressed the audience warning that "there's no such thing as a harmless fling." With its preachy and somewhat scolding tone, the lyric thus failed—despite the craft evident in the first draft. The suggestion was made to try the subject again to *show the effects of cheating* by giving an individual example—written either from the third-person or second-person singular viewpoint: the lyric could then deliver the desired message—that extramarital affairs hurt others—without the singer sermonizing the audience. This lyric resulted from an assignment to write a compact-simile title: During the writer's list-making process to produce a fresh title, "Paper Thin Lies" popped onto the page—giving her a workable approach to infidelity.

Infidelity: Example No. 3 (Verse/Chorus/Bridge)
PAPER THIN LIES

In my bones I felt it—
All the signs were there:
You were cheating, baby,
Having an affair.
Secret conversations,
Whispered on the phone,
Body-building workouts,
Fancy new cologne.

PAPER THIN LIES
PAPER THIN LIES
Any fool could have read
The guilt in your eyes.
Did you want me to know?
Did you want me to see
Through your PAPER THIN, PAPER THIN LIES?

You started wearing skin-tight jeans
A stylist did your hair.
Honey, you were leaving clues
Everywhere.

Must have been a bore
To share my bed—
Wishing you were somewhere
Else instead.

PAPER THIN LIES,
PAPER THIN LIES,
Did you think I'd believe
You were out with the guys?
Wish you'd thought of my pride
Every time that you lied
Those PAPER THIN, PAPER THIN LIES.

Too many nights I waited
Too many dinners burned.
Honey, you are history
As far as I'm concerned!
With your

PAPER THIN LIES, PAPER THIN LIES
You and your see-through
Alibis
I don't have a doubt
I can manage without
Your PAPER THIN, PAPER THIN LIES.

© 1992 Felicia Reymont. Used with permission.

▲ Comment

In her strong opening line, the writer grabs our attention making us eager to know what "the signs" were. Then she satisfies our expectation with some sensory evidence of infidelity. You'll note that Felicia Reymont used her hooky chorus to keep developing the plot, skillfully maintaining her -*ies* rhyme for cohesion and memorability. With the fresh title and sassy treatment, the "music ready" lyric sets its sights on the Top 40 chart.

WrapUp

Sometimes we feel that a subject's been covered—that there's just no new approach. But when you look for one, you'll find it. For example, you could consider the vantage point of the onlooker: a waiter in a small café or a desk clerk in a motel. Or you could consider a telephone device—a call between the executive's secretary and his suspicious wife. . . . The possibilities are as wide-ranging as those of the breakup song, coming up next.

Breaking Up as Plot Device

Tell It Like It Is

Some breakup songs clearly spring from biographical material. Some spring from pure imagination. Others fuse the two. It's certainly not required of a writer to have lived a song. Yet, to engage the empathy of an audience, it *is* required of a writer to tell the truth about human nature. Paul Simon puts it this way, "I try to begin ... with some statement that is true ... something that actually happened or something that I really feel .... Then it's easier to go from that to a universal feeling."

Under the heading "breakup songs," can be included the various phases that lead up to a confrontation or actual leave-taking as well as the post-mortem period that may continue long after the final parting.

Some Estrangement Titles

Hurting Each Other	Could I Leave You?
Just Once	You've Lost That Lovin' Feeling
You Don't Bring Me Flowers	I Don't See Me in Your Eyes Anymore

Some Breakup Titles

You're Moving Out Today	Touch Me in the Morning
Breaking Up Is Hard to Do	D-I-V-O-R-C-E
Separate Ways	How Am I Supposed to Live Without
With Pen in Hand	You
Break It to Me Gently	

Some Post-Breakup Titles

Feelings	Every Breath You Take
All Alone	One Less Bell to Answer
Where Do You Start?	I Get Along Without You Very Well
Where Do I Begin?	Last Night When We Were Young
Can't Smile Without You	What She Wants

Avoid the Pitfalls

Lyric plots of estrangement, breakup, and their aftermath—whether autobiographical or fictitious—often result in first-draft problems. The major syndrome can be characterized as *terminal murkiness*: murky time frame, murky setting, murky motivations, murky emotions.

In autobiographical lyrics the murkiness sometimes stems from a writer's mixed feelings surrounding a recent breakup: Insufficient time has lapsed for the emotional haze to dissipate. In other instances the murkiness comes from the writer's attempt to camouflage the lyric's personal nature. In non-autobiographical lyrics—where a plot's been fabricated to fit a title—the murkiness usually results from the writer's failure to clarify the basic outline of the plot and the motive for

A PLOT SYNOPSIS FORM

Before you start to write, visualize your characters, their relationship, the physical setting for the lyric. Then from the picture you see, fill in the blanks—either literally on this page or simply in your mind.

Singer's gender _____; approx. age _____

Singee's gender _____; approx. age _____

How long has singer know singee? _____

Are they current lovers? _____; former lovers? _____

Married to each other? _____; married to others? _____

If others, specify: _____

When did/is the breakup take/taking place?

_____

What recent event motivated the singer's statement?

_____

Pinpoint the *one* emotion the singer feels

_____

Is the singer alone and thinking? _____

Is it a phone call? _____ A letter? _____

Is the singer talking to the singee who is present? _____

Is the singer "thinking to" the singee who is present? _____

If together, where are they? His place _____; Her place _____

Their place _____; (other) _____

Was the meeting accidental? _____; or requested? _____

If requested, by whom? _____

If another person—an unclarified "he" or "she"—is referred to, what is the relationship to the singer or singee?

_____

(Be sure your writing will make it clear to the listener.)

With what idea/emotion that the singer will express do you expect millions of listeners to identify?

_____

the leaving. In class, when the group is confused as to the circumstances surrounding a breakup lyric. I pose to the writer such questions as: "Who's done what to whom? Are they married or living together? Who's doing the leaving? Where are they?" And so on. Common responses consist of variations on: "I'd never thought about it," and/or: "Well, it *could* be that she . . . *or may be* that he . . . ." I respond, "Nope. Not '*could be* that . . . or *may be* that. . . .' A vague plot produces a vague lyric: Good writing doesn't offer the listener plot options."

Creating a Plot: A Guideline

For an audience to experience a song, the writer must envision the story. True-life breakups result from causes, so too should lyric breakups reflect a cause/effect scenario—however simple. In order to elicit from students more coherent first drafts, I've made up a short prewriting questionnaire, shown on page 172. Having to answer each question will ground your idea/title in a set of circumstances that your right brain can see and your left brain can sequence; the result will be a lyric that your listener can feel.

This prewriting exercise in no way suggests that the lyric itself contains your responses to these questions. It does suggest, however, that only when you yourself *know* the answers are you truly ready to begin to write a lyric that will be coherent and clear.

Establish the Breakup Time

When writing the post-breakup song, it's essential to pinpoint for yourself the moment of the parting in relation to the song: Was it last night, last week, last month, last year? It's unnecessary, of course, to *state* the anniversary date in the lyric. (Put it in only if it's intrinsic to your plot.) The sole purpose of *your* knowing the time frame of the breakup is to enable you to establish and maintain the singer's clear and consistent emotional distance from the event.

The two role-model breakup songs reflect polar-opposite attitudes toward the ended relationship. Not surprisingly, they were written by lyricists polar-opposite in their judgment function. (Cognitive style is more than word-deep). To exercise your powers of analysis, I'll let you try to identify each writer's dominant—thinking or feeling. I'll point out some significant characteristics in the writing, but I'll wait till the WrapUp to divulge their types.

Post-Breakup: Example No. 1 (Verse/Chorus)
EVERY ACHING HOUR

As I sit here by my window
Staring at the moon
A figure by the streetlamp
Cries a lonely tune.
My room is cold and empty
My heart is icy blue
I'm trying not to think of her
But that's all I ever do.

EVERY ACHING HOUR
Every sleepless night
Time can pass so slowly
When there's no one in your life.
The memory of her kiss
Hasn't lost its power
It haunts me every minute
Of EVERY ACHING HOUR.

The wind outside is laughing
Mocking me, I know —
Calling me a pitiful fool
Because I let her go.
I made her feel neglected,
Till resentment grew so deep.
Now loneliness and heartache
Are the company I keep.

(repeat chorus)

© 1991 Noel Cohen and DeAnne Macomson. Used with permission.

▲ Comment

We could certainly characterize this stage as melancholia — with its sense of isolation and self-recrimination. The writer used a subtle device that intensifies the darkness of his room; he referred to the singee as *her* rather than *you*, increasing the feeling of emotional distance. A fine point to remember. I'm sure you noted the instances of metaphor (*my heart is icy blue*) and its subtype, personification (the *wind outside is laughing/mocking*) — telling barometers of the writer's cognitive style.

Post-Breakup: Example No. 2 (AABA)
I DON'T DO WINDOWS ANYMORE

I often think about the day
You packed your things and went.
And I wasn't sure your heated words
Were what you really meant.
So I sat glued to the window
And I listened for the door, but
I DON'T DO WINDOWS ANYMORE.

You stayed away and I became
A mighty angry case.
For hour after hour I'd keep
Staring into space.
I'd gaze out through the window
And at times I'd pace the floor, but
I DON'T DO WINDOWS ANYMORE.

One day I simply told myself
Enough was enough.
The waiting game was not my style at all.
And while I knew that life
Would be sometimes pretty rough.
I could handle it much easier
By standing up tall.

So I got up from the window
And I got my head on straight.
I've things to do and it's true
That I'm doing almost great.
I guess that I can say
That I've evened up the score 'cause
I DON'T DO WINDOWS ANYMORE.

▲ Comment

No taking the blame for the singee's departure, not here, nosiree! The tone is as clear and hard-edged as the window pane through which the singer will no longer look. This singer appears to make decisions with her "*head on* straight," rather than with an "icy blue *heart*." We hear no metaphoric mocking wind, but instead a playful pun on "*do windows*." Clear-minded, practical and decisive.

WrapUp

We see that breakups evoke different feelings and thoughts in different people. As always, the objective is to write the story from your slant and in your style. As Marilyn Bergman told me: "If you have had the pleasure of creating something that makes you feel good—without the market looking over your shoulder—but just *you*—writing to please *you*, then no matter what happens to it, you have had that pleasure of pleasing yourself. If anything happens to it, that's gravy."

You were probably able to identify the most obvious aspect of each writer's style—even if not the whole four-letter type: "Every Aching Hour" was by an introverted/feeling dominant (IN*F*P) and "I Don't Do Windows Anymore" by an extraverted/thinking dominant (ES*T*J). Now on to the best part of breaking up—making up.

Reuniting as Plot Device

Some Background

In our cycle of phases of intimate relationships — attraction, commitment, and disaffection — reuniting's a fitting windup. This strategy includes not only the "making up" plot, but also the somewhat mystical theme that "somewhere, somehow, we'll be together again" as in some of the following titles:

Some Making-Up/Getting-Together Titles

Reunited	Just One More Chance
Don't Give Up On Us	Come Back to Me
The Best Part of Breaking Up	Break Up to Make Up
Another Time, Another Place	Somewhere Down the Road
Somewhere Down the Line	We'll Be Together Again
Somewhere Out There	Love Will Lead You Back
After All	Somewhere

Pinpoint the Motivation

Like the breakup song, a makeup/getting-together-again plot requires having a clear scenario in mind. In other words, when you write about getting back together, you need to know why your leading characters separated in the first place. For example, were they too young ("Our Day Will Come")? Was one involved with someone else ("Somewhere Down the Line")? Were they being separated by long-distance careers ("Somewhere Down the Road")? Incubate.

Prewriting Suggestion

It's possible that the second-person viewpoint — addressing "you" — will be the most effective for this lyric. Decide whether your singer is thinking the words, or talking them to a singee who is present. Picture the scene. Consider, too, if your concept might make an effective duet — if the two people are in accord (as in "Reunited"). This song has been plotted from one person's viewpoint.

Making Up: Example No. 1 (Verse/Chorus/Tag)
READY WHEN YOU ARE

Since the day we said goodbye
I've tried to get you out of my heart.
But I can't stop wond'rin' why
We fell apart.
Like two children with a new balloon
Caught in a tree,
We let go of the string too soon,
We gave up too easily.

I'm READY WHEN YOU ARE
To try our love again,
To give and take and bend
The way I know we need to do.
I'm READY WHEN YOU ARE
To learn where we went wrong
We started out so strong
I think we owe ourselves
A second chance—don't you?

On a scale from one to ten,
Guess we made about an eight or a nine.
In a less than perfect world,
That's doin' fine.
But perfectionists like you and me
Expected more.
Well, I'm wiser than I used to be:
We had something worth working for.

(repeat chorus with tag):
I'm READY to start again
READY to start again
READY to give you my heart again
Please say you're READY too.

By Sheila Davis and Doug James
© 1981 Solar Systems Music/Sumac Music. Used with permission.

▲ Comment

This one started with a colloquialism that I believed hadn't been used as a song title. The next question I asked myself was, of course, what's the scenario? Ready for what? Several potential plots came to mind: 1) Sex: I'm ready when you are to get it on; 2) Love: I'm ready when you are to commit to each other; 3) Making up: I'm ready when you are to get back together. That's the one I decided upon because it held the potential for more drama. In the process of setting the lyric to a "power ballad" melody, Doug James came up with the tag ending to the final chorus which enables the singer to *end* the song (on the open vowel *too*, on a high note) rather than use that old standby for many verse/chorus songs, "repeat chorus to fade." I agree with Billy Joel who once said, "Good songs don't fade, they end."

Here's a student lyric that expresses a similar desire to hold on to a good thing.

Making Up: Example No. 2 (AABA)
ONCE MORE FROM THE TOP

I walked out the door
And knew I'd gone too far.
How could I go when breaking up
Would break my heart.

We have started something here
That's too good to stop.
So let's try again
ONCE MORE FROM THE TOP

We knew how to take
But we were too scared to give.
And you gotta give to get
That's just how it is.
But that was then.
Baby, now I'll give all I got
Just to take it
ONCE MORE FROM THE TOP

We'll find ourselves again,
Define ourselves again,
Remember seasons when
We had it all:
We spent the winter nights
Lying so safe and warm
In a world that was filled with our love.
It's still waiting there for us.

No one said the road was easy.
But that's okay.
We've had our share of growing up
To do on the way.
But now, at last the time is right
So, let's take our shot.
Yes, let's take it
ONCE MORE FROM THE TOP

Lyric by Arlin Udis/Music by Hec Stevens
© 1989 Regina Kaye Music Inc./Seaport Music/Protoons, Inc. Used with permission.

▲ Comment

In this song, the AABA melody came first and evoked from Arline Udis a positive plea that reinforced its inherent emotion. For her title, she drew upon the show business rehearsal term that's become a colloquialism. The winning combination attracted the attention of Judy Torres who chose the song for her debut Profile Records album.

WrapUp

That completes the cycle of intimate relationships as plot strategies. Now on to more devices to help you strike a common chord.

PART EIGHT

More Plot Strategies: The Universal Theme

After our examination of the many sides of the romantic relationship as plot strategy, it's time to expand our song topics to other themes that strike a common chord. In this section, we'll take a look at seven popular topics for song plots including the parent/child relationship, friendship, and music and dance. We'll also draw upon Harvard psychologist Henry A. Murray's list of Fifteen Basic Needs. We've already covered his No. 1—you guessed it—sex. Here we'll include what he labels No. 9 and 10—the need for autonomy and the need to escape. Dr. Murray's list has long served as a guide to advertising copywriters. Now songwriters will be made more conscious of some subjects with built-in listener interest.

The Parent/Child Relationship as Plot Device

Some Background

This theme may strike you as an uncommercial concept. Not so. Most titles below were designed for the pop marketplace. The exceptions: "Papa, Can You Hear Me?" (*Yentl*), "Soliloquy" (*Carousel*) and "Sunrise, Sunset" (*Fiddler on the Roof*).

Some Titles on the Parent-Child Theme

Ships (That Pass in the Night): (Father/son estrangement.)
Leader of the Band: (Son's gratitude to father.)
Men in My Little Girl's Life: (Father watching daughter grow.)
Cat's in the Cradle: (Parenting style repeats itself.)
Homecoming: (Son experiences father/son estrangement.)
My Father: (Daughter fondly remembers father.)
The Portrait: (Daughter addresses dead mother.)
The Living Years: (Son's regret for the unexpressed words.)
Daddy, Don't You Walk So Fast: (Plea to divorced father.)
The Gift of Life: (Father addresses aborted baby's spirit.)
Papa, Can You Hear Me?: (Daughter addresses dead father.)
Sunrise, Sunset: (Bride's father observes passage of time.)
Soliloquy: (Unemployed man fearful of impending fatherhood.)

Finding the Plot Angle

How might you use this strategy to make some statement of both personal significance and universal appeal? Looking over the lyric synopses suggests the range of perspectives and diversity of content: appreciation for good parenting, regret over flawed relationship, anxiety over impending parenthood. The unique nature of the relationship also allows for treatment of other sensitive subjects such as illegitimacy, abortion and homosexuality.

Prewriting Suggestion

When framing your lyric, consider such strategies as apostrophe, the letter, and the phone call: You've already seen in "Thank you, Mama," an example of the usefulness of the phone call device to convey a loving message to a living parent (pages 135-136). Here are three other looks at the parent/child relationship.

Parent/Child: Example No. 1 (Verse/Chorus)
HE'D PLAY "AIN'T MISBEHAVIN' "

My dad was not an easy man to know.
Most of what he felt, he'd never show.

Wasn't much for huggin'—handshakes had to do.
I've wondered who he was my whole life through.
He worked hard, he kept his family clothed and fed.
And he kept his secrets safe inside his head.
The only window on his world of mysteries
Was when he'd sit down after supper at the old piano keys:

HE'D PLAY "AIN'T MISBEHAVIN' " on the baby grand.
He'd walk the bass line up and down with his left hand.
He'd play the right hand in his barroom style,
He'd lean back, close his eyes and smile.
Things he'd never speak, he'd let his fingers say
When HE'D PLAY "AIN'T MISBEHAVIN'."

We kids would gather 'round him on the floor
And watch his fingers fly for an hour or more.
Maybe the music took him somewhere far away.
I only know he'd show a little of his soul every time

(repeat chorus)

Now my father's gone, my youth is long gone too.
I miss the man it seems I barely knew.
But there's one sweet mem'ry burnin' bright and clear
And in my mind there's the echo of the song I still can hear

(repeat chorus)

© 1988 Daniel Fox. Used with permission.

▲ Comment

Dan might have chosen a title like "When My Father Played the Old Songs," and still have written a role-model lyric. Yet his choice of the famous song "Ain't Misbehavin' " illustrates the power of the specific over the general. Not only does it make his song more memorable, it creates a symbolic image to vivify the father's introverted feeling. A pair of balanced metonyms support how he used his hands when he wasn't caressing the keys: *handshakes* replaced *huggin'*.

Worth noting is Dan's choice of rhyme style for "Misbehavin' ": He might have chosen the obvious feminine rhyme mates of *gave in/savin'/wavin'/maven* and so on; but he avoided the potential singsong sound by opting for the subtle device of trailing rhyme: *say/-ha-vin'*. In the pursuit of well-crafted lyrics, every decision counts.

Parent/Child: Example No. 2 (Verse/Chorus/Bridge)
LITTLE HEART
(Verse/Chorus/Bridge Form)
I remember the night you were born
What a thrill it was for me:
When I heard your cry
I'd never heard a sound so sweet.
I remember the first time you stood
And the look that was in your eyes.

Since the day you walked across that room,
Every day's been a new surprise.

LITTLE HEART, LITTLE HEART
You mean so much to me.
LITTLE HEART, LITTLE HEART
You're so beautiful to see
LITTLE HEART, LITTLE HEART
I'm so happy when you're near.
LITTLE HEART, LITTLE HEART
I thank God that you're here.

I love the funny games you play
When you're sittin' on my knee
Like coverin' up your eyes
And sayin' peek-a-boo to me.

And at night when I tuck you in,
And you smile that magic smile
And hug me with a kiss
It makes my life worthwhile.

(repeat chorus)

And when I'm far from home and feelin' low,
I pick up the phone to hear your hello,

(repeat chorus)

© 1989 Cory Morgenstern. Used with permission.

▲ Comment

Simple, direct and heartfelt. The lyric moves from a sound of birth through a progression of achievements — standing, walking, game playing. The bridge does what a bridge should do — present a new thought. True to type, here is the loving appreciation so characteristic of the intuitive/feeling (NF) outlook on life. Although a right-brain dominant for whom maintaining time frames and cause/effect sequencing doesn't come naturally, Cory Morgenstern offers proof in "Little Heart" that, in service to feeling, left-brain skills can be mastered.

Parent/Child: Example No. 3 (Verse/Chorus/Bridge)
MY BROWN SKIN BABY

Come, momma's baby,
Let me wipe away your tears.
This is the day
Many mommas like me fear.
Now you've learned this world
Can be painfully unfair:
You've seen the disappointed looks
At your dark face and hair.

MY BROWN SKIN BABY
Pretty little one.
Believe in yourself.
'Cause you determine who you are,
Not anyone else
MY BROWN SKIN BABY

Color is an issue
In this world in which we live.
There are some who'll judge you
Before they see what you can give.
When someone acts unjustly
You are not to blame.
Hold your head up, honey.
And never feel ashamed.

(repeat chorus)

Go ahead, get angry
Then use that energy
To drive you and push you
To be all you were born to be.

(repeat chorus)

© 1991 Vernetta Cousins. Used with permission.

▲ Comment

This lyric illustrates again that you attain the universal through the particular. Though specifically addressed to a child of color, the lyric delivers a message about self-esteem and self-empowerment for all.

WrapUp

These role-model lyrics should help reaffirm that it's not just romantic love that makes the Top 40 go 'round. If you'd like to see one more parent/child lyric — a dramatic one written for the theater — turn to Strategy 39, pages 235-237. Or if you're ready for some treatments of one of our fifteen basic needs, autonomy, turn the page.

The Need for Autonomy as Plot Device

Some Background

As already pointed out, autonomy—and its components of self-esteem, self-belief and self-empowerment—is considered an inherent human need. Sometimes it's necessary to affirm it verbally. And there's no place like a song—not only as a motto for oneself, but as an anthem for others.

Some Autonomy/Survival Titles

I Am, I Said	Some People
I've Got to Be Me	I Will Survive
It's My Turn	Everybody Says Don't
I'm Still Here	You're Gonna Hear From Me

Prewriting Suggestion

Songs of self-affirmation tend to be a kind of "thinking out loud" to no one in particular. Sometimes the assertion is set in the talking voice and addressed to a particular singee. "It's My Turn," with the second-person plural addressing the collective you, offers yet another viewpoint to consider. Here's a student example.

Autonomy: Example No. 1 (Verse/Chorus)
IT'S MY LIFE

Hey people, I've got something to say.
Please don't take it in the wrong way.
It's just that sometimes I feel kinda wild
And I may act like a foolish child.
But I'm not asking for approval, you see.
You can be you, 'cause I'm gonna be me.

IT'S MY LIFE
I'll live it my way.
Can't be worried 'bout what people say.
IT'S MY LIFE
Whatever I do,
I'm the one who's gotta walk in these shoes.

Says in the Bible, "Don't cast the first stone."
You mind your business, I'll mind my own.
That don't mean we can't be friends.
Without respect, though,
The friendship must end.
I work hard to take care of myself.
I don't depend on nobody else.

IT'S MY LIFE
And you only get one
When it's over Jack, it's over and done.
IT'S MY LIFE
I'll be my own boss.
I'll pay the piper, whatever the cost.

Hey people, I've had my say,
Now please don't take it in the wrong way, but

IT'S MY LIFE
And it's so quickly done.
I can't waste it trying to please everyone.
IT'S MY LIFE
As long as I live
I'm gonna give it all I can give.
IT'S MY LIFE . . .

▲ Comment

In "It's My Life" Noel Cohen illustrates two important writing options: It's all right to use only a part of a verse the second or third time around *and* the words of chorus can vary. The chorus' slight variations, in a sequence of progressively stronger statements, clearly enhances the lyric. Shirley MacLaine might argue with the writer's assertion that we get only one life, but no one will argue with the need for autonomy in it—or *them*.

Autonomy: Example No. 2 (Verse/Chorus/Bridge/Tag)
I'M A SURVIVOR

At work I got a pink slip
The day you packed to leave.
Lord, I asked, what can be next
If bad luck runs in threes?
Into each life some rain must fall;
Well, it's rainin' now as heavy as I can recall.
But when this downpour is done,
I'm gonna find my place in the sun 'cause

I'M A SURVIVOR
And if I'm hurtin' that's okay.
I'M A SURVIVOR
No matter what life throws my way.

Had enough disappointments
For a lifetime and a half.
Though I'm feelin' shaky
I know this too will pass.
I've been hit in the wallet and 'n the heart
But there's no time like now to make a new start.
'Cause

(repeat chorus)

I've got fam'ly 'n' friends
'N' faith to keep me goin'
Till I feel like myself again.
Soon there'll be
A little sunlight showin':
My luck is gonna change.
Though I don't know when, I know

I'M A SURVIVOR
And if I'm hurtin' that's okay.
I'M A SURVIVOR
No matter what life throws my way.
I'll survive, I'll survive—
I'M A SURVIVOR
I'll survive, I'll survive—
I'M A SURVIVOR
(repeat tag to fade)

▲ Comment

No Pollyanna optimism here, but a realistic appraisal of problems with a realistic hope for improvement. Sharon Swerdloff's (sensate/feeling) view of the world is evidenced by her metonymic *pink slip* effect-for-cause introduction to the singer's run of bad luck as well as the metonymic symbols of *wallet* and *heart*. The classic *rain = trouble* metaphor works well as a motif to underscore both current problems (*downpour*) and future promise (*sunlight showin'*). As in all well-executed lyrics, the figurative language serves to support the point, not be the point.

Autonomy: Example No. 3 (Verse/Climb/Chorus)
I AM A BEAUTY

My skin is like black velvet—smooth.
My hips are full and sway when I move.
My bones are big, and my arms are strong.
My back is sturdy from working hard and long.
   I see myself in a positive way
   So when I look in the mirror I have to say:

I AM A BEAUTY
'Cause without any doubt
I feel like a beauty
Inside and out.
The outside may be all
The world can see, but
I AM A BEAUTY
'Cause there's beauty in me.

I treat myself with love and respect.
My weaknesses I try to accept.
And when I act human and things go wrong
I sing myself an un-bluesy song.
   I see myself in a positive way;
   When I look in the mirror I have to say:

(repeat chorus)

I've decided I will personally define
What pleases my eye, and ear and mind.

(repeat chorus)

© 1991 Vernetta Cousins. Used with permission.

▲ Comment

The writer's experience transcends the particular and becomes a message that rings with universality. In a society where facade is often valued over substance, and reality is denied with lifts, tucks and dyes, we can use an occasional reminder that true beauty lies within.

WrapUp

The songs that touch us most are written from conviction rather than contrivance. The three role-model lyrics illustrate the way in which a writer's individual experience and personal truth can be shaped into an art form that resonates with meaning for millions. Now, here comes a plot strategy that combines two basic needs—the need to nurture, and its flip side, the need to be nurtured: The Friendship Song.

Friendship as Plot Device

Some Background

The archetypal friendship song generally reflects a personal statement from one of three attitudes: the offer/commitment of friendship, gratitude for someone's friendship, or a shared appreciation of friendship—a duet.

Some Friendship Titles

Friendship	Bridge Over Troubled Water
Old Friends	Thank You for Being a Friend
Together Wherever We Go	Come in From the Rain
You've Got a Friend	That Old Gang of Mine
That's What Friends Are For	True Colors
Friends	Bosom Buddies
With a Little Help From My Friends	

Tone Is of the Essence

A successful song requires a consistent tone. In offering friendship, the tone can, of course, be playful as Cole Porter's "Friendship," or as heartfelt as Carole King's "You've Got a Friend." Two theater titles illustrate the range of possibilities in friendship duets from appreciative ("Together Wherever We Go") to sardonic ("Bosom Buddies").

Small Craft Warning

A potential pitfall exists with this theme: Be careful to avoid unconsciously including lines that suggest lovers rather than friends, thus muddying the waters of the relationship. The themes "we're-friends-*and*-lovers" and "friends-*have-become*-lovers" fall under the "love-as-plot device." As I continue to emphasize, the ability to make fine distinctions—as we've been making between the thinking and talking voice, literal and figurative language, the themes of sex and love, and now between friends and lovers—is a prerequisite for writing songs as memorable as those just listed.

Prewriting Suggestion

If you happen to be writing for a specific project such as TV, theater, or a children's album—you've already got a character in mind. That simplifies the job of staying consistent both in tone and subject. A pop writer can easily duplicate that context: Purposefully pick someone to *write to* in your mind—someone for whom you feel particular affection—a personal friend, a teacher, a mentor, etc. The image of that person will keep you focused so that you're not led astray—perhaps by a seductive rhyme—into a different tone, or a different subject.

Think about one particular person: Consider the feelings that you've never expressed that could be said effectively in a lyric. You might even make a list of the friendly things you would willingly do—whether realistic, fanciful or outrageously absurd. In an upcoming example, you'll see how that prewriting warmup exercise can generate "a list song."

This incubation period may well produce a title which, as you know, is a strong way to start. The next step might be to consider what song form would best develop your title. All the major forms have scaffolded the subject: The AAA, "Friendship" and "Bridge Over Troubled Water"; The ABAC, "Old Friends"; the AABA, "Bosom Buddies"; and Verse/Chorus, "True Colors." Here's a lyric that was written to music, a slow shuffle in the lilting style of "Can't Smile Without You."

> *Friendship: Example No. 1 (AABAAC)*
> **YOU CAN COUNT ON ME**
>
> When you're gettin' turn downs
> And the world frowns
> YOU CAN COUNT ON ME
>
> In the really bad times
> And sad times
> YOU CAN COUNT ON ME
>
> I'll be there to dry your eyes
> And getcha to smile.
> Betcha then you'll realize
> All your troubles will fade
> In a while.
>
> When you're really hurtin'
> And certain
> Your dream's gone down the drain,
>
> I will run to find you
> And remind you
> That rainbows start with rain.
>
> Promise you'll remember next time
> You feel lost at sea
> You've a friend to turn to—
> YOU CAN COUNT ON ME
>
> By Sheila Davis
> © *1982 Solar Systems Music. Used with permission.*

▲ Comment

One day in the late '70s, noodling at the piano, my left hand began a descending baseline pattern which led to a rather ingenuous melody. It wasn't till several years later that I decided to put a lyric to it. After getting the title, I thought about a particular woman friend—a composer/collaborator for whom I feel great affection—and I wrote the lyric with her in mind. The song was recorded by the Shawnee Chorus and its two-part choral arrangement has become a staple in school choral repertoires.

Friendship: Example No. 2 (Verse/Chorus/Bridge)
I FIND ME A SISTER

When my cat died, my man thought
I was crazy to cry all day long.
He laughed,"Call the preacher,
Put on black. That's the way to mourn."
I got angry at his remark,
But before things went too far,
I said, "Baby, I'm going out."
And I grabbed the keys to the car to

FIND ME A SISTER to talk to—
One to laugh with, and cry with,
And tell me she understands—
'Cause she do!
When my man hasn't a clue,
I FIND ME A SISTER.

Tonight I came home with an attitude
'Cause I'd had a bad day.
And he came home complaining
With nothing positive to say.
This time instead of running out
(Or sitting with my face in a pout)
I called someone on the phone
Who knows what I'm about. I

(repeat chorus)

Most of the time my man is good.
He'd give me the world if he could.
But what I need is for him to be my friend
Until then,

I FIND ME A SISTER to talk to
To laugh with, and cry with,
Someone who'll act like she understands—
'Cause she do!
When my man hasn't a clue,
I FIND ME A SISTER.
'Cause she comes through!

© 1991 By Vernetta Cousins. Used with permission.

▲ Comment

When Vernetta read the first draft of "Sister" in class, there was an audible appreciative response from other distaff writers. In a fresh and distinctive lyric, the writer vivifies a truth that every woman knows but no one has ever put in a song. I'm hopeful it'll make a name for itself in the name of sisterhood.

Here's a playful list song written to a jazz waltz. In this particular version a woman is singing to a woman friend.

Friendship: Example No. 3 (AABA)
COUNT ON ME

You've got a friend who's like Gibralter
COUNT ON ME season after season
I will never falter
COUNT ON ME for the slightest reason:
If the party's gone to pot
And your nerves are in a knot,
Send for me and I'll know what to do.

When your diet's slipping
COUNT ON ME hiding all the candy
When the faucet's dripping
COUNT ON ME being very handy
When your zipper's off the track,
When your psyche's out of whack,
I'll be there to get 'em back for you.

Any old time
I'll come arunning
If you give me a call.
You know that I'm
More than just willing
I'm ready to give my all.

If you're in a blackout,
COUNT ON ME for illumination.
If you throw your back out,
There's no fee for a consultation.
If your partner trumps your ace,
If your lawyer blows your case,
You know who'll be there embracing you.

Some friends appear
Only on birthdays—
For cake, candles, and wine.
I will be near
Come all the "dearthdays"
When life's not quite so fine.

Like Gertrude Stein with Alice Toklas
COUNT ON ME now and ever after—
'Speshly' when you're jokeless;
I'll come by and supply some laughter.

When the chips are really down
And your shrink is out of town —
And no other can be found to see,
Hey, you can COUNT ON ME.

Words by Sheila Davis/Music by Steve Covello
© 1970 Solar Systems Music. Used with permission.

▲ Comment

A melody whose A-section calls for an ababccc rhyme scheme — one that demands frequent (and suggests perfect) rhyme — can be simultaneously daunting and challenging. But it offers a chance to play with both trailing rhyme (*case/ embracing*) and augmented rhyme (*town/found*) as ways to meet the challenge. (More on rhyme schemes in *CLW*, pages 198-201). With its many (twelve) verses written for specific contexts, the song has been performed by a woman to a woman, by a man to a woman, and as a male/female duet. Never let it be said that writing a lyric doesn't require more work than writing a tune!

WrapUp

Those are just a few of the many possible treatments of the friendship theme. If you'd like to see another role-model lyric on the underused aspect of female friendship, check out "Girls Night," in *SLW* (page 162). Or, move on to one of pop music's favorite themes — pop music.

Song, Music, and Dance as Plot Devices

Some Background

Because we so commonly use both *music* and *dance* as metaphoric, euphemistic or symbolic stand-ins for a variety of concepts, those words often appear in lyrics figuratively to suggest something other than their literal meaning. For example, in the title "Make Your Own Kind of Music," *music* acts as a metaphor for "be your own person." In "I've Heard That Song Before," *song*—as in the expression "don't give me that song and dance"—acts as a metaphor for insincere talk. In "Do You Want to Dance?" *dance* acts as a euphemism (metonym) for the four-letter vulgarism for sex. "Dancing in the Dark"—the Dietz/Schwartz standard—symbolically implies that the singer tries to face life's uncertainties with grace.

This strategy challenges you to design a lyric around the *literal* use of music or dance—its charm, its romance, its redemptive power. In addition to using one of pop music's archetypal themes, a secondary benefit accrues from reinforcing the distinction between literal and figurative.

Some Song/Music Titles	Some Dance Titles
Say It With Music	You Make Me Feel Like Dancing
I Love a Piano	Dancing With Tears in My Eyes
Slap That Bass	Dance, Dance, Dance
You and the Night and the Music	I Could Have Danced All Night
Sad Songs Say So Much	Save the Last Dance for Me
Please, Mister, Please	Dancing Queen
This One's for You	Ten Cents a Dance
Sing, Sing a Song	The Carioca
Fascinating Rhythm	The Hucklebuck
Whistle a Happy Tune	The Big Apple
The Old Songs	The Hustle
Without a Song	Breakdance
Song Sung Blue	Vogue

Prewriting Suggestion

As you can see from the foregoing examples, the names of dances—real ("Breakdance") or fanciful ("The Carioca")—top the list of dance plot strategies. Another aspect of music you might treat would be the sheer appreciation of it as evidenced in such songs as "Fascinating Rhythm" and "I Love a Piano." Then there's the power of music to evoke stored emotions ("Please, Mister, Please") or to match current ones ("Clarinet," page 100).

Small Craft Warning

As in previous guidelines, I urge you to discriminate between literal and metaphoric uses of your subject and not to mistake alternating between the two as evidence of "layered meaning." (A rereading of the section on symbol, pages 117-119, may be useful before you begin to write.)

Here's a lyric that transports us into a jazz club.

Music/Song/Dance: Example No. 1 (Verse/Chorus/Climb/Bridge)
SAX MAN

When the room's abloom with cigarettes,
Come and share a drink between your sets.
If you need fortification,
No need for conversation.

You're perspired and tired; you feel your age.
But the years drop off when you take the stage.
As you begin performing
I can see you transforming

And it's Paris again, long before I was born,
I'm transported the minute you pick up your horn.
There's so much that I missed but you bring it all back
Oh yes, I do love the sax.

SAX MAN, do your job,
Make my senses throb
And my spirit soar.
Let the music pour.
Oh, SAX MAN, fill my head with honey,
Fill my ears with pearls.
Guess I'm one of those girls
Who can't resist a SAX MAN.

First you blow as slow as summer rain.
Then as light as bubbles in champagne.
And then your magical bebop
Takes me as high as a treetop.

Now you've found all the secrets I keep in my heart
I don't know how you do what you do with your art:
Turn my soul into flame
Turn my knees into wax.
Oh yes, I do love the sax

(repeat chorus)

Words can never say what you tell me when you play
Volumes of emotion float on every liquid note.

SAX MAN, do your job,
Make my senses throb
And my spirit soar,
Let the music pour.
Oh, SAX MAN, roar like the north wind
And purr like a lamb,
Make me lose all discretion
And forget who I am,
I was brought up a lady
But I don't give a damn.
I just can't resist,
I can't resist a SAX MAN.

▲ Comment

The external details of the smoke-filled room, the aged, perspiring performer counterpoint against the singer's orgasmic reactions to the soloist's performance. "Saxual" music appears to transport Maureen Sugden straight to her limbic system: *Make my senses throb . . . fill my head with honey, ears with pearls . . . turn my soul into flame . . . my knees into wax . . . roar . . . purr . . .*

The lyricist, a former jazz singer and devotee of the late Dexter Gordon ('*Round Midnight*), conjures up the power of music to transport us into another realm. Topped with a simple metonymic title, "Sax Man" paints a memorial musical portrait. Now from jazz in particular to music in general.

Music/Song/Dance: Example No. 2 (ABAC Variant)
TRY A LITTLE MUSIC
(ABAC Variant Form)
TRY A LITTLE MUSIC when confusion
Comes aknockin' at your door.
Play a happy tune when disillusion
Has your chin upon the floor.
Try a cheery hum when you've been dumbish —
Something with a ho, ho, ho,
Try a little strum when life's hum drumish,
Pluck it on your old banjo.

Tap a little toe 'cause you will mope less
When you do an old soft shoe.
Don't give up the ghost when things look hopeless —
Blow it on your old kazoo.
Do re mi is magic on the menu
When you want to chase the blues:
Give a little whistle and you'll see,
This'll be a simple remedy,
TRY A LITTLE MUSIC
Whatcha gotta lose?

TRY A LITTLE MUSIC, that's my theory
When your troubles multiply.
TRY A LITTLE MUSIC when you're weary
'Cause your luck is runnin' dry.
Give yourself a beat when you're defeated,
Try it on your xylophone.
Give yourself a treat when you feel cheated,
Blow it on your old trombone.

Thump upon a drum when hopes has crumpled,
Bang a hearty bam, bam, bam.
What's the use of grumbling when you've stumbled,
Give a tambourine a wham.
When you're up to here in apprehension,
Tense enough to blow a fuse,
Pick a piccolo or castanet,
Toot upon a flute or clarinet:
TRY A LITTLE MUSIC—
Whatcha gotta lose?

Words by Sheila Davis/Music by Paul Murphy
© *1977 Solar Systems Music. Used with permission.*

▲ Comment

The tune, an infectious soft shoe, came first and seemed to require a theme to fit the melody's virtual insistence on interior rhyme. The song, in its 4-part choral arrangement, has become a favorite in elementary schools.

Here's a lyric that combines the subjects of dance and music and illustrates the universal power of both.

Music/Song/Dance: Example No. 3 (Verse/Chorus)
MUSIC IS THE LANGUAGE OF THE WORLD

I got a friend, he likes to dance,
Dance the night away.
He met a girl the other night.
But he didn't know what to say.
He can't speak Spanish,
And she can't speak English,
Yet they danced the whole night long.
That DJ must have been real sharp:
He played the perfect song.
It went like this:

La Musica Es El Idioma Del Mundo.
MUSIC IS THE LANGUAGE OF THE WORLD
La Musica Es El Idioma Del Mundo.
MUSIC IS THE LANGUAGE OF THE WORLD

As she smiled he knew this was a sign
That sparks were beginning to fly.
He found some paper; she wrote her number
As he looked in her deep Spanish eyes.
There was no need for a word to be said
'Cause the rhythm felt so right.
He went home dreamin' of the time
When he would hold her tight.
He went home singing:

(repeat chorus)

Now, my story's got a happy ending;
(Maybe you guessed it at the start.)
He learned some Spanish. She learned some English.
They learned the pleasures of the heart.
So if you find you're at a loss for words
'Cause you don't know what to say,
Let the music take your thoughts
And express them in a special way.
Ole!

(repeat chorus)

Words and Music by Carrie Starner
© 1987 EDC Music (ASCAP). Used with permission.

▲ Comment

The lyric epitomizes the mythic power of music to communicate, and its bilingual chorus suggests both a useful strategy to broaden a song's audience—and a potential trend. In addition to its status as a 1988 *Billboard* Song Contest winner, "Music" was one of three songs performed by Carrie Starner in the syndicated TV series "Rap to Rock" spotlighting the lives and music of emerging songwriter/performers.

WrapUp

If you haven't come up with a song or dance title or concept yet, there's a whole subdivision yet to consider: vignettes about musicians and songwriters. Think about "Piano Man," "Mr. Bojangles," "She Believes in Me," ("He Plays for) Free," "Daddy Sang Bass," "Mr. Tanner". . . .

The Need to Escape as Plot Device

The Background

Although they may appear to be unrelated, the existence of the coffee break, the "happy hour," and the expression "Thank God It's Friday" all ratify our innate need for escape from routine fully as much as the lure of Disneyland or a Royal Caribbean cruise. Naturally, this universally experienced need expresses itself in song.

Some Escape Titles

Up, Up and Away	Somewhere
The Far Away Hills	Let's Get Away From It All
Sailing	Beyond the Blue Horizon
Sail Away	Over the Rainbow
Never Never Land	Escape (Pina Collada Song)
Yellow Submarine	On the Good Ship Lollipop
Downtown	There's a Small Hotel
I Want to Get You on a Slow Boat to China	

Styles of Escape

Some escape songs picture realistically attainable interludes like the bright lights of "Downtown" or the dunes of Cape Cod ("The Pina Collada Song"). Some reflect the singer's romantic longing to run away with a singee ("Somewhere"/ "Small Hotel"). Others fantasize such utopias as "The Good Ship Lollipop." Perhaps more than any other song, the enduring appeal of "Over the Rainbow" testifies to our need to believe that somewhere there's a land where "dreams that you dare to dream really do come true."

Prewriting Suggestion

In case you haven't a getaway plot or title poised for takeoff, some free associating might produce a launchable idea: Try clustering from the word "Escape" encircled in the center of an unlined sheet of paper. Be playful. Let what comes, come uncensored until you fill the page.

Small Craft Warning

Whatever style of escape hatch you choose, beware of blurring the song's innate literary mode: Take care to shape your plot into one of the four major modes: *Realism,* the way you see it actually *is; Romance,* the way you feel or hope it *could be* (if you're lucky); *Fabulation,* the way you imagine it *might be* (though it's highly improbable); or *Fantasy*, a fanciful notion that *can't be*. Choose one: Again, the key words are *discrimination* and *consistency*. (For an extended discussion of the literary modes, see *CLW*, pages 83-86.) Here's an escape lyric that puts desire into action:

Escape: Example No. 1 (Verse/Chorus/Bridge)
MIAMI INTERLUDE

Palmy days and balmy nights
Under semitropical skies.
Steel guitars and sequin stars
Reflected in the ocean in someone's eyes.

I need a MIAMI INTERLUDE
Time to leave the real world behind.
I need a MIAMI INTERLUDE.
I've got a southern destination on my mind.

Fizzy gin and sunburnt skin,
Fragrant jacaranda in bloom.
Coral shells and pink hotels
With a Magic Fingers mattress in ev'ry room—

(repeat chorus)

Hold all my calls—
Cancel each appointment.
I'm puttin' my money into volleyballs
And zinc oxide ointment. I've got my

Radio, I'm set to go
Sink into the sugary sands.
You can reach me at the beach
Soakin' up the sun and readin' Judith Krantz—

(repeat chorus)

© 1986 Maureen Sugden. Used with permission.

▲ Comment

The first verse dives right into the subject and leads quickly to the song title, satisfying that music business caveat: "Don't bore us, get to the chorus." *Palmy* introduces the sunny subject with a pun—clearly suggesting both its meanings— *shaded by palms* and *glorious*. The first verse's compact simile (sequin stars) continues by adjectivizing the drink gin fizz to *fizzy gin* and links the anticipated oral, olfactory and tactile treats by alliteration *fizzy/fragrant/fingers*. *Palmy days/balmy nights* and *steel guitars/sequin stars* present coordinated ideas in a parallel construction for emphasis and memorability. The bridge appropriately gives multiple contrasts: attitude—focusing on 'here and now' rather than 'then and there'; viewpoint— addressing some unseen secretary; rhyme—from masculine to feminine, *appointment/ointment*. The final verse presents a bookend compact simile *(sugary sands)* to link to the first verse's *sequin stars*. The compact metonym song title gets a coordinated metonymic allusion to author *Judith Krantz* — the creator for the creation. The Miami tourist bureau doesn't know what it's missing! Here's a different motive for escape.

Escape: Example No. 2 (AABA Variant)
DISAPPEAR

DISAPPEAR
That's what I'd like to do
Cut out and fly with you
Far from here . . .

DISAPPEAR,
Run from the prying eyes,
Run from the need of lies,
Run to a place where
You can be part of me,
Living and loving free
Far from here . . .
DISAPPEAR . . .

Somewhere,
It must be somewhere,
One piece of sunshine
That we could call our own.
Somehow,
We'll get there,
But now
Don't let the faces that frown on us
Spoil what we share.
Though they look down on us
Try not to care . . .

Hold me near,
Kiss me again and say
We're gonna find a way,
Some way to work it out
Very far from here . . .
Show them that they are wrong
Show them that our love's so strong
That we're
Gonna make
All our fear
DISAPPEAR
DISAPPEAR
DISAPPEAR
© 1986 May Caffrey. Used with permission.

▲ Comment

The classic theme of ill-fated lovers motivates this singer's urge to escape. Given its one-word synopsizing title and focused simplicity of statement, "Disappear" has the potential to speak for a multitude of teenagers. Now, a fresh treatment of a classic situation.

Escape: Example No. 3 (Verse/Chorus)
I WON'T BE IN TODAY

It's five forty-five on my radio clock
The weatherman's callin' for rain.
I roll out of bed in the cold and the dark.
Need some coffee to jump start my brain.
I shave and I shower and throw on some clothes,
Heave a sigh and head out the door.
Soon the boss'll be screamin' and I'll be dreamin'
Of bein' a free man once more.
And I'm thinkin' how sweet it would be
To pick up the phone and say, "Listen to me—

"I WON'T BE IN TODAY.
I won't be in tomorrow.
Won't be in the rest of the week.
I might be in Aruba, might be in Bermuda
Or Puerto Vallarta or Martinique.
I need relaxation, so I won't be returnin',
Till spring, maybe summer or fall.
I've had all I can take; now I'm takin' a break
I'll be workin' on havin' a ball."

Out on the freeway it's bumper to bumper.
(Walkin', I'd make better time).
I got ten miles of traffic jam stretchin' before me
And ten more stretchin' behind.
Guess I'll be here a while, so I manage a smile
And let my mind take me away
To a strip of white sand, a cool drink in my hand
Beside a tropical bay.
Maybe someday I really will go.
I'll call up the boss, say, "I think you should know

"I WON'T BE IN TODAY.
I won't be in tomorrow.
Don't look for me anytime soon.
I might be in Tahiti or Maui or Fiji
Might be in Caracas or in Cancun.
I need relaxation so I won't be returnin'
Till spring, maybe summer or fall.

I've had all I can take; now I'm takin' a break.
I'll be workin' on havin' a ball.

"I WON'T BE IN TODAY.
I won't be in tomorrow
Don't know how long I'll be away.
I might be in San Juan, I might be in St. John.
The Bahamas, St. Thomas or St. Tropez.
I need relaxation so I won't be returnin'
Till spring, maybe summer or fall.
And if I find me a lady, a sweet island baby,
I may never come back at all.
Yes, if I find me a lady, a sweet island baby
I may never come back at all!"

▲ Comment

This lyric exemplifies how to get to the universal through the particular. Fashioning a filmic script of one's man's nine-to-five bumper-to-bumper frustration, Dan Fox, with consummate SF craft, speaks for millions. The changing chorus of "I Won't Be In Today" illustrates how the verse/chorus song can be exploited to the fullest and build to a payoff line — "I may never come back at all!" Sounds to me like a contender for a future airlines commercial.

WrapUp

While title hunting, why not employ the strategy of place names for your jetaway and choose some unsung tropical refuge from the morning alarm. Remember the success of "The Isle of Capri," "Bali Ha'i," "Poinciana," "Tropicana," "Veradero". . . .

An Archetypal Portrait as Plot Device

Some Background

Just as songwriters may use forms of metonym and synecdoche in their lyrics without necessarily being familiar with those terms, so too do they draw upon *archetypes* of all kinds—music forms, plots, characters, settings—without being conscious of it.

A definition: From the Greek word meaning "original pattern," an archetype (ARK-a-type) is a basic model from which copies are made. For example, the basic stages of life are archetypal: birth, adolescence, adulthood, marriage, parenthood, old age and death.

Archetypal Personalities

Certain personality types are considered archetypal: the self-made man, the miser, the bigot, the cowboy, and so on. When you practiced antonomasia (pages 112-113) and started a list headed "Characteristic/Quality," you were drawing on your knowledge of archetypal personalities. And had you listed in your left-hand column those just cited, you might have paired them with such embodiments as: Horatio Alger, Scrooge, Archie Bunker and Roy Rogers.

Archetypal Situations, Settings and Images

In addition to archetypal life stages and personality types, there are archetypal situations: The tension between parent and child, the rivalry between brothers, the search for the father, the young man from the country arriving in the city. Again, common stuff of lyrics—especially story songs.

Then there are archetypal images—particular colors, animals, products, and so on, which have become symbols. For example, white = purity; dog = faithful friend; beer = middle class; BMW = success. These are images that lyricists readily employ. Actually, the forty lyric strategies outlined in this book draw upon forty archetypes—or basic models. So as you've been practicing such plot devices as the inherent need for sex, or friendship or escape, you've been applying archetypal themes.

Being Archetypal by Design

By an archetypal portrait, I mean one that characterizes some basic type familiar to all. So the idea now is to be archetypal by design, rather than by accident. Successful lyricwriting can be said to depend to a great degree on the ability to transform a personal experience into a recognizable (archetypal) situation and setting.

Desperado	Rainy Day Woman
Arthur and Alice	Coward of the County
Foxy Lady	Georgy Girl
Valley Girl	Bad Bad Leroy Brown
Hard-Hearted Hannah	Big Spender
Maneater	Old Hippie
Harper Valley PTA	Cat's in the Cradle
Mr. Businessman	Rose's Turn

The country classic "Coward of the County," for example, came into being from the desire on the part of each of its co-writers, Billy Edd Wheeler and Roger Bowling, to employ archetypal themes: Billy Edd told me of his desire to write about an "underdog—somebody who comes from behind" and of Roger's to tell the story of "a promise." The song embodies both.

Prewriting Suggestion

You might begin your plot/title hunt by checking the Antonomasia page in your ideabook to see how many stock characters you've listed. Then try to add to them. To help get your archetypal entrainment chugging along, here are a few more: the nagging wife, the wanderer, the siren, the big-hearted whore, the braggart, the snoop, the know-it-all, the rebel. . . .

Some archetypal portraits are first-person narratives ("Cat's in the Cradle"); many are written in the second-person talking voice addressing a singer—entreating ("Desperado"), or admonishing ("Gloria"), or warning against a third person ("Maneater"); others are told from the third-person camera eye ("Old Hippie"/ "Arthur and Alice"). Consider your viewpoint options before you begin.

Small Craft Warning

Two inherent pitfalls accompany the archetypal portrait. One is the danger of being judgmental—placing the singer on a court bench looking down on the characterized subject. "Mr. Businessman," a 1968 hit by Ray Stevens, is a rare recorded case in point that accused an entire segment of society of being immoral and neurotic (with their 'harlots' and their 'charlatans'); in this case the recording artist was also the writer, hence no cool editorial eye suggested a toning down of the harsh judgment. Then there are those workshop first drafts which, despite a well-crafted portrait of a recognizable archetype, lack a point. The safeguard is to ask yourself, why do I want to tell the world about this person? With what idea/ emotion do I want millions to identify or empathize? Here's a role-model example that asks us to empathize with the singer's weakness for a drifter.

Archetypal Portrait: Example No. 1 (Verse/Chorus)
THE DRIFTER

He's a six-foot hunk who hails from Amarillo
And anywhere he hangs his jeans is home.
And he shared my dreams and also shared my pillow.
But he rolled on 'cause he's a rollin' stone.

He's a DRIFTER,
He's a dreamer,
He's around a little while
'N' then he's gone.
He's a lover
Who's a loner
'Cause he never got the hang
Of hangin' on.
He's a knight in shinin' Levis
In a rusty, dusty Chevrolet.
He's a DRIFTER,
And Oh, Lord,
I wish he'd drift on back again my way.

He's a tumbleweed who tumbles with the breezes.
He moves around from town to town to town.
'N' his good looks take him anywhere he pleases.
And nobody'll ever pin him down.

(repeat chorus)

When I think he's gone for good 'n' I'll forget him,
He blows on back 'n' needs a place to stay.
And he talks the sweetest sweet talk, so I let him
Take up where he left off some yesterday.

(repeat chorus)

▲ Comment

That's a classic country theme featuring *two* archetypal characters — the waiting woman and the wandering man. Morgan's alliterative opening lines link the main thoughts (*hunk/hails/hangs/home)* and set the style for a lyric notable for its unifying literary devices. They're worth identifying because they're worth emulating:

- *Alliteration*: drifter/dreamer, lover/loner, blows/back
- *Contiguous rhyme*: rusty dusty
- *Paragram*: anywhere he hangs his *jeans* is home; knight in shining *Levis*
- *Parallelism*: shared my dreams/shared my pillow
- *Polyptoton*: rolled on/rollin', tumbleweed/tumbles, sweetest/sweet
- *Sequential Pun*: hang of hangin' on

Archetypal Portrait: Example No. 2 (Verse/Chorus/Bridge)
SATAN IN A SATIN DRESS

There's a sexy lady running 'round destroying men
A hard-hearted Hannah with a devilish plan,
A maneater posing as an innocent gal
You better beware of this *femme fatale*.

She's SATAN IN A SATIN DRESS.
She'll mesmerize you with her kiss.
She'll seduce you with her sweet caress.
She's SATAN IN A SATIN DRESS.

Like Lorelei, she'll lure you from the shore
With a siren song you've never heard before.
She'll steal your heart and leave you lost at sea.
And I oughta know, 'cause she did it to me.

(repeat chorus)

She's like that Foxy Lady you've heard about,
A real Dolly Dagger, so you better watch out.

(repeat chorus)

© 1991 Cory Morgenstern. Used with permission

▲ Comment

Topped with an original and compelling title, Cory Morgenstern's archetypal portrait weaves into the warning the titles of four (!) well-known *femme fatale* songs—"Maneater," "Foxy Lady," "Hard-Hearted Hannah," and "Dolly Dagger." And by additionally linking the legendary Lorelei to his roll call of fatal females who metaphorically *lure ... and leave you lost at sea,* the writer further strengthened his archetypal design.

WrapUp

Consciously thinking in archetypal terms serves as a safeguard against writing the "private" lyric which, though meaningful to the writer, lacks identification for the audience. The next strategy takes archetype to the ultimate.

The Famous Person as Plot Device

Some Background

Dotting the lyrical landscape with allusions to famous people adds both charm and memorability to a song: *rich as Rockefeller* ("Sunny Side of the Street"); *Where have you gone, Joe DiMaggio?* ("Mrs. Robinson"); *The nimble tread of the feet of Fred Astaire.* ("You're the Top"). Each, of course, symbolizes an archetype.

Taking the allusion to the ultimate results in a lyric designed around a famous person who, for some particular reason, has captured a writer's interest. If the lyric resounds with a universally understood message, it may also capture the public's interest.

Songs Featuring the Famous

American Pie (Buddy Holly)	Joe Hill
Elvis and Marilyn (Presley and Monroe)	Black Velvet (Presley)
	Missing You (Marvin Gaye)
Candle in the Wind (Marilyn Monroe)	Roy Rogers
	James Dean
Judy Blue Eyes (Judy Collins)	Vincent (van Gogh)
Amelia (Amelia Earhart)	Abraham, Martin & John (Lincoln, King, Kennedy)
When Smokey Sings (Robinson)	
Will, Mickey and the Duke (Mays, Mantle, and Snider)	

Employing this strategy enables you to express an aspect of your view of the world in a distinctive and memorable way.

Prewriting Suggestion

Think of a famous person, past or present, who's exerted some impact on you. Your chosen subject can be from any realm — the arts, sciences, sports, politics — whatever. A quick way to narrow the field is to ask yourself: With what famous person, dead or alive, would I like the chance to spend an hour? In that hour you might want to praise their work, pick their brain, show your appreciation, or possibly, tell them off. Having students ask that question of themselves tends to speed up the selection process. It also tends to touch the heart of their personal concerns as you're about to see in three lyrics that evolved from this exercise.

When you've made your choice, think about which of the viewpoints will best serve your subject. Some famous-person tributes use apostrophe (second-person) for their one-way dialogues ("Vincent"/"Amelia"/"Candle in the Wind"); the third-person approach worked well for "Abraham, Martin & John"; and the first-person narrative proved effective for "American Pie." Test out different viewpoints until one feels right. Do the same with song forms: Would a chorus add to or detract from your desired effect? And so on with the AAA and AABA.

Small Craft Warning

Two points: 1) The subject of a pop song should have acquired sufficient celebrity status to be known by the general public; 2) To help your listener experience the song from the beginning, establish the singee's identity in the opening lines.

Focus on a Famous Person: Example No. 1 (Verse/Chorus)
A LIGHT IN THE FOREST

Concord was growing in quiet desperation
While you searched the woods for a simpler way—
Pine for the fire and berries for supper
And truth for the pages you wrote every day.

Henry, you gave us A LIGHT IN THE FOREST,
Simple reflections on Walden Pond.
Henry, you gave us A LIGHT IN THE FOREST,
Destined to shine on the world beyond.

Your hut by the road is now a pile of rubble
Where pilgrims contribute one stone at a time.
For two years you lived all alone in the forest,
You made it your home—we've made it a shrine.

Henry, you gave us A LIGHT IN THE FOREST,
Brilliant reflections shimmering on.
Henry, your life was A LIGHT IN THE FOREST,
Destined to shine on the world beyond.

You died believing your life was a failure
(Verses and journals all written in vain).
But a hundred years later, your light is still shining
And millions of people are touched by your flame

Because you wrote the book about living—
Respecting nature, and protesting war—
And you wrote the book about passive resistance
That Gandhi would quote while he sat on the floor.

Henry Thoreau, you're A LIGHT IN THE FOREST,
An eternal flame burning brightly today
For the wonder of man and the wonders of nature.
Your life is a beacon to show us the way.

© 1988 Rick Swiegoda. Used with permission.

▲ Comment

By having his opening lines incorporate such well-known allusions to Henry Thoreau as *Concord, quiet desperation* and *woods*, the writer immediately identified the subject of the song. Its metaphoric title phrase, that translates to "insight into life's complexity," also evokes the literal house in the forest where Thoreau lived for two years. The theme of *light* is further heightened throughout the lyric with such metaphoric links as *reflection/shine/brilliant/shimmering/flame/burning brightly/beacon.*

Apostrophe enabled the writer to avoid stating to the listener his beliefs in "simplified living . . . respecting nature, and protesting war"; instead his message is obliquely couched in an "overheard conversation" with Thoreau. The instant pun "you wrote the book," which simultaneously expresses the literal meaning and the colloquialism "to be an expert," gives further evidence that puns, although *generally* humorous, are not *inherently* humorous.

This lyrical tribute by a sensate/feeling (SF) writer to an archetypal symbol of self-sufficiency and anti-materialism, illustrates my theory about the innate correspondence between a writer's type and dominant trope: Not only does the favored trope manifest itself in discrete instances within a lyric, it often reflects itself in the lyric's central theme—in this case, symbol.

Focus on a Famous Person: Example No. 2 (Verse/Refrain/Bridge)
MOTHER TERESA

Another day dawns in Calcutta
And the rising sun reveals
A city of the sick and the starving
Who know how poverty feels.
Through the filthy streets comes a figure in white,
A wrinkled woman, her face shining bright.
Every morning she comes like the dawn
With hope in her hands.

Reaching out with the love of the Lord she serves,
Reaching out with the love every soul deserves,
She sees her world through the eyes of the One
Who died for the lost and lowly.
And she knows the life of the least of them is holy.

There's an ancient man sprawled in a doorway.
There's an orphaned child's pleading cry.
There's a world that wants to forget them,
But *she* can't pass them by.
She takes them in, and she does what she can—
Dresses their wounds and holds their hands
And she'll tell you it's only a drop
In the ocean of need.

(repeat refrain)

They suffer day after day.
The monsoon tries to wash them away.
But the poor will always be there,
And as long as she lives she will care.

Another night falls in Calcutta
And the glow of a candle reveals
Rows of simple beds where life flickers and fades,
Where love alone still heals.
Mother Teresa prays for each one —
The beggar, the leper, the motherless son.
She blows out the candle and the light
Of hope fills the room.

(repeat refrain)

© 1989 Words by Daniel Fox/Music by J.R. Dennis. Used with permission.

▲ Comment

Here we have a tribute to a living symbol of humanitarianism. The spiritual aspect of the theme is heightened by the motif of light that opens the first verse — the images of a *figure in white*, the *shining face*, the *dawn*. The last verse brings the motif full circle, *the glow of a candle* and *the light of hope*.

The lyric's serious tone is further supported by the use of occasional *run-on* lines — the two lines ending with the word *reveals*. Instead of having the thought of the line end with the rhyme as in the more common *end-stopped* line, this device makes the thought run on past the rhyme into the following line, requiring the listener/reader to wait longer for its full meaning. (For a discussion of run-on and end-stopped lines, see *CLW*, pages 220-221.)

The writer's identification of his character, first by the name of the city with which she's become linked and further as "a figure in white," — the substitution of the color for the apparel, a nun's habit — again represents a sensate/feeler's fondness for symbol and metonym. Worth mention is a striking metaphor: "a drop in the ocean of need."

Dan Fox strengthened his structure by opening-line repetitions (anaphora) *Reaching out with love/Reaching out with love* and *There's an/There's an.* With the melodious interplay of alliteration and assonance in the refrain*: *eyes/died/lost/lowly/life/least/holy*, the lyric hardly requires music.

---

*A note on refrains: Let's make a distinction between the terms chorus and refrain: The chorus of a verse/chorus song both summarizes its plot and contains its title; without it there would be no song. In "Mother Teresa," if the repeated section were deleted, the lyric would still be complete because its verses tell the entire story; the repeated section serves solely to amplify what the verses have stated and thus is more accurately termed a refrain.

Focus on a Famous Person: Example No. 3 (Verse/Chorus/Bridge)
MAYA ANGELOU

You know why the caged bird sings —
Offers song when she's suffering.
Just like you, she survives against the odds.
She lifts her voice when times get hard —
You write your way through.

Maya, MAYA ANGELOU
Your words dance and your words cry
To identify with you soothes my soul
Maya, MAYA ANGELOU.

Poems so rhythmic I hear the conga drum
Thumping out ancient African wisdom.
Like the Good News, honey, you tell the truth.
My heart feels happy and my spirit moves
'Cause your writing lifts me so . . .

(repeat chorus)

It seemed my life hit bottom one day
But you gave me the courage and the strength to say
"And still I rise."

(repeat chorus)

▲ Comment

Incorporating Maya Angelou's book title (*I Know Why the Caged Bird Sings*) into the opening line serves to establish the author's identity before the chorus hits. Vernetta's use of light rhyme (*sings/suffering; drum/wisdom*) and consonance (*odds/hard*) enhances the conversational voice and feeling tone of the lyric which perfect rhyme might have diminished.

In contrast with the sensate details of the first two lyrical tributes, this lyric's more abstract language —*pain, suffering, sorrow, courage, strength* — reflects the literary style more common to the *intuitive/feeler*. But the feeling function, shared by all three lyric writers, expresses a common appreciation for those they esteem: the two (fact-oriented) sensate writers acknowledge the influence of a single human life upon millions of people; whereas the intuitive/feeler — the most personal writer of the four cognitive styles — acknowledges the redemptive influence of a single human life upon her own.

WrapUp

"A Light in the Forest," "Mother Teresa," and "Maya Angelou" exemplify the injunction to "find your voice." As those lyrics demonstrate, when we write from our personal truth, we write with conviction and originality — free from the clichés and collective generalizations that make so many pop songs sound manufactured rather than created.

This strategy has evoked from students paeans to such diverse personalities as Mozart, Martin Luther King, Jim Croce and Freud. I encourage you to take the time to identify one significant influence upon you and translate your feelings about that person into a lyric.

This ends our tour of some of the major universal concepts which can serve to augment your lyric ideas. Next we look into a few special markets and themes.

More Plot Strategies: Genres and Special Markets

As you've seen throughout the book, the breadth and depth of subject matter available to a lyricist can transcend the narrow confines of the often formulaic pop marketplace and its injunction: "Bring us hit songs."

The first six sections focused on strategies that serve the thematic and stylistic need of Top 40 radio. But the range of role-model songs indicates other venues of creative satisfaction such as country, folk, Christian, cabaret and theater.

To further expand your stylistic potential, let's explore some alternate markets and touch on a few special themes such as the Christmas song—coming up next.

The Christmas Song as Plot Device

Some Background

It would seem that the best Christmas songs have all been written: There's nothing new to be said about chestnuts and eggnog and snowflakes and tinsel and reindeer and carols and Saint Nick. The standards have said it all. Yet, every year, come late November, new Christmas songs hit the airwaves to make their bid for public acceptance.

Despite the limitations of the subject, inventive songwriters seem to find a fresh approach, a new angle, an untried scenario, yet another way to say "It's Christmastime once more."

Some Perennial Favorites

White Christmas	Rudolph the Red-Nosed Reindeer
Frosty the Snowman	Home for the Holidays
The Christmas Song	I'll Be Home for Christmas
The Little Drummer Boy	Santa Claus Is Coming to Town
My Two Front Teeth	I Saw Mommy Kissing Santa Claus
Silver Bells	Have Yourself a Merry Little
It's Beginning to Look a Lot Like	Christmas
Christmas	

Barry Manilow's 1990 yuletime entry, "Because It's Christmas," made the charts by combining a strong melody with a statement we hadn't yet heard: "It's Christmas for all the children, and the children in us all"—an unassailable truth about the holiday's universal appeal. The song's initial success suggests it just might join the ranks of Christmas standards.

Another viable approach is the novelty song—that bit of whimsy or fantasy that encourages a producer or artist to gamble that it might generate enough airplay to make it "happen"—at least once. As we know, the offbeat may not only create a hit, it may create a standard: "(All I Want for Christmas Is) My Two Front Teeth," "I Saw Mommy Kissing Santa Claus" and, of course, one of the most successful songs of all time, "Rudolph the Red-Nosed Reindeer." Hardly a season goes by without a newspaper story about the song that virtually supported its creator (Johnny Marks) for over four decades!

Prewriting Suggestions

So there are several approaches you can consider: 1) Send a message that reflects a universal truth that has somehow eluded other writers; 2) Create a novelty/ fantasy situation; or 3) Come up with a distinctive title and go from there. The first role-model song used the title approach.

Christmas Song: Example No. 1 (Verse/Chorus)
"SANTICIPATION"

They've sent their letters to Santa
With a list they know by heart.
Left carrots for the reindeer,
Hung stockings above the hearth.
Children glow this Christmas Eve
Knowin' St. Nick is near.
They toss and turn through the night
Wonderin' when he'll appear
'Cause they've got

"SANTICIPATION"
"SANTICIPATION"
They can hardly wait for that jolly guy
With the reindeer that really fly.
Boys and girls all around the world
Have "SANTICIPATION" tonight.

Their minds are filled with visions
Of gifts they hope to see.
Leavin' their beds to walk the halls,
They keep peekin' under the tree.
They tiptoe to their window
To watch the sky for Santa's sleigh.
They listen for the jingle bells
That say he's on his way.
'Cause they've got

(repeat chorus)

© 1989 Lyric by Laresa Forbes/Music by Kathy Durrett. Used with permission.

▲ Comment

Drawing on a wordplay technique described in Strategy No. 9 (page 71), Laresa Forbes created a fresh title. It compresses *Santa* and *anticipation* into a portmanteau coinage that has the potential to make Webster along with *palimony*. Putting into practice Ira Gershwin's famous guideline "A Title/Is vital./Once you've it,/Prove it," the writer proves her title with a plot development that's simple, direct and clear. Who could ask for anything more. The song caught the attention of a Nashville publisher and earned for the team their first songwriting contract.

Here's a viewpoint about the holiday season that is far from clichéd.

Christmas Song: Example No. 2 (AABA Variant)
IT'S THE RED AND GREEN SEASON AGAIN

IT'S THE RED AND GREEN SEASON AGAIN,
The season when goodwill endorses
The sending of holiday cards by the dozens
To nonpaying clients and obnoxious cousins.

Your hands are stained blue; your tongue tastes like dead horses.
IT'S THE RED AND GREEN SEASON AGAIN, ah yes!

IT'S THE RED AND GREEN SEASON AGAIN
When charity makes us stand taller.
The kids' Christmas list isn't hard to compute now:
They just want an Apple, but it's not a fruit now
So the wife's promised mink shrinks to cuffs and a collar.
THE RED AND GREEN SEASON — what stress!

A toast to the green of the U. S. dollar:
Your credit expands as your wallet grows smaller.

IT'S THE RED AND GREEN SEASON AGAIN,
The season of wassail and good cheer!
So hang up the mistletoe, drag in the Yule log!
You'll know that you've had enough holiday eggnog
When you're really seeing those *eight* tiny reindeer!
THE RED AND GREEN SEASON AGAIN, oh boy!

It's "Joy to the Worldly," on an untuned piano,
And the "Unholy Night" of the church choir soprano!

IT'S THE RED AND GREEN SEASON AGAIN,
When grownups wish they were still children,
While loudly complaining they hate to go through it,
And yet they all know that's it's worth why we do it:
A glass of warm milk and a cookie or two — it's
The perfect reward, and amen,
For THE RED AND GREEN SEASON AGAIN.

© 1990 Nancy Louise Baxter. Used with permission.

▲ Comment
The metonymic title, substituting the holiday's symbolic colors for the term itself — introduces a playfully irreverent collage of traditional and offbeat yuletime images. Fresh and inventive — and true: That's why we smile — in recognition.

WrapUp
So it appears that there are still new angles to find and new scenarios to write. Consider that no brain ever existed exactly like yours. What that means is that you experience Christmas differently from anyone who has ever lived. Think about what you personally feel about it and then, drawing upon a particular design device, say something that no one's said before. For example, no one yet has used a letter to Santa from a homeless child . . . or apostrophe to address the manger in Bethlehem . . . or personification to become a pine tree being chopped down or . . . or. . . .

The Children's Market

Children's Songs and Type

Nowhere perhaps is the link between personality type and writing style more evident than in the prevalence of feeling types among children's writers. The reason's easy to see: Qualities of empathy and caring make the feeling dominant ideally suited to relate to the child with songs that teach, encourage and inspire.

The *intuitive*/feeler's (NF) lyric often reflects both a playful attitude and a fantasy situation. The *sensate*/feeler (SF) style may draw more on realistic settings along with colorful sensate details. Writers with an extraverted preference tend to enliven lyrics with gestures, movements and sound effects. Of course, every type can and does write for children and each brings its own distinctive qualities and values to the lyrics.

The Market

Writing for children has become a burgeoning field with multimedia possibilities, such as the book/cassette/video combo. Sometimes children's songs are written on assignment from book publishers or film producers. To break into the market, resourceful songwriters often generate original projects and then shop them to outlets such as Disney World, Sesame Street and Scholastic Inc.

Categories of Children's Songs

Children's songs include such general categories as lullabies ("Hush Little Baby"), sing-a-longs ("Frog Went A-Courtin' "), activity songs ("Where Is Thumb-kin"), and learning songs ("Every Day We Grow-I-O"). Because leaders in the educational field have discovered more about the learning and therapeutic values of music, publishers now seek songs for special purposes such as enhancing reading skills and enlivening math or geography lessons.

Music and the Brain

We know that music activates the ancient limbic area of the brain and that the songs we learn at an early age remain deeply embedded in our memory. As lyricist Yip Harburg once observed, "Words make you think a thought; music makes you feel a feeling. But a song makes you *feel a thought*." And it's that felt thought that apparently we remember the longest: "Pins and needles, needles and pins/That's where all the trouble begins." (I still remember the words to Irving Caesar's cautionary songs that I learned in my first-grade classroom.) The following song titles reflect their diverse sources—film, TV and theater.

Some Children's Songs

Animal Crackers in My Soup	On the Good Ship Lollipop
Pins and Needles	Heigh Ho, Heigh Ho
I'm Flying	Davy Crockett
When You Wish Upon a Star	Sing, Sing a Song

Ding-Dong! The Witch is Dead
Big Rock Candy Mountain
Whistle While You Work
Hans Christian Andersen
Supercalifragilisticexpialidocious

Chim Chim Cher-ee
Talk to the Animals
It's Not Easy Being Green
Neverland

Writing for Children: Some Guidelines

Target Your Age Group

To write a successful children's song requires focusing on the specific age for which it's targeted. That age range will, to a large extent, limit the content, the message and the vocabulary of the lyric. For example, a lyric vocabulary designed for seven-to-nine-year olds would be too sophisticated for the three-to-five set. Similarly, ten-year olds would require much hipper language than six-year olds.

Keep Your Language Style "Age Appropriate"

First drafts are often rendered unbelievable by phrases not yet in the vocabulary of the song's target age; for example, in a first-grade song, ". . . I talked the matter over with Mom." That's not a six-year old's way of expressing that thought. Similarly, a child that age cannot make an abstract judgment such as "I know we all must be lonesome some time."

Sound is seductive: Beware of sounds leading you into inappropriate thoughts. For example, in a nap-preparation song for the nursery school set, the rhyme agent *find* spawned the line, "time to *unwind*," a metaphoric concept beyond the comprehension of the four-year old's literal brain.

The success of the novelty song "Supercalifragi . . .", reflects the undeniable appeal of the exaggerated. But in the main, children's lyrics thrive on short words that are easy to grasp and sing ("Some day I'll wish upon a star and wake up where the clouds are far . . ."); visual words with colors and shapes and textures ("on the sunny banks of peppermint bay"); nonsense syllables ("Chim, Chim Cher-ee"); alliteration (". . . the wicked witch!"); and puns (". . . *Which* old *witch*?").

Identify the Song's Purpose

In addition to gearing your vocabulary to your target audience, have a clear idea of the song's single purpose: Is it to entertain, to produce an effect (like going to sleep), to teach a skill, for instance, numbers? Any song subject—can be treated from many angles. If writing a Halloween song, for example, you might decide: "This lyric will describe the fun of dressing up on Halloween," *or* "This lyric will encourage children to trick or treat for a charitable cause," *or* "This lyric will warn children of the potential danger of eating unwrapped treats before they get home." Limit your lyric to making one point.

Narrow your Focus

Keeping a narrow focus can be an especially hard task for right-brain dominants for whom it's natural to see and to link similarities. I remember a first draft of a song aimed to help children develop good dental habits; it was marred by playful references to elephant's teeth and vampire's teeth (unrelated to the song's practical message) which thus had to be extracted in the second draft. To safeguard against the intrusion of unrelated ideas: Write at the top of your lyric sheet a concise statement on the one point your song will make.

A good guideline: *Narrow the range of the subject and develop with examples.* Here's an example of that principle in a song designed to teach vowels.

Children's Song: Example No. 1 (Verse/Chorus w/Intro Verse)
SING A SONG OF VOWELS

You and I are singing
Right this very minute.
And every word we're singing
Has a vowel sound in it.
As we look at pictures
Of words that we all know,
We'll sing their special vowels
Pointing as we go.

SING A SONG OF VOWELS
Of A, E, I, O, U
SING A SONG OF VOWELS
Because it's fun to do.

First comes A:
A as in angel
A as in gate
A as in sail, and pail and plate.
A as in cape and grape and sleigh
And now we know all about A sounds.

Next comes E:
E as in eel
E as in ear
E as in leek and beak and beer.
E as in deer and tear and bee
Now we know all about E sounds.

Next comes I:
I as in pie
I as in kite
I as in ice and mice and light
I as in dime and lime and tie
Now we know about I sounds.

(repeat chorus)

Next comes O:
O as in oval
O as in toast
O as in sew, and toe, and ghost
O as in goat and boat and bow
Now we know all about O sounds.

Next comes U:
U as in moon
U as in flute
U as in two and shoe and boot
U as in pool and spool and zoo
Now we know about all about U sounds.

(repeat chorus)

▲ Comment

The song, designed by a teacher for young children, incorporates large cards placed around the room that the children can point to as they sing. It illustrates how a successful children's song limits the theme and develops by examples. The words make the lyric easy to sing as well as make their grammatical point.

The next lyric is part of a book/record project created by a successful team of children's writers.

Children's Song: Example No. 2 (Verse/Chorus w/Intro)
MAKE A FACE

You can make any face
The funnier the better
It takes a little practice
So let's try it all together.

Wanna be a monkey
Climbin' up a tree,
Reachin' for bananas?
Simply follow me:
Put your tongue inside your lip,
Then jump up and down,
Scratch you head just like a chimp
And make a squeaky sound.

MAKE A FACE, a monkey face
It's easy as can be.
Now erase it and replace it
With another magic'ly.

Wanna be a fish
Divin' in the sea?
Or swimmin' in a fish bowl?
Simply follow me:
Put your lips together
Pucker up like this.
Move 'em up and down
Now give a swishy kiss.

MAKE A FACE, a fishy face
It's easy as can be.

Now erase it and replace it
With another magic'ly.

Wanna be a monster
Like creatures on TV?
Who can be the scariest?
Simply follow me:
Stretch your mouth with fingers
Into a ghoulish grin.
Give a very spooky yell
And goosebumps will begin.

MAKE A FACE, a monster face
It's easy as can be.
Now erase it and replace it
With another magic'ly.

MAKE A FACE, any face
That matches one you see.
Then erase it and replace it
With another magic'ly.

© 1991 June Rachelson-Ospa/Jody Gray/Phil Goodbody. Used with permission.

▲ Comment

"Make a Face" comes under the category of activity song. The design, with its repeated motifs of the question and instruction, makes the idea both easy to grasp and to memorize. The vocabulary is playful with sounds like *fishy/swishy/ghoulish/spooky*. The lyric exemplifies the ENFP personality: imaginative, outgoing, enthusiastic — and motivational. After the fun of making silly faces and sounds, a self-empowering message resonates: You can be whatever you want to be.

The next example combines two genres — writing for children and writing for the Christian market; it thus creates a product for a special market: Children's Christian songs.

Children's Song: Example No. 3 (AABA Variant)
A SNAKE NAMED LARUE

There once was A SNAKE NAMED LARUE
The only way he knew to get here and there
Was slither, slither.
All LaRue knew how to do was slither.

One day LaRue saw a bird,
And wondered just why in the world is it
Birds could go flying, flying.
He slithers below while they go about flying.

LaRue told the bird,
"You must truly be God's favorite creature —
To be able to fly up so high
Where no one can reach ya.

And a snake in the grass is surely
God's lowliest creature.
And God mustn't like me 'cause I only
Slither, slither.
Look how you fly while I only slither!"

The bird took LaRue in his claws.
Gently he lifted and soared through the sky:
They were flying, flying.
Before LaRue knew it, the bird had him flying.

And the bird said, "LaRue,
You were there on the ark with Noah.
If God had thought less of you,
You'd have been left on the shore.
Here in the kingdom,
There is no higher or lower.
Though I'm able to fly
It's just my way to slither, slither.
And I 'slith' when I fly
And you fly when you slither."

LaRue thanked the bird for the flight,
Said goodnight and turned with delight as he
Started to slither, slither.
LaRue seemed to fly through the grass as he slithered.
There once was A SNAKE NAMED LARUE.

Words and music by George Wurzbach
© 1990 Bright Side Music (BMI). Used with permission.

▲ Comment

"A Snake Named LaRue" brings us a tale of two polar-opposite archetypal animals—the snake, representative of unconscious instinct, and the bird, symbolic of inspirational and creative thought. In "LaRue," George Wurzbach presents a *fable*—a tale, often about animals, that teaches a moral. Because it suggests something more significant than it explicitly states, a fable can be considered a special form of symbol—thus a subtype of metonymy. As its young listeners are being entertained by the story of the snake who gets skyborne by a friendly bird, they're unconsciously assimilating larger concepts about their uniquely individual gifts, their interconnection with others, and their ability to transcend limitations. *"I 'slith' when I fly/And you fly when you slither"* gives children a memorable motto to engender both self-esteem and brotherhood. This musical parable is part of the children's cassette "Sunday Morning Songs" which George Wurzbach arranged and produced.

WrapUp

If you feel a pull toward writing for children, be encouraged to do what these writers have done and to create your own projects. It's a good foot-in-the-door method to gain credibility for future assignments from film and TV producers. And now on to another special genre: The Comedy Song.

The Comedy Song as Plot Device

Charm Songs Vs. Comedy Songs

Many standards by Cole Porter, Rodgers and Hart and the brothers Gershwin come under the heading of *charm song*: "Let's Do It," "Bewitched (Bothered and Bewildered)," "Let's Call the Whole Thing Off." The playful tone, the clever rhymes, the semi-serious situation treated lightheartedly exude charm. You've read examples of the genre in several role-model lyrics—"Acapulco," "In the Thick of Getting Thin" and "Hey, Mr. Murphy." They made us smile—but not *laugh*. Writing a *comedy* song is a serious enterprise.

Some Theory on Humor and the Comedy Song

The essence of humor lies in exposing the maladjustment between people and their environment. Its essential ingredient is incongruity. As Stephen Sondheim succinctly put it, "Comedy is about character, not cleverness." A comedy song evolves, not from a joke, but from the character and his or her situation. Because a successful comedy song is rooted in truth, it makes audiences laugh, not just once, but time and time again.

So, the major requisite for a comedy song is some inherent disparity between the singer's situation and the attitude or tone taken toward it. Hence, its lyric may also include some discrepancy in the way the sound of the words combines with the sound of the music: Allan Sherman had a genius for paradoxical pairings like fusing the French folk melody "Frère Jacques" to a conversation with the Jewish "Sarah Jackman," ("Howze by you?"). You'll find a prime example of the paradoxical in "Lizzie Borden" from the revue *New Faces* (reprinted in *CLW*, pages 182-184), in which the language and tone taken toward "chopping your momma up in Massachusetts" were appropriately inappropriate to the act of matricide.

Because a comedy song emanates from a situation, it follows that most of the best-known ones originated in the plots of Hollywood or Broadway musicals or revues.

Some Classic Comedy Songs

Adelaide's Lament	Take Back Your Mink
Gooch's Song	I'm Just an Ordinary Man
Miss Marmelstein	The Ballad of the Shape of Things
The Boston Beguine	On the Steps of the Palace
Lizzie Borden	Agony
Sarah Jackman	Hello Mudduh, Hello Faddah!

The universally recognized subject of a camper's letter home put Allan Sherman's "Hello Mudduh, Hello Faddah!" on the pop charts (1963). But the majority of the foregoing songs—because of their theatrical origins—are less familiar to the general public.

The Personal Comedy Song

Many of the titles just cited exemplify a subtype of humorous lyric known as the *personal comedy song*. Here the singer has a complaint about a problem—a misfortune, or perceived disaster—which s/he takes seriously. In addition to being in the throes of a problem, the character must also possess two characteristics—sincerity and naiveté. The combination acts as the yeast to make the laughter rise. In case you're not familiar with the plots of the examples, here are a few synopses:

- "Adelaide's Lament" *(Guys and Dolls)*: Waiting for fourteen years for her fiancé to marry her has (incongruously) given Adelaide psychosomatic ailments. She naively stumbles over the terms as she reads a medical book.
- "Miss Gooch's Song" *(Mame)*: After being advised by her mentor to go out and "Live!," she did. And she (naively) got pregnant: Now she wonders how to get from here to maternity.
- "I'm an Ordinary Man" *(My Fair Lady)*: The learned Professor Higgins is naively unaware of both his own egocentricity and lack of ability to understand the opposite sex, as he enumerates the flaws in females.
- "Agony" *(Into the Woods)*: In a duet two princes bemoan the unattainability of their two hearts' desires—Rapunzel (locked in a tower) and Snow White (asleep in a glass box). Their total seriousness juxtaposed with their ludicrous situation creates the laughs.
- "On the Steps of the Palace" *(Into the Woods)*: Cinderella, as she tries to flee the advances of the prince, seriously ponders how to solve the (incongruous) predicament of one of her slippers being stuck to the tarred steps of the palace.

Rhyme and Rhythm and Humor

Rhyme plays an important role in comedy lyrics; frequent, contiguous and internal rhyme, along with incongruous sound pairings, contribute to laughter. When using frequent rhyme as a feature, aim to place the more unusual of the rhyme pair last *(tunics/eunuchs)*. Because both frequent and clever rhyme suggest reasoned thought, their use would be inappropriate to convey certain emotional states; for example, to help convey disorientation or hysteria, little or no rhyme would be the better approach—as you'll see in the first student example. (The theory of rhyme gets complete coverage in *CLW*, pages 185-212.)

You can also manipulate rhythm for humorous effect. For instance, Sheldon Harnick in the comedy song "Boston Beguine," set the tale of a dowdy, inhibited woman's flirtation on the Boston Common to a sensuous beguine rhythm; the paradoxical mating played a major role in the song's success. (*CLW*, pages 214-242, delves into the theory of rhythm and meaning.)

Prewriting Suggestion

How to begin to generate a comedy idea? Think situationally: Ask yourself who might have what kind of *real* problem? If you're used to writing mostly attitudinal lyrics—emotions without a plot—it will help to move to your left-brain sensation function to think more specifically and realistically. For example, what if a waitress were in love with a married patron. . . . Ask yourself, how do I show the singer's naive attitude toward her problem? What might be the disparity or discrepancy the lyric could play off? Picture how she would behave to the diner as she tries to attract him and simultaneously to act in a professional manner? When you come up with a situation that appeals to you, walk around with it—picture the scene. Let it incubate.

Humor and Song Form

About song forms: Essentially, all song forms can work; the effect you're seeking will determine your choice. The AAA proved ideal for "The Ballad of the Shape of Things" (reprinted in *CLW*, page 39); the AABA with an introductory verse and with multiple encore "choruses" perfectly fit "Take Back Your Mink" *(Guys and Dolls)*; the V/C served to raise the laugh meter in "Agony" *(Into the Woods)*. To determine the best form for your concept, study the best comedy songs.

Small Craft Warning

Be mindful that jokes, like rhymes, should be placed in "ascending order of punch" (Sondheim). Ideally a payoff comes in the last line—which is why comedy songs are frequently written last line first. Remember too that a comedy song requires that the singer take the problem seriously. Avoid having the character laugh at her/himself. Comics don't laugh: Consider Chaplin, Keaton, W.C. Fields, Laurel & Hardy. *We* laugh at *their* difficulties.

Some Background on Lyric No. 1

The first example was written for a dinner theater show. The singer, a single woman in her thirties, breathlessly rushes into her therapist's office. Her agitation is apparent during her nonstop monologue. Occasionally, she checks her watch noting how little time is left in the session. The lyric was designed as a rapid-fire patter song. To get the intended effect, read *very fast* without pausing at the end of a line.

Comedy Song: Example No. 1 (AAA Patter Song)
CONTACT LENSES

Wait a minute, Dr. Klutchky
While I make a small adjustment
I've just gotta get this lens out
'Cause the other one is missing
It got lost while I was waiting
And I really oughta find it
'Cause I'm almost blind without it
But I hate to waste a second
(Though I know it's not my hour)
But I've gotta lot to tell you:

I've just broken off with Roland
Now I'm having trouble breathing
Which I know is symptomatic
Of a co-dependent conflict
With a fear of separation
And a pattern of denial
Oh, what good are contact lenses
When you keep on losing one!

(Spoken): Seventeen minutes!

Now I know it's not the lenses
'Cause they're just another symptom
Of the problem I've been having
With my unresolved aggression.
Please excuse me for a second—
I remember seeing something
Kind of shiny near the table.
I could run right out and get it;
It'll only take a minute
And I really want to find it.
What if someone doesn't see it?
They could step on it and break it.
God! I hate these freaking lenses—
They go foggy when you're crying
And they stop your eyes from breathing
But my mother made me get them
And whenever I don't wear them
My left pupil starts to cross.

[Spoken]: Four minutes!

Mother said that girls with glasses
Always end up in a file room
So I wore those lousy lenses
And I ended up with Roland
Till last night when I decided
I am through with men forever,
But I got these palpitations
And I simply had to see you,
So this fellow who was waiting
Handed over his appointment
As I dropped the other lens out
And there wasn't time to find it
But who cares 'cause I don't want it
'Cause I'm changing my whole image:
I'll get aviator goggles
With those lavender reflectors.

[Spoken]: One minute!

And I'll be a whole new person
No more tears and palpitations
Boy, I'm really glad I came here
I just knew that you could help me
And I'll be on time next Tuesday;
I'm so grateful, Dr. Klutchky:
And thank you
For all your
Advice!

1978 Words by June Siegel/Music by Irwin Webb. Used with permission.

▲ Comment

The singer's been portrayed as both naive, and having a problem which she's certainly taking seriously. I'm sure you experienced how the rapid meter and the virtual absence of rhyme contributed to the humorous effect. The spare end-sound links — *Klutchky/adjustment, missing/waiting, get it/minute, get them/wear them* — were achieved through the minor accents of light and unstressed rhyme. In the song's ironic payoff, the self-deluded singer thanks her doctor for giving the advice that she actually gave to herself. In her memorable portrait of a hysteric, June Siegel leaves us with a bit of wisdom as appropriately subtle as her rhymes.

Some Background on Lyric No. 2

The second role-model song comes from a theater piece in progress — a musical, *Quilt*, based on that awesome tapestry of over 15,000 handmade squares united in a traveling tribute to those who have died of AIDS. Jim Morgan's original book and lyrics fuse fact and fiction in a focus on the surviving friends and family of AIDS victims and the manner in which their lives have changed. This song is based upon a true experience of a clinical psychologist whose professional colleague Tedd died of AIDS. She is getting ready to go for the first time to a quilt workshop where friends of victims make panels to add to the constantly growing quilt. This lyric is the first part of a four-part "through joke" that continues to pop up at various spots in the show.

Comedy Song: Example No. 2 (AABA Variant)
KAREN'S SONG

(Karen is an attractive thirty-five. She enters carrying a large shopping bag and acting hyperanxious. She takes several deep breaths, trying to gain control of herself.)

Try to be calm.
Try to be clear.
Try to identify present emotions:
They're panic and fear.

Try to be calm.
Try to be cool.
Try to proceed in an orderly fashion
And not be a jittering fool.
Well, I decided to do it.
And now I must follow it through.
Although I'm not sure
What I'm going to do.

I should be calm.
I should get dressed.
I should relax, get my alpha waves going
Because I am stressed
Try to detach.
Try to unwind.
Try to begin to get into a steady and
Orderly, rational mind.
Although I long to be steady,
I'm ready to tear out my hair.
What's more I don't know
What I'm going to wear.

What do you wear when you're going to go
To the Gay and Lesbian Center?
Why do they have the Quilting Workshop there!
How do you dress when you're spending the day
At the Gay and Lesbian Center?
When you want to look like you fit in?
But not like you really belong!
Wrong:

Homophobia!
I know! I know! I know!
But that isn't a problem!
Don't make it a problem!
(Well, it's sort of a problem.)
All right, it's a problem.
Acknowledge the problem.
Let go of the problem.
You're late. Get dressed and go—
Calm-ly.

What do they do?
What will I see?
What if there's only one heterosexual there
And it's me?
What if I am?
Hey, it's okay.
But what if someone comes on to me
Thinking because I am there that I'm gay!

Oh, how distressing! I know I'm obsessing, but
What if it's true?
I'm so full of 'what *if*,'
I don't know *what* to do.

What if someone I know sees me go
In the Gay and Lesbian Center?
What if I have to use the bathroom there?
What if I *die* and I lie on the floor
At the Gay and Lesbian Center?
And my parents must come for the body?
And I don't know how I could ever explain?
Wrong!

That's ridiculous!
I know! I know! I know!
So stop wasting time creating dramas
It's late. Get dressed and go.

I have the cloth.
I have the thread.
I have the lab coat — the one with the stencil
That says Doctor Tedd.
I have the pins.
I have the glue.
And in my bag there're a couple of
Two-point-five-milligram Valium too.
I've got my feelings and fears
Which I'm trying like mad to subdue.
And I wish I knew
What I'm going to do.
At the new
Gay and Lesbian Center.
Aaaaaaaaaaaaaaaaaaaaaaaahhh (She screams)

© 1991 Words by Jim Morgan/Music by Michael Stockler. Used with permission.

▲ Comment

That's what you call/having technique/. Having the art and the craft/that can fashion a draft/that is funny and sleek. That's what you call/skillful design,/where anaphora starts or epistrophe ends/each appropriate line. Okay: Enough. (But metric patterns can pattern you!) Anyway, epistrophe (e-PIS-tro-FEE) is the mirror image of anaphora — where end-of-line repetitions substitute for rhyme: *problem/problem/problem*. That's a sound device to reinforce and intensify the singer's obsessive state. Another is "obsessive" (three-line) rhyme. Anaphora, of course, also emphasized the singer's need to control herself: *Try to be/try to be, I should/I should, What if/what if, I have/I have.* Jim Morgan also chose the perfect way to lend punch to the final verse: he *r*eemphasized her obsession by extending the *oo* rhyme for two more lines: *glue/too/subdue/knew/do/new.* The lyric exemplifies Sondheim's dictum: "Comedy is about character, not cleverness."

Some Background on Lyric No. 3

"Bruce," the next comedy song illustrates how frequent, close and audacious rhyme leads to laughs. Written and performed by the songwriter/entertainer John Wallowitch, "Bruce" adopts the persona of the late diva of high couture, Diana Vreeland, fashion editor and curator of costumes of the Metropolitan Museum of Art. The slow, romantic melody is incongruously fused to the ascerbic advice she offers a male friend:

Comedy Song: Example No. 3 (ABAC w/Intro)
BRUCE

Dear One,
Your life is a waste.
My advice is *feel* and *think*
Or you'll end up on the shelf.
Dear One,
You know *I* have taste
Let Diana Vreeland
Help you save you from yourself.

BRUCE, wherever you go
Whatever you do, Bruce,
I'm thinking of you, Bruce,
And worrying so.
Make sure you're not wearing
That tacky green gown.
And burn up that wig and those
Joan Crawford pumps you limped
Into town upon, with Yvonne.

BRUCE, I'm not one to mock
A civilized frock, Bruce.
You're wedded to schlock, Bruce,
To sequins and sleaze.
That gold lamé jumpsuit
With wimple, is simply an also ran.
You look like a hag, Bruce.
Now don't be a drag, Bruce.
When aping a woman,
Dress like a man!

BRUCE, you've got to reduce!
Spruce up that caboose, Bruce!
Or wear something loose, Bruce:
You're lacking "Allure."
Get off the Godivas
And Nesselrode pies
And banish your Gloria Vanderbilt jeans

They seem to be undersize!
Thunder thighs!

BRUCE, you've read too much Proust—
You're getting "confeust" confused, Bruce,
We are not amused, Bruce.
Your wardrobe is gauche:
Don't emulate Nancy, or Jackie,
You're acting just as I feared.
My heart has an ache, Bruce,
Please give me a break, Bruce,
For *haute couture's* sake, Bruce,
Shave off your beard!

BRUCE, I've run out of juice.
I'm praying to Zeus, Bruce,
Don't ever wear puce, Bruce,
It's not *de rigueur*.
Last night at the Met
You looked like a troll.
And who were those mean looking
Awful old queens resembling some
Bus-and-truck *Cage Aux Folles*?

BRUCE, You use too much rouge.
I can't stand your lipstick.
To really be hip, stick
With something pastel.
I don't mind your handbag,
Those earrings, that beauty mark
On your knee. But
You're making me blue, Bruce
I'm pleading with you, Bruce,
Don't call yourself Sue, Bruce
Stick with Marie.

Words and music John Wallowitch
© *1983 Sky Witch Music. Used with permission.*

▲ Comment

John Wallowitch, who critics have compared to Cole Porter and Noel Coward, writes for a cosmopolitan following that dotes on his French idioms and "in" references. Enjoying the song depends to a degree on an awareness of Diana Vreeland's high profile for impeccable taste. A few footnotes might also be in order here to enhance your enjoyment of a second reading: *Allure* was the name of Vreeland's elegant fashion magazine; *Godiva* is a brand of expensive chocolates wrapped in gold foil; *La Cage Aux Folles* was a Tony-award winning Broadway musical about the relationship between two male lovers—one of whom was a transvestite. The other allusions were broader in scope—from Nancy (Reagan) to Jackie (Onassis) and Joan Crawford to Zeus. *Nancy* and *Jackie* are instances of synedoche — the part (first name) for the whole (both names).

The line *"We* are not amused," evokes Queen Victoria's famous remark in which, referring herself, she used the "royal" *we,* a characterization of Ms. Vreeland's sense of regality. Wallowitch, in performing, purposefully stumbles over "confeust" and then corrects himself: This is an actual literary device, a form of repetition by correction *(epanorthosis)* that Stephen Sondheim used to humorous advantage in the comedy duet "Agony."

The most fun comes from both the close positioning and odd combinations of sounds: *reduce/caboose/Bruce/loose, juice/Zeus/Bruce/puce.* The mosaic rhyme *lipstick/hip, stick* is made more enjoyable because of the comma in between. Fun too comes from the instant pun in "Don't be a *drag,"* simultaneously conveying a *bore* and *in a woman's dress.* If I had my druthers, I would druther close the lyric with the line "Shave off your beard," but the (recorded live) laughter of John's cabaret and TV audiences attests to the wisdom of his ending the song as he does.

WrapUp

In proportion to the huge body of popular music, the inordinately small number of well-known comedy songs seems to suggest that the ability to write funny lyrics is a special knack — a rare turn of mind — or brain. Don't be surprised then if you find this strategy daunting. But at least "Bruce" should reinforce for you that subject matter has no bounds. If you'd like to hear more innovative comedy songs, I highly recommend John Wallowitch's album, *My Manhattan* (DG Records), as a home course in the art of lyrical humor.

The Social Statement as Plot Device

Some Background

Sometimes when the headlines get too much and we feel overwhelmed by humanity's failings, a song results. The act of writing serves to lessen a sense of frustration. The biggest satisfaction, of course, comes from getting the message to the public. When the songwriter is also a recording artist, then the world readily gets a "Jack and Diane," or an "Allentown" or "Another Day in Paradise." When you're a nonperformer writer, the process may be a bit slower, but your statement can still get out there as "40-Hour Week for a Living" and "Who Will Answer" attest.

Some Social Statement Songs

Eve of Destruction	The Times They Are A-Changin'
Blowin' in the Wind	Jack and Diane
Brother, Can You Spare a Dime?	Where Have All the Flowers Gone?
Another Day in Paradise	Big Yellow Taxi
Who Will Answer	40-Hour Week for a Living
Allentown	Little Boxes
In the Year 2525	We Are the World
Discipline	Give Peace a Chance

Attitude Equals Style

A song's style results from the writer's attitude toward a given event or ongoing condition; it may be appreciative, wistful, critical or outraged. For example, "40-Hour Week" is a country tribute to the unsung working class; "Where Have All the Flowers Gone?" a folk lament on the effects of war; "Discipline," a pop plea for safe sex in the era of AIDS.

The Satirical Song

Somewhere between social protest and the comedy song, lies the realm of satire. The satirist is a kind of self-appointed guardian of standards, ideals and truth — of moral as well as aesthetic values — who takes it upon him- or herself to censure human foibles and vices in the hope of correcting them.

In the following examples of satirical songs, the writer points a ridiculing finger at such perennial blemishes on the complexion of society as stage mothers, gauche tourists, unethical politicians, and the snobbish rich.

Some Satirical Songs

A Little Tin Box	Politics and Poker
Merry Little Minuet	Why Do All the Wrong People Travel
When the Idle Poor Become the Idle Rich	Don't Put Your Daughter on the Stage, Mrs. Worthington

Depending upon your familiarity with theater songs, many (or even all) of those titles may be unfamiliar to you. Because in satire the emphasis is on the words rather than the tune or groove, the genre's more commonly found in theater and cabaret where the performer has the listener's full attention.

Satire and Personality Type

A satirical bent requires several qualities: an observance of concrete realities, tough-minded cause-effect thinking, a valuing of propriety and lawfulness, and an impulse to set the world to rights. In other words, the characteristics of an STJ. If you share those attributes, you're likely to have a flair for satire. (As did the writer of "Have a Nice Day.")

If, on the other hand, you're the polar-opposite NFP, it's quite possible that you'll find this attitude somewhat alien. You'll see.

Prewriting Suggestion

Here's a prewriting approach used by Hank Williams, Jr., "I watch TV and read the newspaper and try to keep up with things. And I get mad a lot. I try to put that in a song." Sounds to me like the perfect preparation for writing "a song with social significance," as Harold Rome satirically put it.

First choose a subject of genuine personal concern. The question to ask yourself would be, What element of society arouses my indignation or censure. What lights my ire? Subjects can range from annoyance at bus passengers who exit at the entrance door to outrage at the malfeasance of elected officials.

Small Craft Warning

Writing successful satire requires that your subject be sufficiently familiar to your audience to give your comic barbs instant recognition. Be mindful, too, of your intended marketplace. Quite naturally, that marketplace will be the genre of songs that you like best—folk, pop, R&B, country, cabaret or theater. To help keep your writing consistent in style, imagine a particular recording/performing artist singing your words. Here's a student song tailored for cabaret.

Social Statement Example No. 1: A Satire (Verse/Chorus)
KILL AND TELL

A lady and her lover
Had a king-size brawl one day
And she became too furious
To simply walk away.
So she drilled him full of bullet holes
And left him on the floor.
Now publishers from everywhere
Are lined up at her door.
'Cause when you

KILL AND TELL,
No crime goes unrewarded.
Just KILL AND TELL,

The public loves it sordid.
A story that is gory
Will be sure to sell
And you'll reap a heap o' glory
When you KILL AND TELL.

Then there was the feller
Who got tired of his wife
And laced her wine with arsenic
Thus cutting short her life.
While out on bail awaiting trial
He made a pile of dough
Giving interviews on Donahue
And the Oprah Winfrey show.
'Cause when you

KILL AND TELL,
No crime goes unrewarded.
When you KILL AND TELL,
You're flashbulbed and recorded,
And you can bet your autographs
Will also do quite well
As celebrity mem'rabilia
When you KILL AND TELL.

So if you aim for instant fame,
Here's what you have to do:
Go out and do somebody in.
(The choice is up to you.)
And while you're in your prison cell,
Write down each juicy *de*tail
And the story you produce
Can go for thirty dollars retail.

Then the book'll be translated
And you'll sell the movie rights,
And the ads'll be on billboards
And the title up in lights.
And your face will make the cover
Of *People Magazine:*
Just break one small commandment
And spill a lot of beans
'Cause when you

KILL AND TELL,
No crime goes unrewarded.
I can't oversell
The honor *I'm* accorded:
With a limo to my interviews

And a mike in my lapel,
I make a lively living
Telling how to KILL AND TELL.

© 1991 Rebecca Holtzman. Used with permission.

▲ Comment

With a happy rhythm and frequent perfect rhyme, the lyric spoofs both the public's appetite for the sordid and the media's glamorization of crime. The tone takes an appropriately irreverent attitude toward human life as the plot cheerfully exaggerates the potential rewards of committing murder. The specificity of name dropping—Oprah Winfrey, Donahue, *People Magazine*, and the verbifying of *flash-bulb* add both to the lyric's enjoyment and memorability. Rebecca Holtzman, an ESTJ, brings her extravert's (E) love of action and people and places to her STJ indignation over one of society's less admirable qualities, to produce an original lyric topped with a paragram title.

Some Background on a Theater Piece

This next role-model example of a social statement comes from *Quilt*, the show from which you've already seen the comedy lyric, "Karen's Song." This lyric draws upon the biographical data from two true stories.

Social Statement Example No. 2: A Theater Piece
VICTIM OF AIDS

(Mrs. D'Angelo (Dee-AN-je-lo) is a middle-class woman in her late forties. Behind her is seen a 6' × 3' quilt panel showing a top hat, tap shoes and sheet music. It reads "Tommy Dee." She sings:)

Thomas Patrick Anthony D'Angelo, the third,
Could dance just like Gene Kelly and sing just like a bird.
We don't know where he got it from 'cause if his dad or I
Would sing or dance, the dogs would howl and little kids'd cry!
At talent shows and musicals, we'd watch our gifted boy
And see he was a messenger—a messenger of joy.

Thomas Patrick Anthony D'Angelo, "the three,"
Went to New York City, changed his name to Tommy Dee.
And what he did at home, he soon was doing on Broadway.
And then we got the letter where he told us he was gay.
This took some getting used to, but in time, with love, we knew
If Tommy had accepted this, then we'd accept it too.

But I prayed, Dear God,
Don't let my son become
A VICTIM OF AIDS.

"Thomas Patrick Anthony D'Angelo, your son,"
That's how he signed the Christmas card along with David Dunn.
When they arrived together at Christmastime that year
We all approached the meeting with anxiety and fear.

But Dave was just like Tommy, intelligent and fun;
Our Tommy'd found a lover, and we'd found a second son.
Dave and Tommy telephone us every Sunday night.
So when they called on Thursday, I feared something wasn't right.
They said they'd had a blood test, about a month ago
And had they tested positive? The test results said, "No!"

Thank God!
My son would not become
A VICTIM OF AIDS

We laughed and cried and laughed some more
Because the news was great.
And then we said goodbye
And they went out to celebrate . . .

(Breaking the song structure — speaking:)

And a black Cutlass Supreme
Pulled up beside them asking directions
Tommy and Dave went over
The doors flew open and four men jumped out
Swinging bats and boards
And one had a knife.
Hitting them again and again and again and again and again

Dave got away and ran.
He found a police call box.
Five minutes later the police arrived
And drove to the scene of the attack.

They found the body beaten and stabbed
And beside the body written in blood
The words . . .
"AIDS fags die."

(She pauses, then resumes singing)

Thomas Patrick Anthony D'Angelo, the last,
Was struck by a disease with a well-established past.
Acquir'd immune deficiency was not my Tommy's fate:
He died from fear and ignorance and violence and hate.
These acquir'd deficiencies contaminate and spread
Till sanity, humanity, and Tommy Dee are dead.
And one by one
We all become
A VICTIM OF AIDS
(Pointing to herself)
A VICTIM OF AIDS
(Looking at her son's Quilt Panel)
A VICTIM OF AIDS

© 1991 Lyric by Jim Morgan/Music by Michael Stockler. Used with permission.

▲ Comment

Jim Morgan reveals the salient facts verse by verse in an easy-to-follow, step-by-step way: Tommy's an aspiring dancer who moves to New York, changes his name, reveals his homosexuality to his parents who accept it and who celebrate his escape from the HIV virus. To communicate all that biographical data in four verses requires making every word count. No flab, no unneeded word. The lyric's opening-line motif—*the third*/*"the three"*/*my son*/*the last*—strengthens the song's framework as it helps underscore its ironic climax.

Jim's intuitive/thinking (NT) style is evident not only in the irony that under-girds the story but in the lyric's inspiring message. (The INTJ, especially, often manifests a strong sense of personal mission.) This powerful piece attracted the attention of the producer of "Here's to Our Friends," a revue to benefit AIDS research, and has already found an appreciative audience in the revue's successful run at New York's supperclub, Eighty Eights.

WrapUp

Writing a social statement not only affords you a means to express a pressing issue—whether amusingly satirical or movingly powerful—it affords the public a focused bit of clarity in an often chaotic world.

The Inspirational Song as Plot Device

Perhaps the greatest reward of songwriting lies in the implicit knowledge that our songs wield the power to affect positively with lyrics that can provide emotional support and hope and inspiration.

Every song conveys a message. The kind of message your song conveys will, of course, embody your personal values: Paul Overstreet, "I write songs that encourage people to work out their problems and remain faithful to their marriage vows and things like that." Tracy Chapman, "The message I'm trying to convey is positive and hopeful." Bruce Springsteen, "If I'm doing my job right, I help people hold on to their own humanity."

Some Songs That Inspire

I Believe	We Shall Overcome
Let's Get Together	Ac-cent-tchu-ate the Positive
Impossible Dream	Pick Yourself Up
Climb Every Mountain	Let the Sunshine In
He Lives	You'll Never Walk Alone
Second Wind	The Blizzard
It's a Wonderful World	When You Wish Upon a Star
Say It Loud, I'm Black and I'm Proud	

Prewriting Overview

Songs that exhort, encourage, and foster a positive outlook can employ all viewpoints, voices and forms. Such songs often use the plural "we" and "you" in talking to or about the world at large as in "We Shall Overcome" and "You'll Never Walk Alone." Then too, they can couch the message subtly within a first-person narrative as does Judy Collins' dramatic narrative, "The Blizzard."

The first example of a positive message is a lyric that developed from a melody. The music, built on a slow stepwise ascending motif, resonated with inspiration and suggested its title.

Inspirational Song: Example No. 1 (AABA)
NEVER LET GO OF YOUR DREAM

You were born with a dream
That lies deep in your soul
You were born with a need
To reach out to a goal.
Swear by all that you know
You will NEVER LET GO OF YOUR DREAM.

When the road seems too long
And your hopes turn to clay,
That's the time to be strong—
With a will there's a way,
Tho' the way may be slow,
You must NEVER LET GO OF YOUR DREAM.

If you're living
Without trying
That's not living—
Just a slower way of dying.
So whatever else you do,
Hold on tight to what you want and you
Will wake to greet one

Great golden morn
When the world seems to say:
"This is why you were born,
Here it is! Here's your day!"
You will reap all you sow,
Make your cup overflow
If you NEVER LET GO OF YOUR DREAM.

Words by Sheila Davis/Music by Tommy Zang
© 1977 Solar Systems Music. Used with permission.

▲ Comment

You probably noticed that the words in the bridge flow right into the last A
section: The music's bridge had originally ended on a D above middle C and then
leapt down to E to start the final verse; I suggested to my collaborator that,
instead of holding that E for four beats, we make it a dotted quarter note and let
the melody descend stepwise in eighth notes to link to the first note of the final
A section—hence the words ". . . will wake to greet one . . . ." It led to a more
effective lyric.

The song, recorded by the Shawnee Choir, and printed in three different choral
arrangements, has become a graduation standard. Far more satisfying than any
royalty statement is the knowledge that my lyric message has touched young lives
in a positive way. Perhaps the biggest satisfaction has come from requests by a
number of high school graduating classes to reprint the lyric in their yearbook as
its theme.

Some Background on a Theater Song

The next lyric is from *A Rock Carol,* a modern-day adaptation of Dickens' *A Christmas Carol.* The scene, Christmas afternoon at the Cratchit home. Tim Cratchit, a
handicapped nine-year old is in his wheelchair. The family has been playing a
little catch and Tim, standing up to go for a ball, falls. He bravely asserts that
someday he'll get well and walk again:

Inspirational Song: Example No. 2 (AABA)
SOMEDAY I WILL WALK WITH YOU

I believe in Santa Claus
I just know he's real.
I believe in stuff that I can't see
But I can feel.
I believe in Superman
And flyin' off with Peter Pan.
Nothin' is impossible to do.
Way down deep inside 'a me
I believe it's true:
SOMEDAY I WILL WALK WITH YOU.

I believe the good guys always win—
Sooner or later.
I believe believin' in The Force
Will beat Darth Vader.
I believe in Indiana Jones,
And Mr. Spock and Twilight Zones
And wishing on a star makes dreams come true.
But I don't have to wish because I know
(I really do)
SOMEDAY I WILL WALK WITH YOU.

I don't know how I know it
But I know it.
I don't know why I feel it
I just feel it.
I don't know where it comes from—
This stuff that I believe—
All I know is I believe.

Yes, I believe that Tinkerbell
Comes back alive by clappin'.
She lives if we believe in her—
I've even seen it happen!
And so God bless us every one.
I'm in Your hands, Thy will be done.
Anything is possible to do:
I believe that somehow, someway,
SOMEDAY I WILL WALK WITH YOU.

© 1989 Words by Jim Morgan/Music by BJ Leiderman. Used with permission.

▲ Comment
The lyric reflects the writer's clear focus on the age of his character. For example, the allusions to such children's favorites as Superman, Peter Pan, *Star Wars* and Indiana Jones were suitable (and instantly recognizable). And Tim's thoughts and emotions were expressed in a language style appropriate to a nine-year old.

No small lyricwriting accomplishment. His bridge, in fine contrast to the specific names listed in each A, makes *general* statements.

Another point worth noting is Jim's understanding of the truism "When you mean the same thing, use the same word" (H.W. Fowler). Hence we hear the forcefulness of purposeful repetition (*I don't know how I know it/But I know it*) throughout the bridge. Amateurs seek synonyms.

By integrating Dickens' famous Tiny Tim quote, "God Bless us every one" and a line from the Lord's Prayer, "Thy will be done," the lyric builds to a strong climax. It is axiomatic that an audience is drawn to a character struggling to overcome some negative force. Creating this tension in a lyric helps to evoke audience empathy: By identifying with the singer's struggle, we are ourselves uplifted.

A Fine Point of Craft

It's worth noting here a hallmark of a well-crafted song: it's impossible to switch the order of any of its parts. Good writing demands that each part arrives in linear order—setup, development, resolution. All the book's role-model lyrics meet that criteria: No interchangability possible. It might be useful to put your own lyrics to the same test: If you find that any verse can trade places with any other, it reveals redundancy and the need for further revision.

WrapUp

In discussing her epic lyric "The Blizzard," on "Sunday Morning," Judy Collins commented: "It's about getting up and going on with your life after whatever trauma that happens to you—whether it's a physical trauma, an emotional trauma, a spiritual trauma. It's about transcending and surviving."

Songs of 'transcending and surviving' can be as lighthearted as Dorothy Fields' "Pick Yourself Up," as playful as Johnny Mercer's "Ac-cent-tchu-ate the Positive," or as stirring as Oscar Hammerstein's "Climb Every Mountain." The style is the writer. It's your uniqueness of mind and spirit that will make your songs as memorable as those.

Coda

Write yourself. Write your value system—always remembering that your brain has two sides—the right with its images, and insight and feeling, and the left with its clarity and logic and structure. By uniting the best of both sides, you'll give the world songs to live by.

The Circle of Wholeness

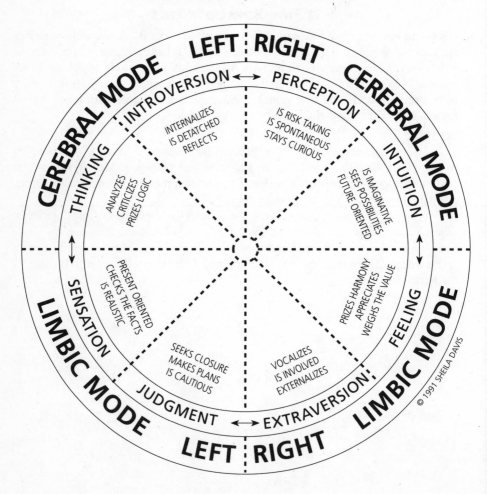

(The page numbers after lyricists' names refer to the post-lyric comments.)

(Page numbers for definitions are in bold type.)

Sheila Davis is a teacher,
lecturer and consultant on
personality type/brain dominance
and the creative process. For a
schedule of upcoming seminars,
contact:

Songcraft Seminars
441 East 20th Street, Suite 11B
New York, NY 10010-7512
(212)674-1143